Winslow Homer
Force of Nature

Christine Riding, Christopher Riopelle
and Chiara Di Stefano

NATIONAL GALLERY GLOBAL, LONDON
DISTRIBUTED BY YALE UNIVERSITY PRESS

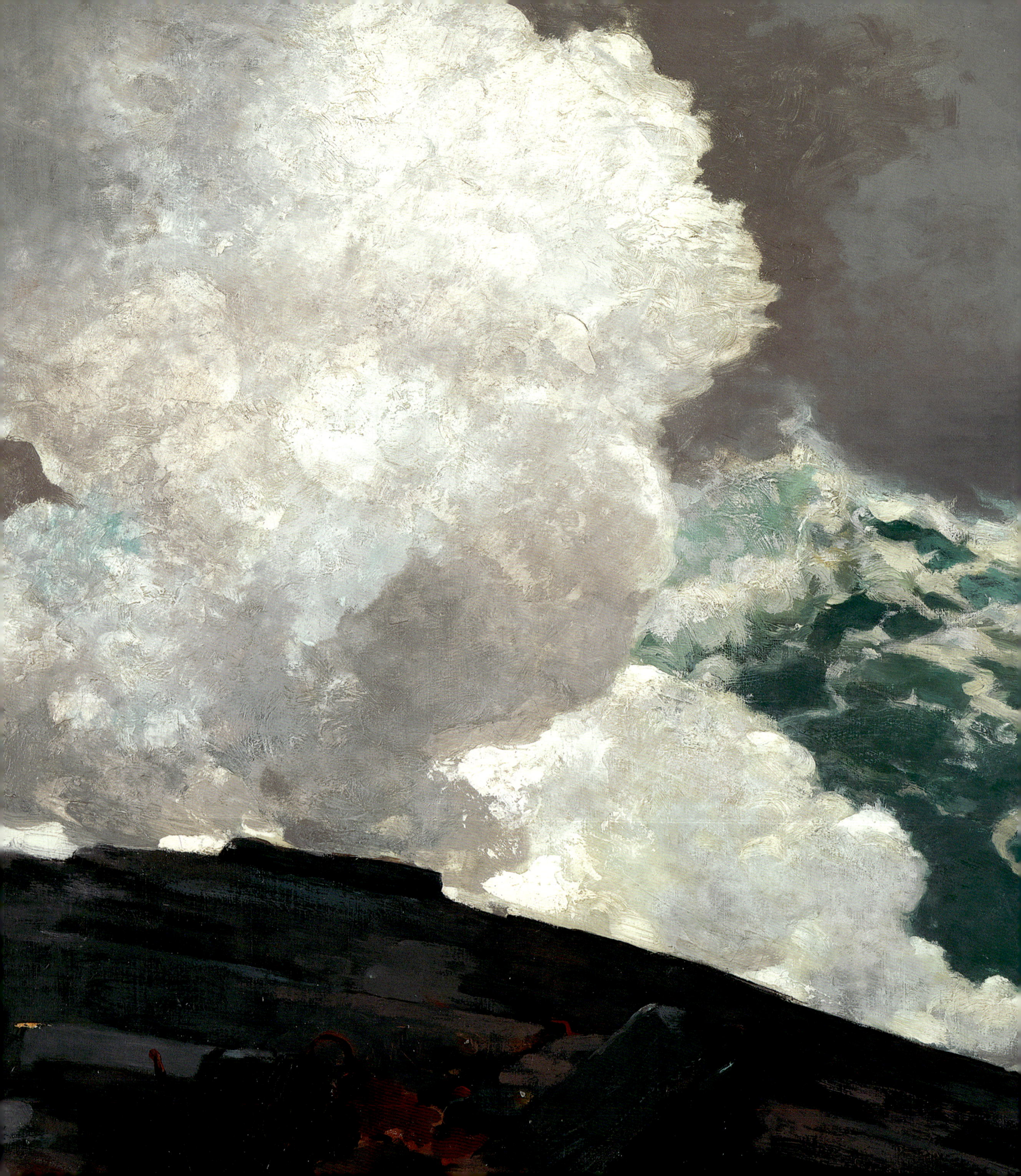

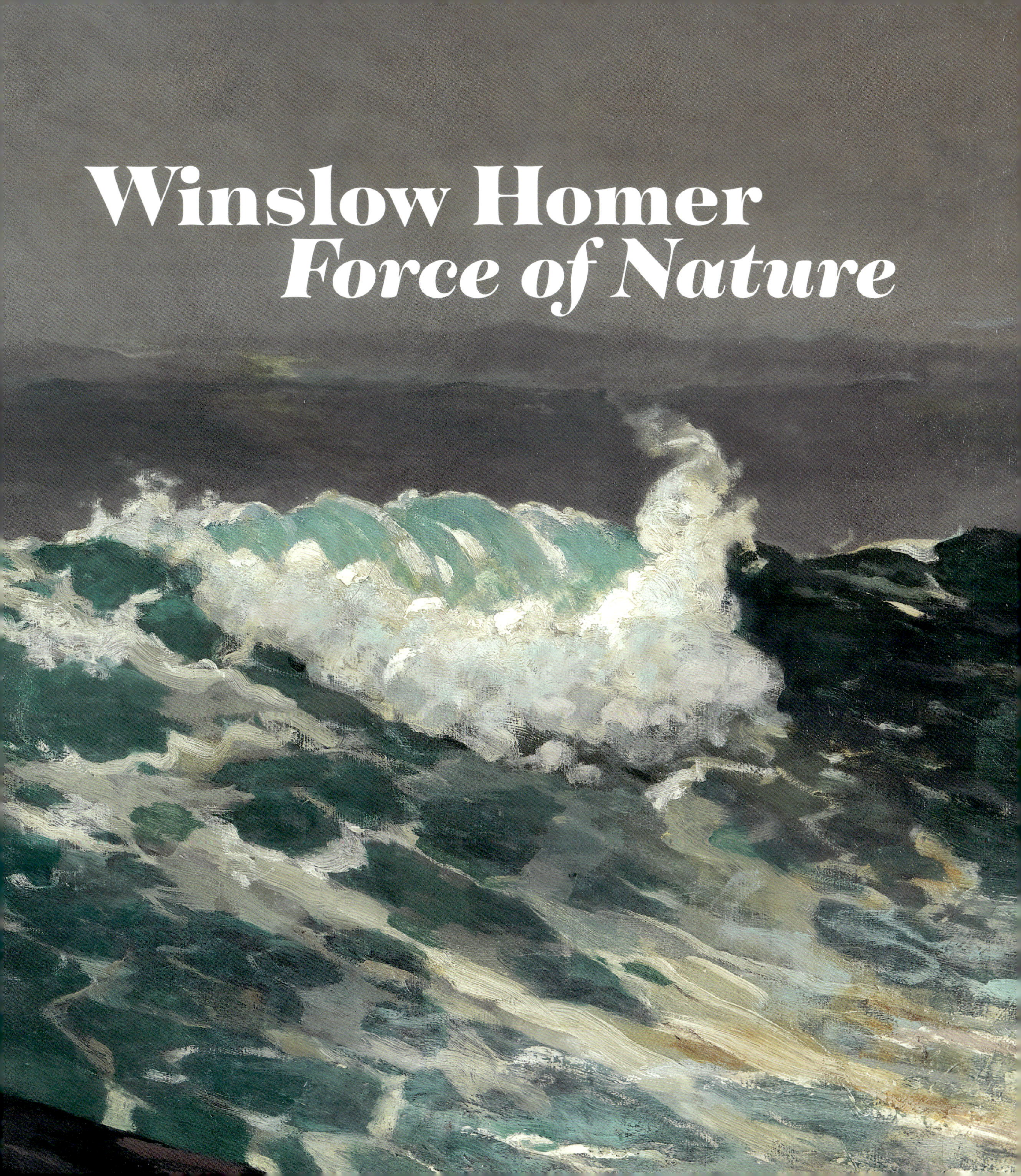
Winslow Homer
Force of Nature

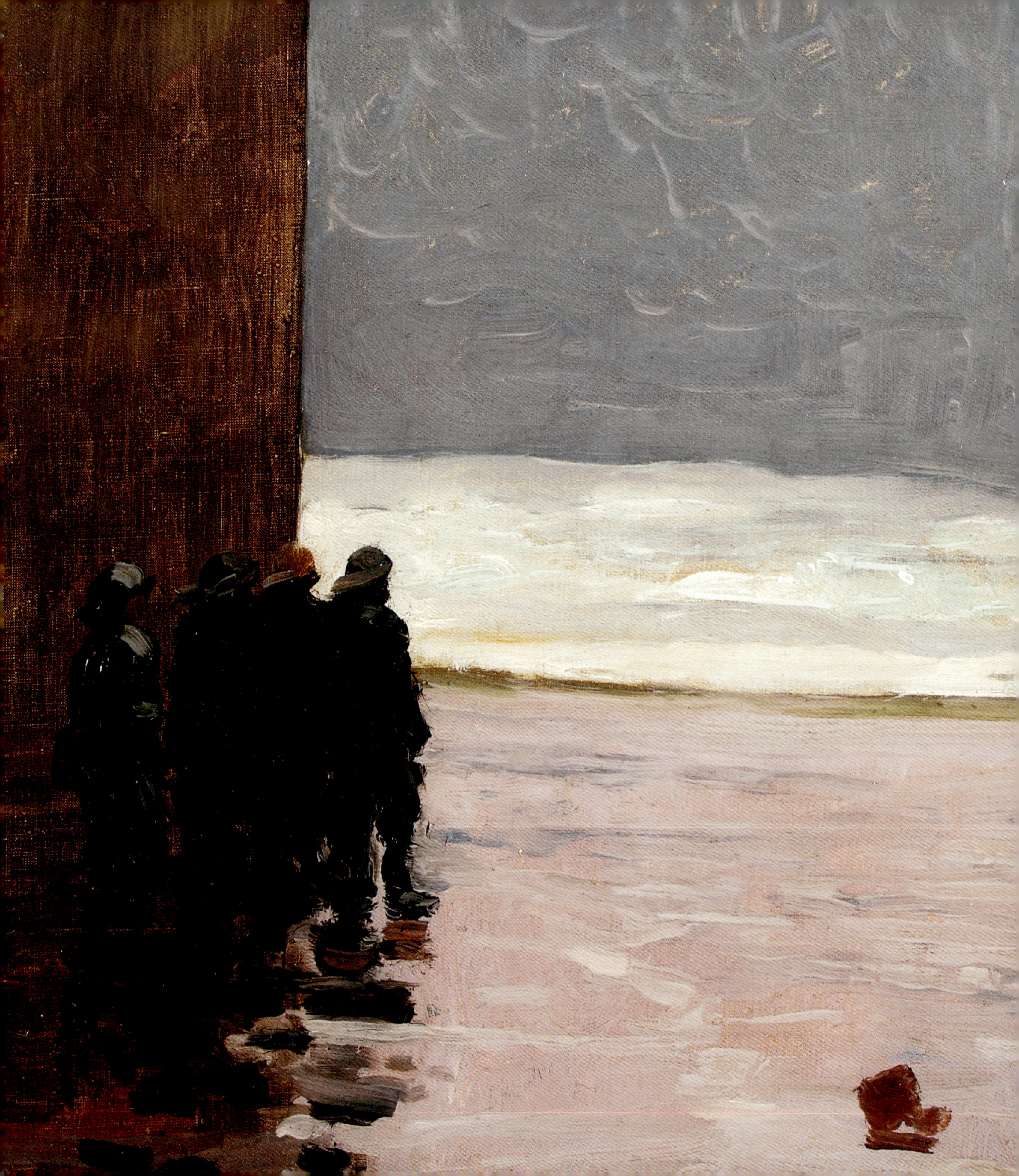

Contents

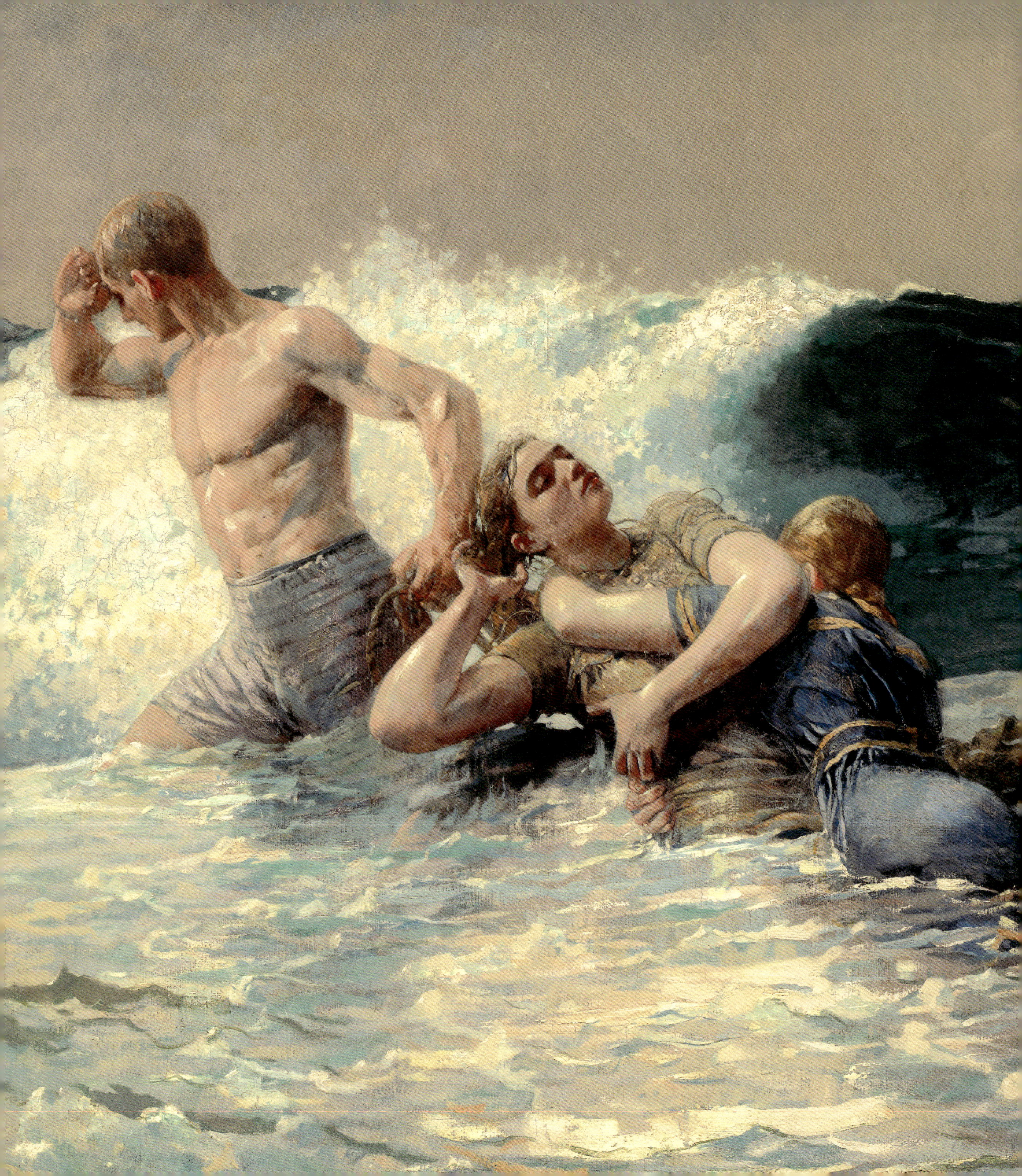

Director's Foreword

Winslow Homer (1836–1910) is one of America's most celebrated and admired painters. Yet in the UK he remains largely unknown, in spite of an extended stay in Cullercoats near Tynemouth on the North Sea from 1881 to 1882 and an oeuvre that includes a significant number of paintings of English scenes. Not a single work by Homer is to be found in a UK public collection, and this is only the second exhibition devoted to his art following the pioneering display held at the Dulwich Picture Gallery in 2006 focusing on his marine subjects.

An exhibition of Homer's work at the National Gallery hardly needs any justification. Throughout his career, he addressed not only the complex social and political issues of his era – war, slavery and imperialism – but also more universal concerns about the fragility of human life and the power of nature. His thoughtful approach to the depiction of race, natural phenomena and the environment remains relevant to current societal concerns in both the USA and our own country. *Winslow Homer: Force of Nature* reflects an ongoing commitment to include American art within the Gallery's wider international mandate, and the project's focus on the Atlantic world provides a relevant context for examining historical and contemporary Anglo-American dialogues.

The collaboration with colleagues at the Metropolitan Museum of Art, with whom this exhibition was conceived, has been enormously stimulating. The Met holds one of the most comprehensive collections of Homer's work, and we are grateful for the large number of loans we have received from them, including his most famous painting *The Gulf Stream*, acquired in 1906, a few years before the artist died. We would like to express our gratitude to all the lenders to the National Gallery's exhibition.

We would like to thank the Terra Foundation for American Art and White & Case LLP for their support of the exhibition in London, following their assistance with *Winslow Homer: Crosscurrents* at the Metropolitan Museum of Art in spring 2022. We are also grateful to Gregory Annenberg Weingarten and GRoW@Annenberg, Ocean Outdoor and the Dr Lee MacCormick Edwards Charitable Foundation for their support of the exhibition, as well as to Athene Foundation for their generous support of both the exhibition and the accompanying catalogue.

Gabriele Finaldi, Director
The National Gallery, London

Opposite Detail of fig. 55

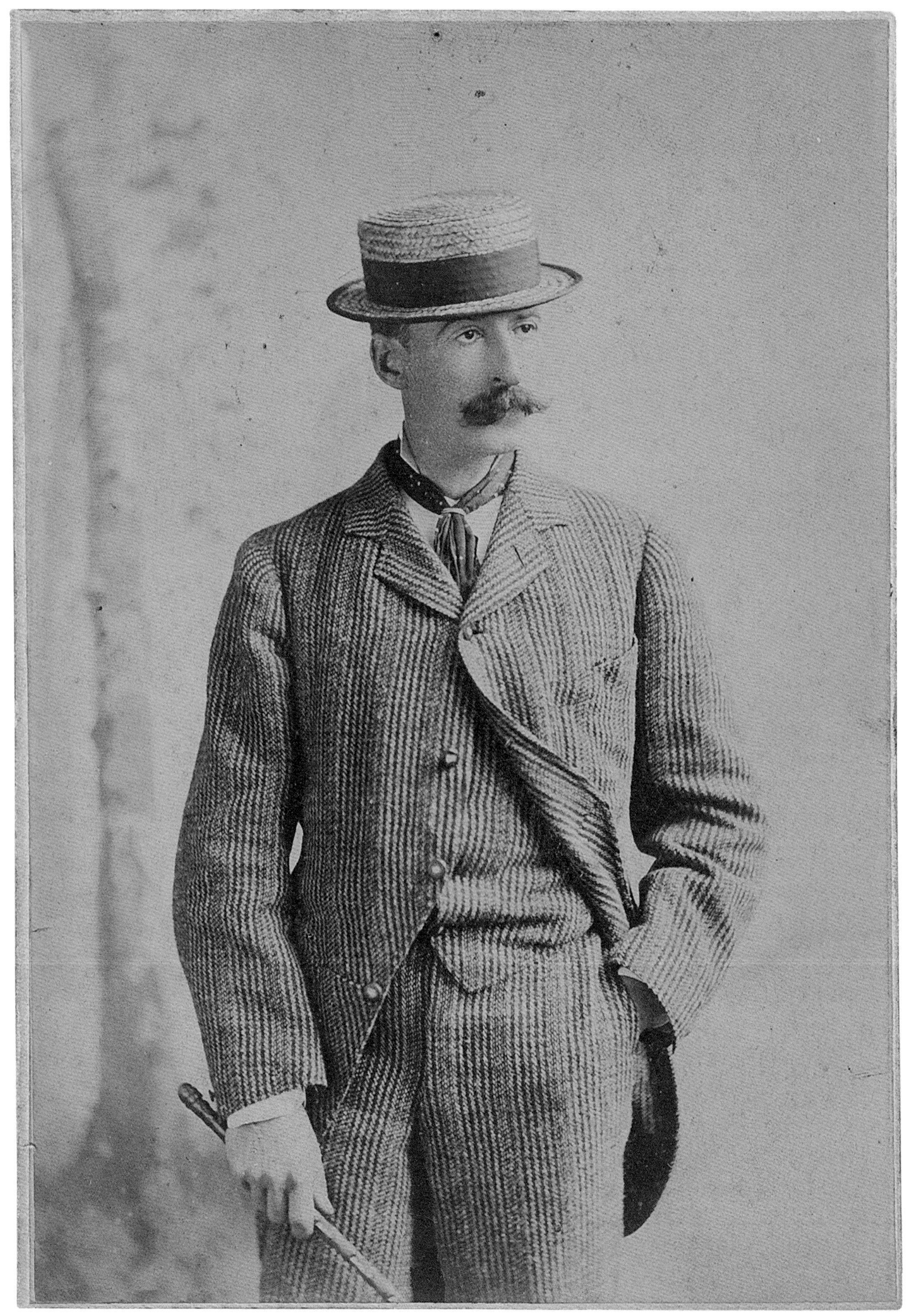

A Sketch of the Artist

Christine Riding

During his lifetime, Winslow Homer (1836–1910, fig. 1) was perceived by his fellow Americans as one of the most original and accomplished artists of his generation. After a meteoric rise in the 1860s, primarily via pictures focusing on the American Civil War, Homer would go on to establish himself as the great chronicler of contemporary life in the USA; his main rival in this regard was American realist Thomas Eakins (1844–1916). Consequently, a wealth of material and analysis has been generated about him. One oft-quoted comment from Homer, first relayed by painter Eugene Benson (1839–1908), stated that artists 'should never look at pictures', but should 'stutter in a language of their own'.[1] This has been taken as a declaration of artistic independence – on style, subject and focus – despite the clear historical influences and contemporary consanguinities in Homer's work. More recently, there has been an emphasis on reassessing his career objectives and legacy, as well as the artist's historiography, such activity being directed most intensively towards his iconic representation of a Black sailor adrift in a dangerous sea: *The Gulf Stream* (1899, fig. 84).

Perhaps in response to ever greater public scrutiny, Homer was notably protective about his private life and working practice, even refusing to divulge information to his first biographer, Boston art critic William Howe Downes (1854–1941). This reticence undoubtedly encouraged the reputation, still prevalent today, that he was a recluse in later life, intent on seeking out isolated places to immerse himself in sublime nature and elemental forces, thus epitomising the notion of the heroic male artist. Whether such mythic identities are wholly deserved or strikingly outmoded, Homer was responding to an era of profound change, challenge and conflict, and remains to this day a tremendously powerful and resonant artist within the canon of Western art.

Fig. 1 Winslow Homer in New York, 1880, albumen silver print by Napoleon Sarony (1821–1896), 14.9 × 10.8 cm. Bowdoin College Museum of Art, Brunswick, Maine. Gift of the Homer family

Starting Out

Homer was born in Boston, Massachusetts, on 24 February 1836. His father, Charles Savage Homer, a hardware merchant who gave up his business to seek his fortune in the gold rush when Winslow was just 13, and his mother, Henrietta Benson Homer, a talented amateur watercolourist, were from long-established New England families. Both encouraged their son's artistic talents, but undoubtedly Homer's mother had a greater influence on his early development and continually supported him until her death in 1884. When he was six years old, Homer and his family moved to the rural suburb of Cambridge, a place often credited with nurturing his lifelong passion for the outdoors. In 1855, he entered an apprenticeship at John H. Bufford and Co., a lithographic printing shop in Boston. There he learned on the job, designing travel cards and sheet music covers, and developing his visual skills.

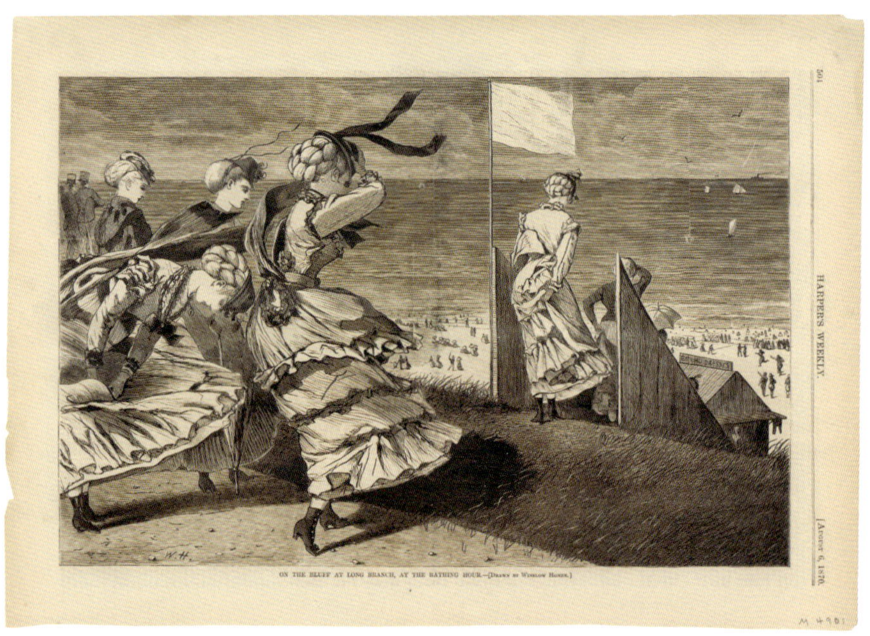

Fig. 2 *On the Bluff at Long Branch, at the Bathing Hour*, 6 August 1870, *Harper's Weekly*, vol. 14, wood engraving on newsprint, 22.4 × 34.7 cm. Sterling and Francine Clark Art Institute, Williamstown, Massachusetts (1955.4487)

The work was conventional and overtly commercial, but this period of Homer's life was to have a significant impact on the direction of his career, not least in being the point at which he decided to become a painter. Furthermore, his early designs of city and rural social scenes, mostly translated into marketable wood engravings, are characterised by defined outlines, simplified forms, dramatic contrasts of light and dark, and animated figure groupings – qualities that were to remain important to his art.

After finishing his apprenticeship in 1857, when he was about 21 years of age, Homer went on to become a leading freelance illustrator of periodicals, an activity he sustained for nearly 20 years. The work consisted of designing wood engravings primarily for two newly founded illustrated newspapers, *Ballou's Pictorial Drawing-Room Companion* in Boston and *Harper's Weekly* in New York, both of which targeted an emergent middle-class readership (fig. 2). In 1859 Homer settled in New York, then the artistic and publishing centre of the USA, opening a studio in the Tenth Street Studio Building, which was the first modern facility designed specifically for artists. Among the tenants were Frederic Edwin Church (1826–1900) and other Hudson River School painters. Homer also enrolled on art classes at the National Academy of Design between 1859 and 1864, drawing from life models, and, in 1860, began exhibiting his work. Such activities were supplemented in 1861 by a brief course of private instruction in basic oil-painting techniques, given by French artist Frédéric Rondel (1826–1892). Even so, like many of his artist contemporaries, Homer was primarily self-taught in oil and, later, watercolour.

War and Peace

Of all the challenges and tensions within the USA during Homer's early life, the most profound can be broadly characterised as that between the abolitionist North, loyal to the Union, and the slave-holding Southern states (the Confederacy), which threatened to secede. By April 1861, the American Civil War had begun. One outcome of the national crisis was the enormous public appetite for news, information and images, and Homer was well placed to respond to the growing demand. In October that year, he was sent to Washington, DC by *Harper's Weekly* as an artist-correspondent with the Union Army, reporting on the Washington encampments of General George B. McClellan and the Army of the Potomac, the principal Union Army in the eastern theatre of the war.[2] Homer returned there independently the following spring when McClellan embarked on a campaign to take Richmond, Virginia, spending five weeks travelling with the army. A further trip in 1864 probably involved visiting Virginia and witnessing the Battle of the Wilderness, the Battle of Spotsylvania Court House and the early days of the Siege of Petersburg. All of these experiences sharpened his observational abilities: detailing uniforms and equipment, soldiers in action and repose, and so on. Homer set to work on a series of war-related oil paintings based on his eyewitness sketches that marked a significant shift in his artistic ambitions and established his reputation (to quote a review of 1865 in the *New York Daily Tribune*) as 'the best chronicler of the war'.[3]

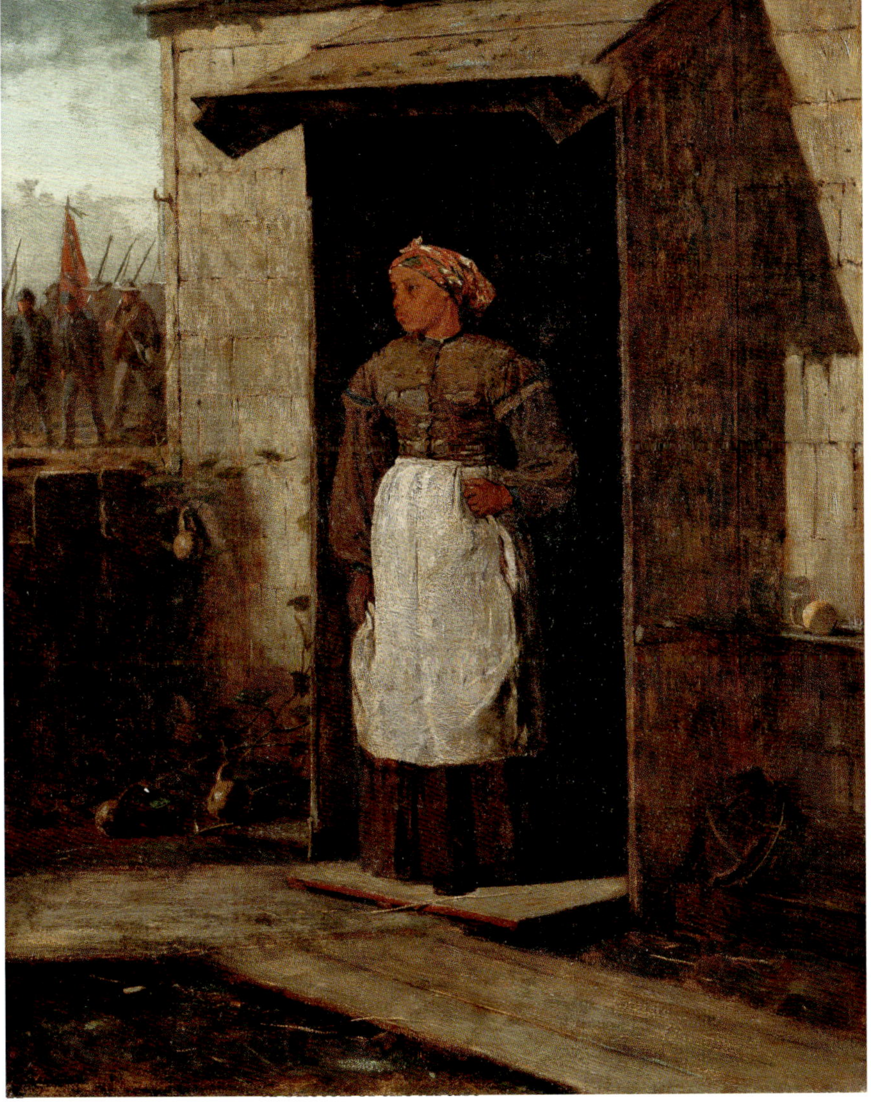

Homer's decision in 1863 to take up oil painting was in part a response to the inherited academic hierarchies that promoted the idea that serious painters worked in this medium, demonstrated by the fact that most highly regarded American artists of the mid-century, whether in landscape, figure, portrait or still-life genres, were oil painters. By working in this medium, therefore, Homer was elevating his Civil War subject matter, which often focused on the routine and mundane, covering camp life, military hospitals, trenches, women's wartime experiences and the home front. Importantly, the works represented the ordinary soldier on both sides, particularly those created just before and after hostilities ceased in 1865. Homer exhibited such subjects every year at the National Academy of Design from 1863 to 1866: for example, the now celebrated *Home, Sweet Home* (about 1863, National Gallery of Art, Washington, DC); his first large-scale painting of the Civil War, *Pitching Quoits* (1865, Fogg Art Museum, Cambridge, Massachusetts); *The Veteran in a New Field* (1865, fig. 26) and *Prisoners from the Front* (1866, fig. 27). Each painting signalled the artist's increasing awareness of the profound impact and legacy of the war, including the experience of Black Americans, whether soldiers, enslaved people or civilians. A prime example is *Near Andersonville* (fig. 3), which shows an enslaved woman watching as Union prisoners are marched to their incarceration by armed Confederate soldiers, the inference being that her emancipation was at that moment in grave doubt. The public attention and critical acclaim Homer

Fig. 3 *Near Andersonville*, 1865–6, oil on canvas, 58 × 45.7 cm. The Newark Museum of Art, New Jersey. Gift of Mrs Hannah Corbin Carter, Horace K. Corbin, Jr, Robert S. Corbin, William D. Corbin and Mrs Clementine Corbin Day in memory of their parents Hannah Stockton Corbin and Horace Kellogg Corbin, 1966 (66.354)

received at this time, occasionally accompanied by quick sales of his works, also demonstrated that his dual role as a commercial illustrator and a fine artist were compatible, even opportune. Indeed, his works in oil and watercolour were promoted as published illustrations, exemplified by one of his first oils, *Sharpshooter* (1863, fig. 24), which appeared as a wood engraving entitled *The Army of the Potomac—A Sharp-Shooter on Picket Duty, from a painting by W. Homer Esq.*

New Horizons

Now lauded as an exciting new talent, Homer was elected an Associate of the National Academy of Design in 1864, then a full Academician in 1865. Thus, by the end of the war, his career as a painter can be said to have fully launched. As a sign of his growing artistic confidence, and no doubt because two of his Civil War paintings – *The Bright Side* (1865, fig. 14) and *Prisoners from the Front* – were included in the 1867 Exposition Universelle in Paris, Homer set sail for Europe in December 1866. He stayed for some 10 months in the French capital and its environs, visiting the musée du Louvre and other museums and galleries, as well as artists' studios. He did not study formally in France, instead focusing on landscape painting while continuing to work for *Harper's Weekly*, producing scenes of everyday Parisian life. Of course, American artists had for some time embraced and reimagined European art, whether historical or contemporary, for the USA, and many considered a voyage to Europe as a rite of passage. Some of Homer's contemporaries, such as Frederic Edwin Church, the brothers Edward (1829–1901) and Thomas (1837–1926) Moran, who were born in England, and other painters of the Hudson River School, took their cue from Joseph Mallord William Turner (1775–1851) and the British landscape tradition, while others looked principally to France, inspired by the realism of Gustave Courbet (1819–1877) and his circle, and Jean-François Millet (1814–1875) and the Barbizon School, who were pioneers of the naturalist movement in landscape painting.[4]

Homer's stay in Paris coincided with fresh artistic developments – his interest in depicting natural light, for example, parallels that of the early impressionists – but they seem not to have had any significant influence on the character of his work, and he was already a practising plein-air painter in the USA. This was in direct contrast to American expatriates James Abbott McNeill Whistler (1834–1903) and John Singer Sargent (1856–1925), who were fully engaged with the French avant-garde and would also forge careers in London. Clearly, Homer shared the same subject interests as his Parisian counterparts and echoed their use of flat, simple forms, shaped in France by an appreciation of Japanese design. On balance, Homer's own highly individual style was arguably closer in spirit to Edouard Manet (1832–1883) than to Claude Monet (1840–1926). Homer could have seen examples of Manet's paintings, such as the notorious *Le Déjeuner sur l'herbe* (1863, musée d'Orsay) and the 1864 American Civil War subject *The Battle of the USS 'Kearsarge' and the CSS 'Alabama'* (fig. 16), at the French artist's private pavilion erected near to the Exposition Universelle.[5] However, the main subject of Homer's paintings while in France was rural life, perhaps showing a natural affinity with Millet, whose influential paintings of rural labourers, *The Gleaners* (fig. 4) and *The Angelus* (1857–9), now in the musée d'Orsay, were also on display at the Exposition Universelle. Although any direct influence by Millet would quickly fade, there is no doubt that the quiet dignity and stature that he instilled in his figures would remain with Homer for the rest of his career.

After returning to the USA in October 1867, Homer continued to develop his images of contemporary American life, particularly scenes of childhood and young women at leisure, notably at Long Beach, New Jersey. His uncle's mansion in Belmont, Massachusetts, was the inspiration for a number of his earlier illustrations, and, later on, his paintings, including several of his 1860s croquet pictures (fig. 15). The game, a recent English import, was immediately popular, providing women with a rare socially acceptable opportunity to compete in an outdoor sport on an equal footing with men. Homer's rural scenes of farm and factory life, of children playing and at school, and young adults courting included *The Country School* (Saint Louis Art Museum) and *Old Mill (The Morning Bell)* (Yale University Art Gallery), both from 1871. His popular *Snap the Whip* (fig. 28), painted the following year, was exhibited at the 1876 Centennial Exhibition in Philadelphia, Pennsylvania, alongside his now celebrated marine painting *Breezing Up (A Fair Wind)* (1873–6, fig. 32), which came out of a summer trip Homer had made to the seaport of Gloucester, Massachusetts, in 1873. It shows an adult with three boys, one of whom is holding the tiller, collectively steadying the boat as it lists against the wind. The *New York Tribune* wrote, 'There is no picture in this exhibition, nor can we remember when there has been a picture in any exhibition, that can be named alongside this.'[6] One reason for this effusive response is unquestionably the inherent national symbolism of the painting, exhibited 100 years after the Declaration of Independence of 1776.

Fig. 4 Jean-François Millet (1814–1875), *The Gleaners*, 1857, oil on canvas, 83.5 × 110 cm. Musée d'Orsay, Paris

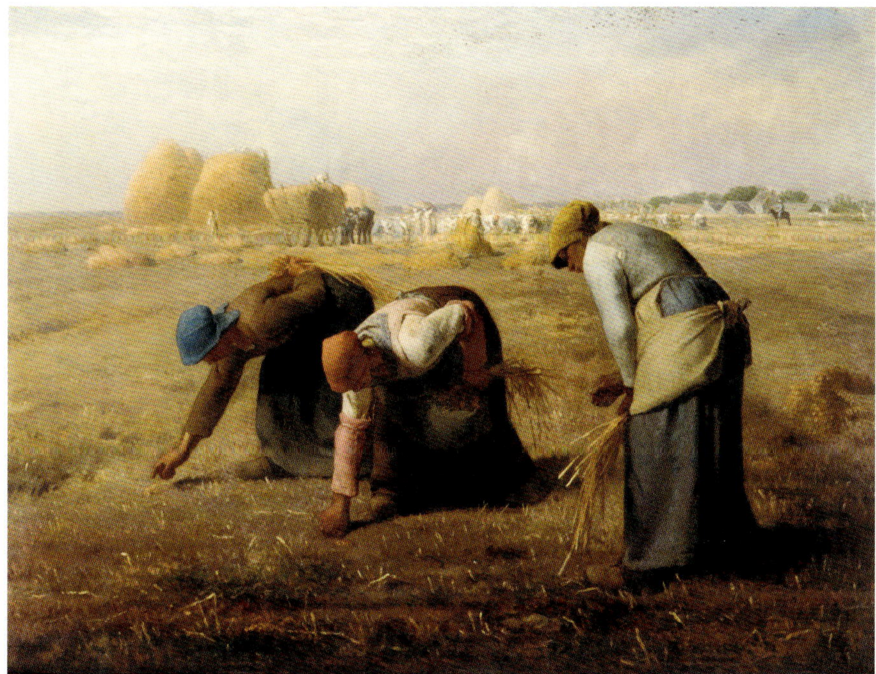

While such imagery chimed with the wave of commemorations and nostalgia for a more innocent time that swept American society after the Civil War, it equally resonated with the collective concern felt towards the next generation after so many young men had been killed and injured. Homer's straightforward, unaffected sensibility towards his subject matter is equally evident in the paintings he created after probably two visits to Virginia in 1876 and 1877, which focus on the post-war lives of formerly enslaved people and include *The Cotton Pickers* (1876, fig. 34) and *Dressing for the Carnival* (1877, fig. 36). The silent tension between two communities, both struggling to understand their present and their future, is dramatically evoked in Homer's painting *A Visit from the Old Mistress* of 1876 (fig. 35), which shows an encounter between a group of four freed slaves and their former mistress. It has been noted that the composition mirrors that of *Prisoners from the Front* (1866, fig. 27) and that the formal similarity between the standing figures implies the sense of balance the nation hoped to achieve in the challenging years of the Reconstruction (1865–77, see p. 37).

The late 1860s and the 1870s were a time of tremendous artistic experimentation and prolific and varied output for Homer. In addition to expanding his skill in oils, he began to create watercolours on a regular basis from 1873, itself a reflection of more recent developments in American art. Up until the mid-1860s, watercolour had been the most popular and broadly accessible medium in the USA. Its widespread use, however, had led many in urban art circles to dismiss it

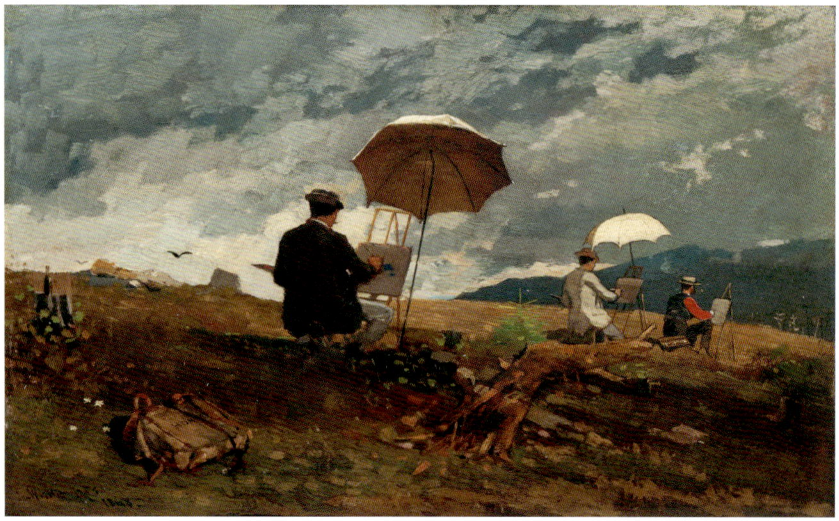

Fig. 5 *Artists Sketching in the White Mountains*, 1868, oil on panel, 24 × 40.2 cm. Portland Museum of Art, Maine. Bequest of Charles Shipman Payson (1988.55.4)

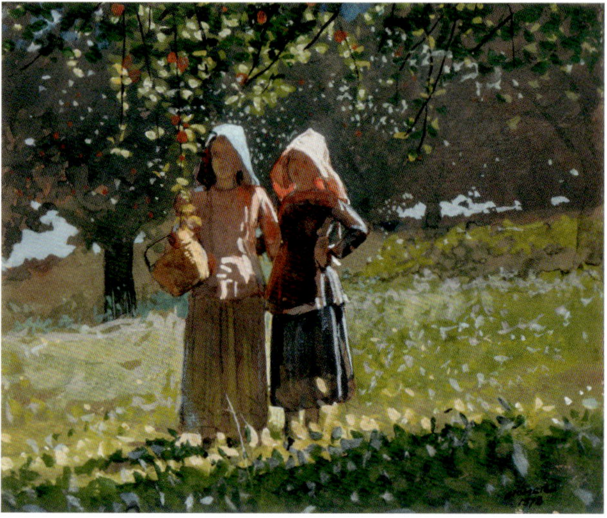

Fig. 6 *Apple Picking*, 1878, watercolour and gouache on paper, laid down on board, 17.8 × 21.3 cm. Terra Foundation for American Art, Chicago, Illinois. Daniel J. Terra Collection (1992.7)

as a 'ladies' medium', or demeaned by its association with amateurs and commercial illustrators and designers.[7] This perception changed rapidly, not least with the founding of the American Watercolor Society in 1866 and the staging of its first public exhibition in New York the following year. By the 1880s, the most adventurous American artists, Homer included, were watercolourists. In stark contrast, the medium was long established in Europe and especially in the UK, where generations of professional watercolourists, numerous watercolour societies and dedicated exhibitions, and a sophisticated collectors' market, had flourished since the early nineteenth century. Tellingly, many watercolour practitioners in the USA were British born, had British heritage or an affinity with the culture, like Homer, who was from Boston's predominantly English community.

Watercolour was the ideal medium for Homer to explore effects of light and atmosphere and expressive handling, and from the beginning his technique was fluid, assured and varied in style. In the years that followed, he would expand the perceived limitations of the medium in increasingly bold and colourful paintings, becoming an acknowledged master and innovator. Homer's watercolours were based on material and ideas he gathered on his regular working vacations, beginning with a summer stay in Gloucester, Massachusetts, in 1873, an example of which is *A Basket of Clams* (fig. 31), followed by visits to other popular seaside resorts in Massachusetts and New Jersey, and vacations spent hunting and fishing in the Adirondacks in rural New York and the White Mountains of New Hampshire (fig. 5). His growing confidence in the medium was such that by 1875 he had given up working as a freelance illustrator, determined to make a living solely from his output in oil and watercolour. At the same time, Homer seems to have been less driven by narrative, focusing instead on aesthetic concerns of light, air and vibrant colour. He spent the summers of 1878 and 1879 at a farm near West Point in New York that was owned by Lawson Valentine, a varnish manufacturer and one of Homer's most important patrons. Among the works created there were numerous watercolours and sketches of young people and children in open-air settings, such as *Apple Picking* (fig. 6). At this point, Homer's watercolours (as was already the case with his oil paintings) were being recognised for their stylistic independence; as one commentator noted, he has 'a style all his own, and with a vigour and individual accent that puts him away from other artists in a quite separate department'.[8]

It is at this point in Homer's career, from the late 1870s, that press reports began to appear remarking on his increasingly reclusive behaviour and speculating as to the causes, whether personal or professional. In the summer of 1880, he returned to Gloucester, this time staying not in the town but in a lighthouse in the harbour of Ten Pound Island. The proximity to the ocean appealed to Homer, who was from a seafaring heritage, and his close engagement with the dynamics of sea and sky, and the challenging lives of fishing communities, would provide a rich source of themes and inspiration. However, it has also been suggested that Homer was wearying of representing scenes of leisure, especially those showing fashionable middle-class women at the seaside, and so settled on pursuing a new direction in his art. The initial encouragement for him to travel abroad, this time to the UK, may have come from his 1876 painting *The Cotton Pickers* (fig. 34), featuring two Black female fieldworkers carrying harvested cotton. It was Homer's first work to be exhibited in the country, at the Royal Academy, London, in 1878, and was submitted by the original owner, known only as an English cotton merchant. Other incentives may have been closer to home, particularly given the renewed critical interest in and identification with British art in the USA, and the widespread recognition that the British excelled not only in the watercolour medium but also, as a maritime nation, in the art of the sea.[9] Inevitably Turner loomed large in these discussions, not least because his influence had already been felt in landscape art in the USA since the 1820s, and was given fresh impetus mid-century through the published writings of influential art critic and stalwart Turner champion John Ruskin (1819–1900). Furthermore, examples of Turner's work were crossing the Atlantic, including *Slave Ship* of 1840 (fig. 17), which Homer saw in New York after it was acquired from Ruskin in 1872 by wealthy American collector John Taylor Johnston (1820–1893), who owned Homer's *Prisoners from the Front*.[10]

Whatever the reason, in March 1881, Homer set sail for England on his second and final trip to Europe. The British Museum is the only art venue Homer is known to have visited in London, where he looked at old master drawings, notably those from the Italian Renaissance, as well as Greek and Roman sculpture (see p. 57). Given this unique opportunity, he would surely have visited other museums and public and private art galleries, including the National Gallery, already much admired for its Renaissance paintings, such as *The Baptism of Christ* (after 1437; acquired in 1861) by Piero della Francesca (about 1415/20–1492), which may have assisted in transforming Homer's figuration.[11] Of equal importance, given the direction Homer's art would take, the National Gallery was at this time the primary venue for displays from the Turner Bequest of 1856, which was particularly rich in seascapes and coastal scenes in oil and watercolour.[12] The presence of *The Fighting Temeraire* of 1839 (fig. 7) and *Snow Storm – Steam-*

Fig. 7 Joseph Mallord William Turner (1775–1851), *The Fighting Temeraire tugged to her last berth to be broken up, 1838*, 1839, oil on canvas, 90.7 × 121.6 cm. National Gallery, London (NG524). Turner Bequest, 1856

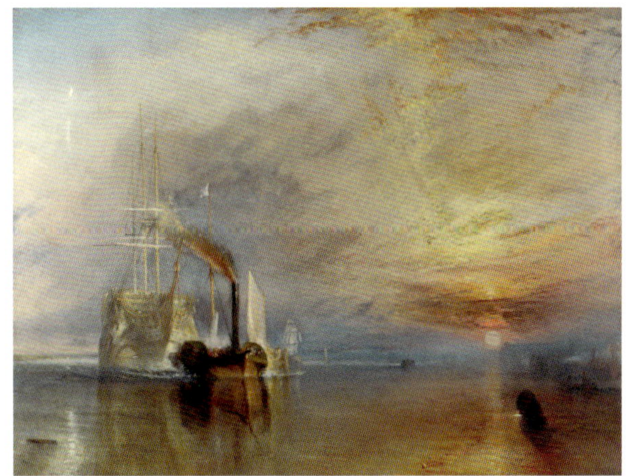

Boat off a Harbour's Mouth of 1842 (Tate) alone demonstrated how Turner's example could accommodate a variety of artistic concerns and traditions using thoroughly contemporary subject matter, as well as act as an exemplar for a distinct and powerful artistic identity forged through first-hand observation of the sea and maritime activity.[13]

After staying in London for a short time, Homer travelled north and settled in Cullercoats, a coastal village near Tynemouth on the North Sea. He remained there from the spring of 1881 to November 1882, a period of intense artistic activity that contrasted with Homer's previous sojourn abroad, and during which time he became ever more sensitive towards and admiring of the strenuous and courageous lives of the village's inhabitants. This was particularly true of the women (fig. 8), whom artist Robert Jobling (1841–1923) described as 'the working bees' and 'Stout hardy creatures'.[14] Much of the material he created in Cullercoats and Tynemouth, mainly sketches and watercolours, thus focuses on the working men and women, imbued with a grandeur that was new to Homer's art, alongside a more constrained and sober palette that contrasted with the spontaneity and brilliance of his American subjects of the 1860s and 1870s. Moreover, the oil paintings, whether started in England or after his return to the USA, were perceptively larger and more ambitious, just as his robust fisherwomen bore little resemblance to the stylish females of his earlier works.

Fig. 8 *Perils of the Sea*, 1881, watercolour and graphite on wove paper, 37.1 × 53.2 cm. Sterling and Francine Clark Art Institute, Williamstown, Massachusetts (1955.774)

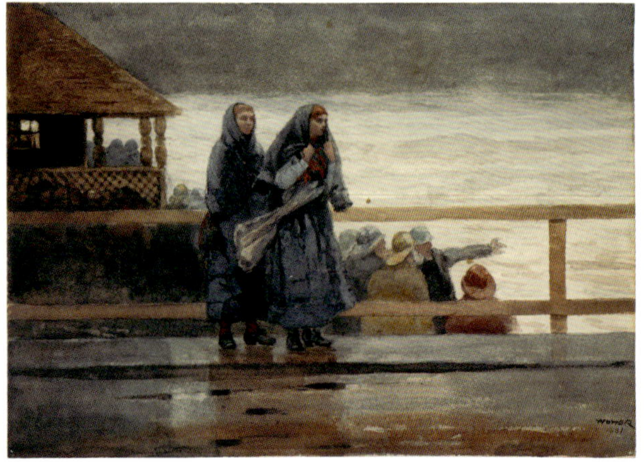

Coming Home

When Homer returned to New York in November 1882, both he and his art were greatly changed. Last seen at the American Water Color Society in 1881 showing startlingly bold, impressionistic marine imagery, in January 1883 he presented large, finished compositions.[15] The new monumentality and seriousness of these English subjects, alongside the forceful, sculptural modelling of Homer's figures, is exemplified in *Inside the Bar* (1883, fig. 45), which centres on a lone woman striding into the wind, with dramatic contrasts of light and dark, and broad washing and lifting to create fast-moving storm clouds. One reviewer in *The Art Amateur* journal described the work as a 'masterpiece', noting how 'the grand gravity of the picture shows how easily at need water-color art can rise out of the reproach of frivolity'.[16]

Perhaps buoyed by such public endorsement, in the summer of 1883, Homer made his first extended stay at Prouts Neck, Maine, a peninsula 10 miles south of Portland. There he lived on his family's estate in the remodelled carriage house only 20 metres from the sea. He had acquired his first cameras while in England and continued to make and collect photographs as part of a wider artistic exploration. In *The Artist's Studio in an Afternoon Fog* (fig. 9), for example, he employed elements from photographic views of his studio, such as the crop, the blur of the background and the flatness of the composition. During that same summer, Homer visited Atlantic City, New Jersey, to observe the shipwreck rescue

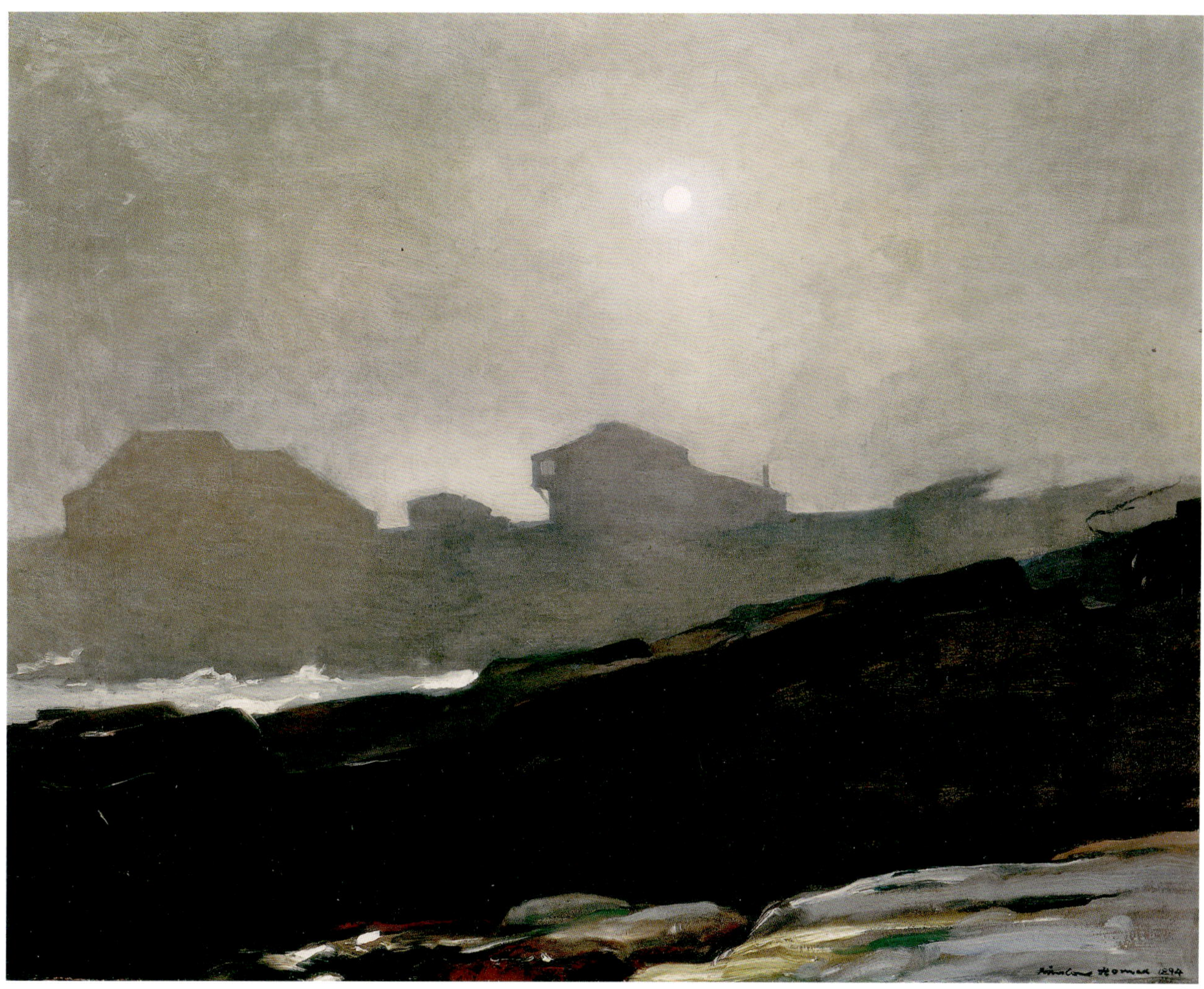

Fig. 9 *The Artist's Studio in an Afternoon Fog*, 1894, oil on canvas, 61 × 76.8 cm. Memorial Art Gallery of the University of Rochester. Gift of Marie C. and Joseph C. Wilson. R. T. Miller Fund (1941.32)

teams operating there. Two major oil paintings were the result. The first to be completed was *The Life Line* (1884, fig. 51), which, when shown in the National Academy of Design exhibition of 1884, effectively reversed the previous year's negative reaction to Homer's *The Coming Away of the Gale* (see p. 58).[17] Its purchase by influential collector Catharine Lorillard Wolfe (1828–1887) for the substantial sum of $2,500 during the exhibition preview made headlines. The second painting was *Undertow* (1886, fig. 55), depicting the dramatic rescue of two female bathers by two male lifeguards, also a notable success when it was shown at the Academy in 1887 (see p. 68). Since late 1883, Homer had made his home in Prouts Neck, where he could devote himself to the dominant theme of his late career: the struggle of human beings against nature. In 1885 alone, he produced a series of paintings on this universal subject: *The Herring Net* (fig. 49), *The Fog Warning* (fig. 52) and *Lost on the Grand Banks* (fig. 50), all inspired by the daily toil and vulnerability of North Atlantic fishermen. Contrary to his reputation as a recluse, Homer would continue to visit New York and Boston regularly, as well as Florida, the Caribbean and Bermuda (see pp. 82–6), with summer and autumn hunting trips to the Adirondacks and Canada, which were the sources of a remarkable series of watercolours (fig. 10). In these, he replaced the muted greys, blues and greens representing the storm-tossed sea of Prouts Neck with a more radiant palette, further expanding his technique and subject matter. By 1890, he had built a strong base of critical opinion and patronage that recognised his watercolours were as much an integral part of his artistic achievement as his oil paintings.

After focusing on the heroic and often fatal encounters between humans and the elements, Homer began to reduce and then remove figures from his seascapes in the late 1880s. By dedicating whole canvases to evoking the physical properties of sea, sky and coastline, he made nature itself the chief protagonist of his art (see pp. 110–21). In their dynamic compositions and richly textured passages, his late seascapes, such as *Sunlight on the Coast* (1890, fig. 88) and *West Point, Prout's Neck* (fig. 11), capture, in the most visceral way, the dynamics of water crashing and receding. For Homer's contemporaries, such paintings were the most effusively admired of all his work, appreciated for their virtuoso brushwork and emotional intensity. Even those major paintings from this period that centre on people and living creatures, such as *Hound and Hunter* (1892, fig. 57) and *Right and Left* (1909, fig. 59), seem to concentrate on their struggle in the face of overwhelming forces (see pp. 69–70). Indeed, the Darwinian battle for survival is the central theme of Homer's *Fox Hunt* of 1893 (fig. 58), his largest painting, which depicts a flock of starving crows descending on a fox slowed by deep snow (see p. 70). It was immediately purchased by the Pennsylvania Academy of the Fine Arts, his first painting to enter a major American museum collection.

Fig. 10 *Hudson River, Logging*, 1891–2, watercolour over graphite on wove paper, 35.6 × 52.4 cm. National Gallery of Art, Washington, DC. Corcoran Collection (Museum Purchase) (2014.136.171)

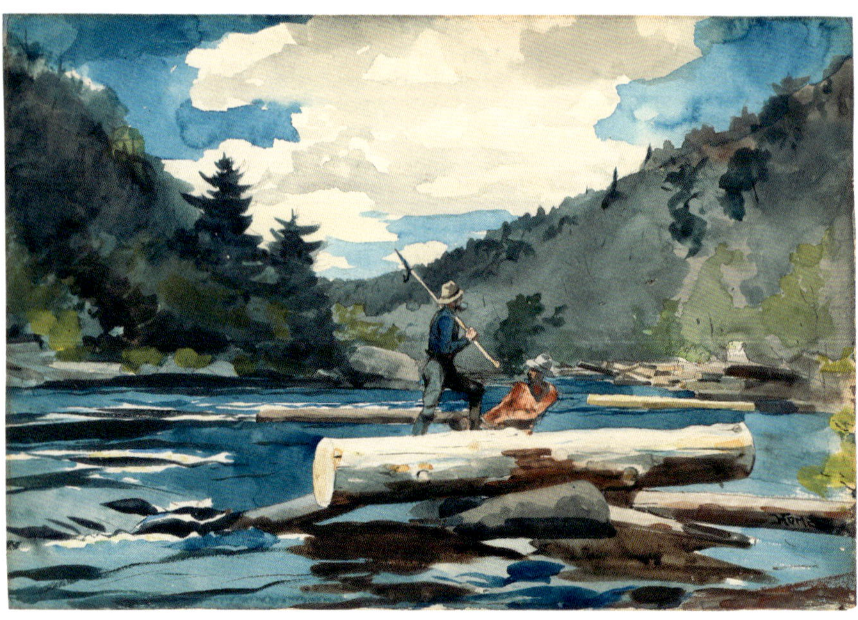

One of his last, and now celebrated, paintings on the theme of 'the figure and the sea' is *The Gulf Stream* of 1899 (reworked by 1906, fig. 84). This extraordinary work of art, showing a Black sailor drifting in a damaged boat surrounded by sharks and an impending storm, represents nature at its most voracious and destructive, while also acting as a commentary on the historical associations between the sea and the transatlantic slave trade (see pp. 102–4).[18] Some measure of its perceived importance can be gleaned from its inclusion in the Academy's winter exhibition of 1906, when the jury took the extraordinary step of writing to the Metropolitan Museum of Art before the exhibition opened, advising them to acquire the painting.

Homer's death on 29 September 1910, when he was arguably the most celebrated artist in the USA, inspired memorial exhibitions and the further purchase of his works for public collections in New York, Boston and Washington. Indeed, the enthusiasm shown by American institutions and

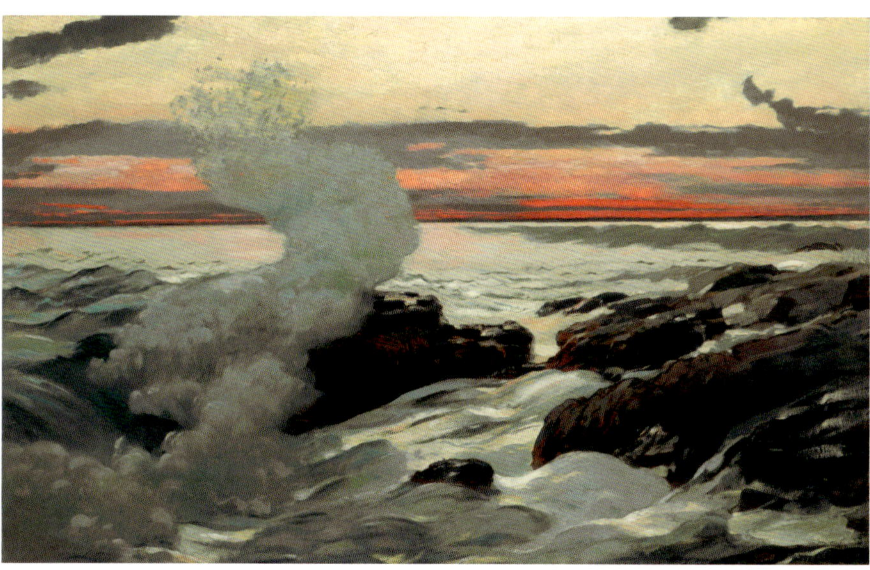

Fig. 11 *West Point, Prout's Neck*, 1900, oil on canvas, 76.4 × 122.2 cm. Sterling and Francine Clark Art Institute, Williamstown, Massachusetts (1955.7)

collectors for obtaining his oil and watercolour paintings has meant that today very few are held outside the country. And if any further evidence were needed of Homer's status in American art and culture, his studio in Prouts Neck, Maine (fig. 85), declared a National Historic Landmark in the 1960s, was acquired in 2006 by Portland Museum of Art. Interestingly, the artist remains relatively little known in the UK, this despite his extended stay in England in the early 1880s, itself the focus of a recent exhibition, *Coming Away: Winslow Homer & England* (2017–18), staged at US venues only. In the exhibition catalogue for *Winslow Homer: Poet of the Sea*, held at the Dulwich Picture Gallery, London, in 2006, Ian Dejardin and Elizabeth Glassman opined that the lack of awareness in Europe of 'such a beloved icon of American art ... seems astonishing, almost perverse'.[19] The present exhibition at the National Gallery, in partnership with the Metropolitan Museum of Art, aims to redress this imbalance still further, applying current scholarship and new perspectives, to bring to light the extraordinary beauty, power and subtlety of the art of Winslow Homer.

1 Benson 1865.
2 Wood 2010, p. 18.
3 *New York Daily Tribune*, 3 July 1865, p. 6. See Giese 1990, pp. 15–32.
4 Named after the village of Barbizon in the Forest of Fontainebleau, France, the Barbizon School was a group of artists focusing on landscape painting, paving the way to realism.
5 On Homer's first European trip, see C. Riopelle, '"These Works Are Real": Winslow Homer and Europe', in New York 2022, pp. 84–92.
6 'Fine Arts, National Academy of Design—Fifty-first Annual Exhibition', *New York Tribune*, 1 April 1876, quoted in Kelly et al. 1996, p. 314.
7 See New York 1998.
8 See Foster 2017, p. 210.
9 See C. Riding and R. Johns, *Turner & the Sea*, London 2013, pp. 11–23.
10 Homer's signature appears in John Taylor Johnston's guest book on 11 April 1872. See S.L. Herdrich, 'Crosscurrents: Conflict, Nature, and Mortality in Winslow Homer's Art', in New York 2022, p. 141.
11 See Worcester and Milwaukee 2017–18, pp. 21–4.
12 The opening of an extension to the Trafalgar Square building in 1876, known as the Barry Rooms (Rooms 32–38 and 40), enabled the National Gallery to reunite the entire bequest in one place.
13 See Riding and Johns 2013, pp. 241–5.
14 A. Watson, 'After the Herring', *Magazine of Art*, 1882, quoted in Sunderland 1988, p. 25.
15 *Illustrated Catalogue: Sixteenth Annual Exhibition of the American Water Color Society, Held at the Galleries of the National Academy of Design*, New York, 1883. On this occasion, Homer's Cullercoats watercolours were highly praised by the press.
16 Strahan 1883, p. 81.
17 See, for example, *The New York Herald*, 7 April 1884, quoted in Philadelphia 2012, p. 112.
18 London and Giverny 2006, pp. 22–3. See also M. Rediker, *The Slave Ship: A Human History*, London 2007, pp. 37–40.
19 London and Giverny 2006, n. p. [p. 10].

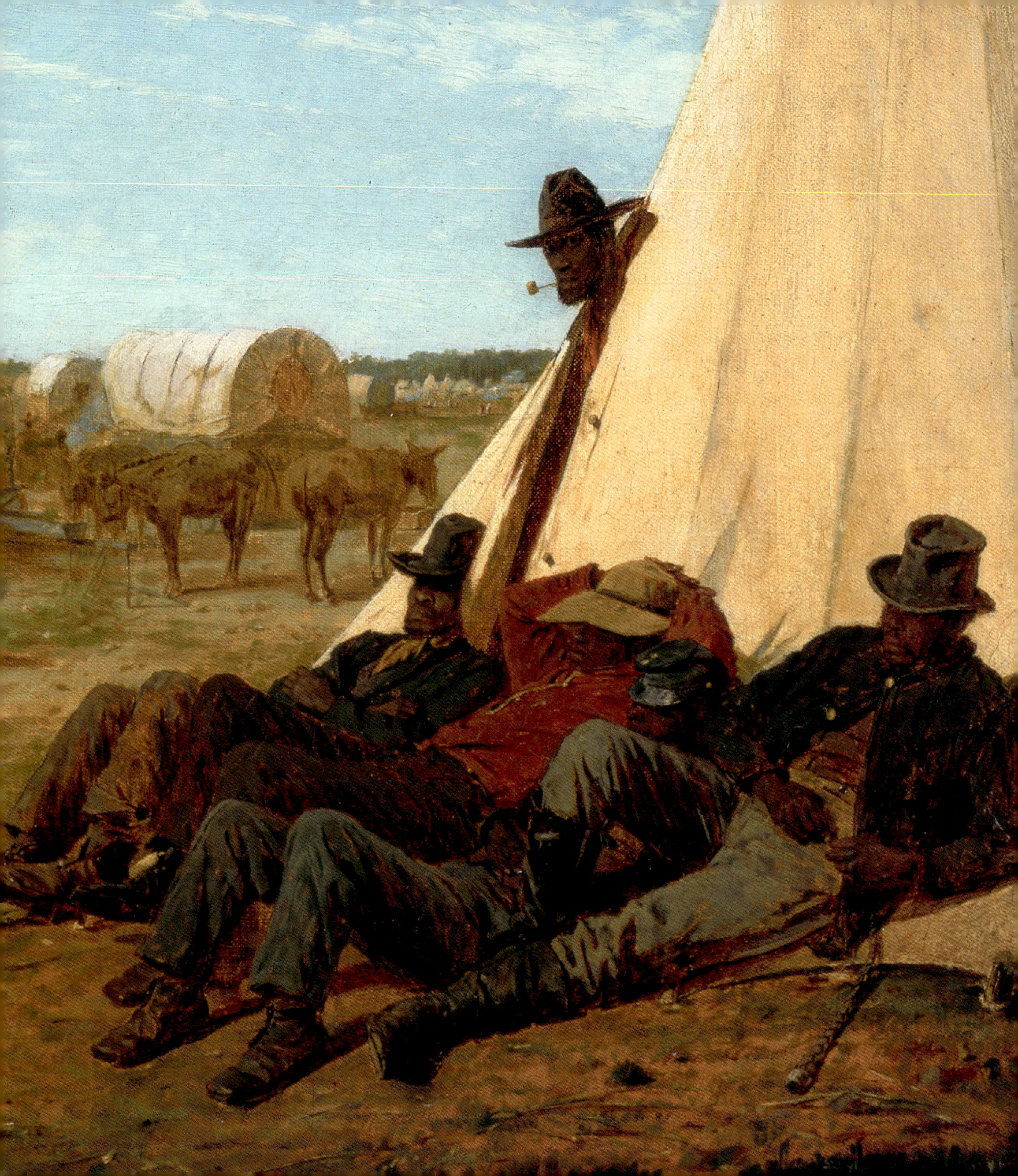

A Master Theme in Homer's Art: Conflict

Christopher Riopelle

The Atlantic world was in turmoil during the second half of the nineteenth century. Simmering tensions regularly erupted in conflict. On one side of the ocean, three long-standing empires – Britain, France and Spain – jostled for control over vast areas of Africa, Asia and the Americas. Everywhere, colonial subjects increasingly resisted European hegemony. In June 1867, France's brazen efforts to impose a puppet emperor on Mexico – the Austrian Archduke Maximilian – were overthrown by local Republican forces, the bumbling impostor executed by firing squad (fig. 12). That same year, exactly 260 since the founding of the Jamestown colony in 1607,[1] Britain largely ceded control over North American territory with the establishment of the Dominion of Canada – relatively peacefully, although Indigenous peoples do not concur. Earlier tossed from South America by national liberators like Simón Bolívar (1783–1830), Spain was losing its grasp in the Caribbean too.

To the west, between 1861 and 1865 a new young imperial power, the USA, fought a bloody civil war to abolish slavery and re-establish internal unity. At the same time, it expanded inexorably westward, assembling awesome industrial might and flexing military muscle. Slavery lingered in Brazil and Cuba until the late 1880s. The Cuban War of Independence (the last of three liberation wars) against Spain began in 1895, leading to American intervention in 1898. Separately and somewhat later in 1898, the USA went to war against Spain in the Philippines; the USA won both conflicts, eclipsing Spanish imperial power. Indigenous peoples, formerly enslaved members of the African diaspora, waves of immigrants to the New World, women: all became increasingly active in forging their own destinies in the ever more globalised world order then taking shape.

Winslow Homer was a witness to these tumultuous events. Born in Boston, he travelled the length of the East Coast observing America in peace and at war. On two occasions he visited and painted in Europe, experiencing the influence and antipathy circulating like the Gulf Stream and its associated currents back and forth across the Atlantic. He explored the tropics and Cuba, paying particular attention to the lives of Black men and women, as he had done earlier in the USA. He depicted fishermen, hunters and farmers extracting livelihoods from America's teeming abundance. He saw how nature itself, sometimes violent, at other times benign, seemed to provide its own commentary on the rhythms of life and death. He observed with awe, finally, how ordinary people responded to trying circumstances in war and peace with innate resolve and everyday heroism. His art absorbed numerous influences, ancient and modern, American and foreign, but was never derivative. He was endlessly alert to wider currents – social, political and aesthetic. His unflinching analysis of conflict in all its manifestations was a vital constant of his artistic vision, and a guarantor of his growing popularity.

Opposite Detail of fig. 14

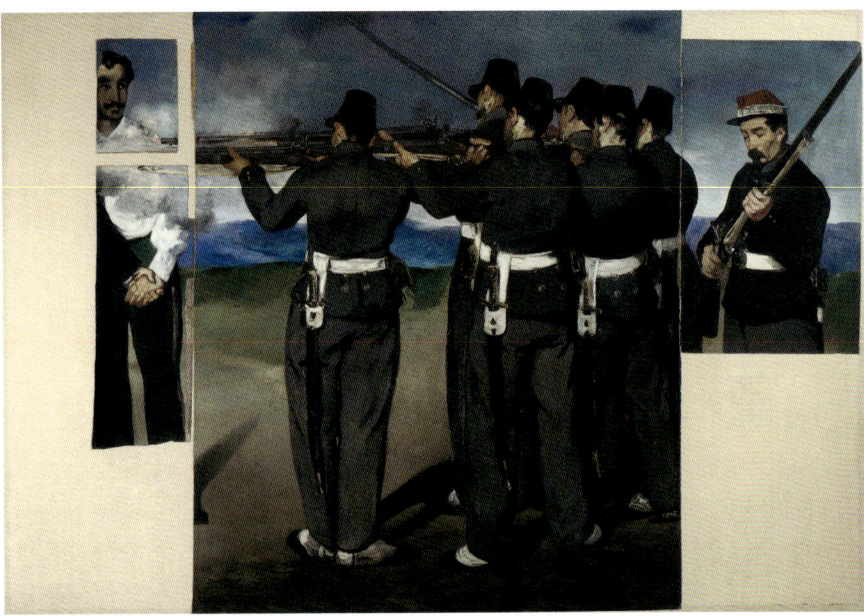

Fig. 12 Edouard Manet (1832–1883), *The Execution of Maximilian*, about 1867–8, oil on canvas, 193 × 284 cm. National Gallery, London (NG3294)

From Fields of War to the Champ de Mars

Homer's vision had been forged in the crucible of the American Civil War. Sketching scenes of conflict for publication in the popular press, he came to understand the raw, visceral power of reportage. He captured highly resonant moments in which the vast conflict was epitomised by one or a few representative figures, learning in the heat of battle to edit down to the pith of a motif. The skill stayed with him when he turned to painting; he would always remain what French poet and critic Charles Baudelaire (1821–1867) extolled as a 'painter of modern life'.[2] A Union (Northern) sharpshooter picks off enemies from high in a tree (1863, fig. 24). A vainglorious Confederate (Southern) soldier, perhaps knowing the cause has been lost, climbs a hillock in *Defiance: Inviting a Shot before Petersburg* to dare just such a sharpshooter to take him out (1864, fig. 25). Here, too, Homer taught himself to move seamlessly from anecdote to symbol. In an image as powerfully concise as any agrarian allegory by Jean-François Millet, *The Veteran in a New Field* shows a Union soldier, returned from war, at last free to harvest grain from his own sun-dappled land (1865, fig. 26).

The moment of Homer's decisive intersection with wider geopolitical and geocultural currents came some 18 months after the end of the Civil War, in Paris. In 1866, a select group of critics and collectors, primarily prominent New Yorkers, was choosing works by American artists to be shown at the Exposition Universelle in the French capital the following year. It would be the largest display of American art yet seen in Europe and they selected two Homer paintings. At the time, the USA was at a crossroads. The Civil War had ended in Union victory on 9 April 1865. The emancipation of enslaved peoples in the South, proclaimed by President Abraham Lincoln on 1 January 1863, could now be enacted. Lincoln himself did not live to see it; shot by assassin John Wilkes Booth on Good Friday 14 April 1865, he died the following day. Henceforth, however, the USA would assume a newly prominent role on the international stage. Even the gentlemen choosing art for the Exposition knew that they played their own small part in shaping the face America now turned to the world.[3]

Frankly, art was the tip of the American iceberg in 1867 Paris. Rather, the USA staked its claim to new-found confidence and consequence primarily on industry and transport. Thomas Eakins and Homer would become in the following decades the leading American realist painters of their day. Yet Eakins, a student in Paris in 1867 and an indefatigable letter writer to his Philadelphia family, never mentioned the paintings at the Exposition, instead waxing lyrical about 'the [American] Locomotive the Press speaks about … I can't tell you how mean the best English, French and Belgian ones are alongside of it.' Perhaps for the first but not last time, America also displayed its genius for popular entertainment. Just as impressive to Eakins was the American soda water fountain. '[Its] fame has spread.... The soda water man is said to have already made a fortune.'[4] Meanwhile, pianist and composer 'Blind Tom' Wiggins (1849–1908), born on a Georgia plantation, thrilled critics as 'the Black Liszt'.[5]

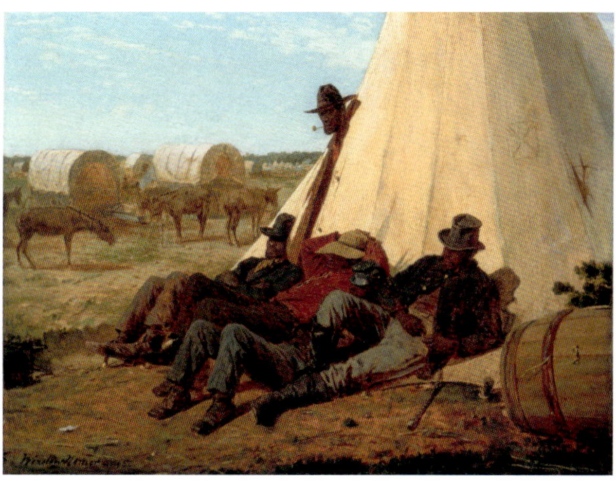

Nonetheless, Paris was the undisputed world capital of the fine arts and the American examples shown there – in the same vast building on the Champ de Mars as the mighty locomotive; some 11 million visitors passed through its doors during the six-month fair – were meant to argue for an American cultural sophistication commensurate with its industrial heft. Paintings depicting its distinctive landscapes took pride of place; Frederic Edwin Church's monumental *Niagara* of 1857 (fig. 13) won a silver medal. Several of the 82 canvases, however, including both Homers, pointedly showed scenes from the recent Civil War. Others presented benign images of post-war African American life. That the Union had won the conflict and now pursued a new course – and implicit in it that Emperor Napoleon III's France, seeking to re-establish influence in the Americas through its Mexican misadventure, had erred in tacitly supporting the losing side – was made abundantly clear.

Homer's two paintings neatly sustained the larger argument. *The Bright Side* of 1865 (fig. 14) shows three Black

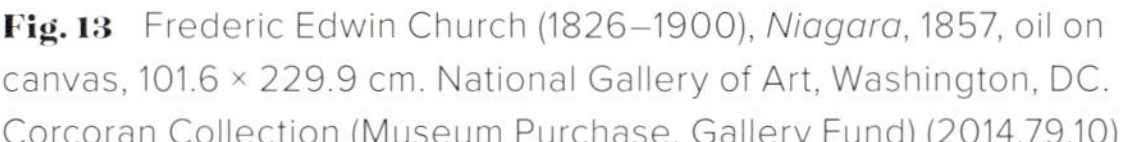

Fig. 13 Frederic Edwin Church (1826–1900), *Niagara*, 1857, oil on canvas, 101.6 × 229.9 cm. National Gallery of Art, Washington, DC. Corcoran Collection (Museum Purchase, Gallery Fund) (2014.79.10)

Fig. 14 *The Bright Side*, 1865, oil on canvas, 32.4 × 43.2 cm. Fine Arts Museums of San Francisco. Gift of Mr and Mrs John D. Rockefeller 3rd (1979.7.56)

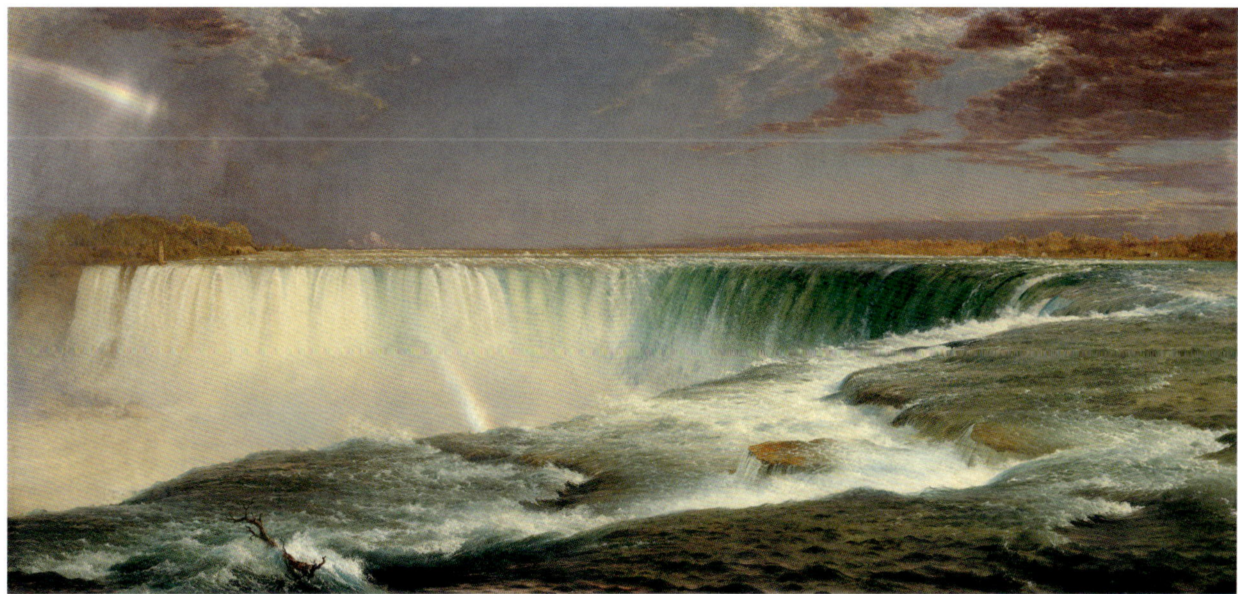

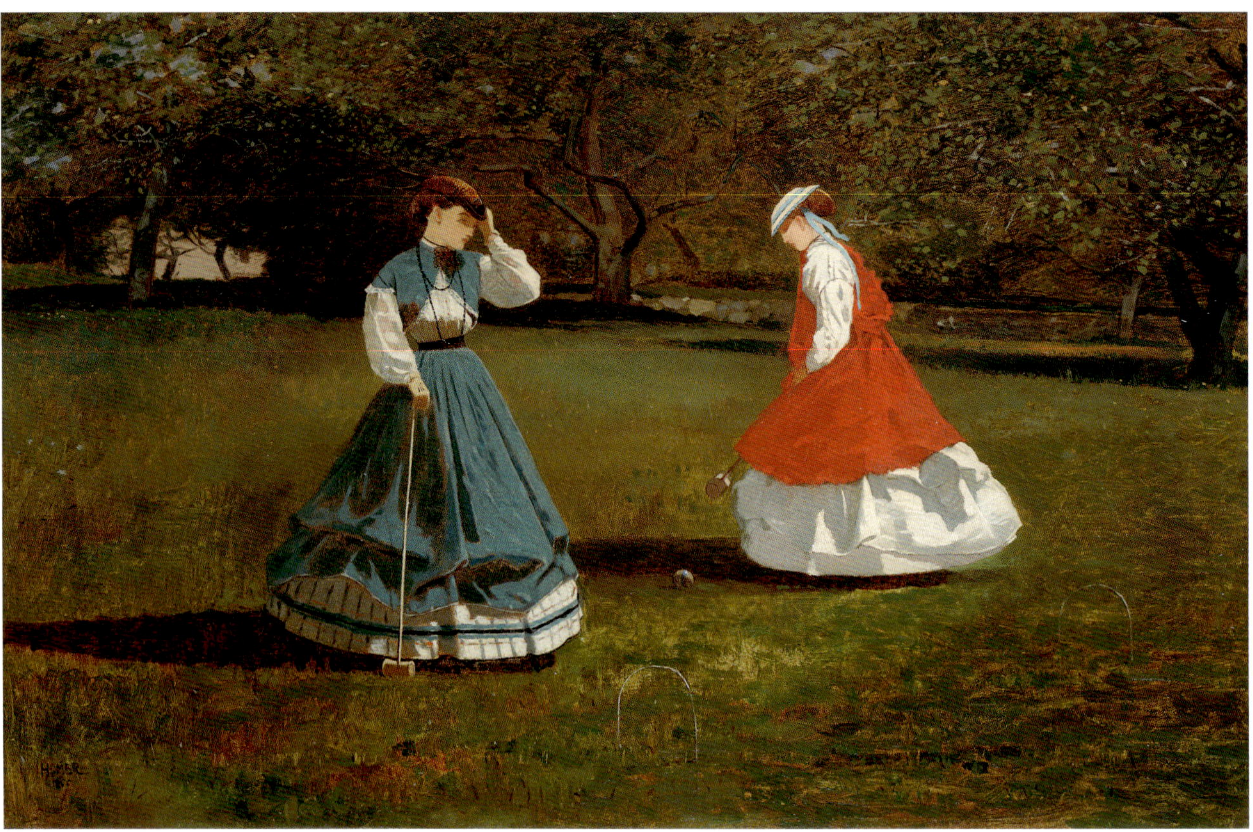

Fig. 15 *A Game of Croquet*, 1866, oil on canvas, 60.3 × 87.9 cm. Yale University Art Gallery, New Haven, Connecticut. Bequest of Stephen Carlton Clark, BA 1903 (1961.18.25)

teamsters employed by the Union Army resting from their labours during a lull in fighting. In the midday sun, they lie against a tent from which a fourth looks out to ascertain that danger is momentarily at bay. The painting made the point (of which European audiences might have been largely unaware) that African Americans participated in the conflict leading to Union victory and universal emancipation. *Prisoners from the Front* of 1866 (fig. 27) is the most ambitious of Homer's Civil War paintings. It shows Confederate troops, including a dashing, blonde-haired officer, hand on hip, who have been brought before their captor, a resolute Union officer, in the final days of conflict. The Southerners and their Northern opponent meet, however, on level ground; there is a hint here of the reconciliation that must come with peace. Said one European critic: 'This painting is real.'[6] Another compared its detailed reconstruction of an historical event to the works of French academic master Jean-Léon Gérôme (1824–1904)! High praise indeed for an unknown American at an Exposition where the powerful Gérôme was no less than Commissioner of Fine Arts. We can only intuit Eakins's frustration at this remark: Gérôme was his teacher, whose attention Eakins felt with increasing desperation he could never quite capture or retain.

Late in 1866 Homer determined to follow his canvases to Paris. In fact, he arrived in the French capital almost four months before the Exposition opened, so eager was he finally to see Europe (a long-standing ambition) and to test himself against contemporary French and international art. In Paris, formal experiment and the questioning of academic formulae were rife as artists sought innovative ways to depict the complex and confusing forces of modernity. Perhaps to a greater extent than most American-based contemporaries, Homer was at home with such works by the Barbizon painters and Gustave Courbet. His interest had begun early as naturalist works by Millet and contemporaries began to appear in Boston and New York in the 1850s. A taciturn man who wrote little, Homer produced relatively small and unadventurous paintings during his time in Paris.[7] Nonetheless he was exposed there to a gamut of ambitious and challenging artistic production, not least early French impressionism with its bright, pure colours applied in unmodulated blocks of pigment. Such bold use of paint, however, had already begun to appear in Homer's bucolic scenes of leisurely sociability before he had even left for France, as in *A Game of Croquet* of 1866 (fig. 15). He also saw works at the Exposition Universelle from almost every country on earth in one of the largest displays of contemporary art ever mounted to that time.

Fig. 16 Edouard Manet (1832–1883), *The Battle of the USS 'Kearsarge' and the CSS 'Alabama'*, 1864, oil on canvas, 137.8 × 128.9 cm. Philadelphia Museum of Art. John G. Johnson Collection, 1917 (cat. 1027)

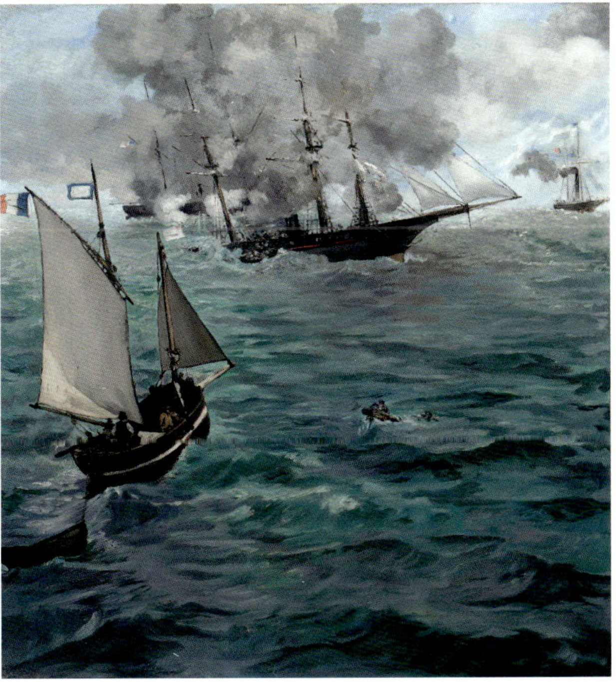

Surely, he sought out the works of Courbet and Manet as well, both of whom audaciously set up private displays of their most radical canvases on the edge of the Exposition's grounds. As a chronicler of the Civil War, he would have been particularly fascinated by the latter's depictions of sea battles between Union and Confederate ships off the west coast of France, such as *The Battle of the USS 'Kearsarge' and the CSS 'Alabama'* of 1864 (fig. 16). Here was a Frenchman addressing the very topic on which Homer's American fame was based. He may too have seen, set in distant Mexico, Manet's coruscating *The Execution of Maximilian* (fig. 12), as topical as a front-page headline. Manet exhibited it in a Paris shop window that spring until the authorities shut down the display.[8] In Paris, then, Homer saw not so much a new way forward for his art but rather confirmation of the path he had already begun to take across the Atlantic. Current events, real life, raw conflict, controversy, bold colour: these were the stuff of a truly modern art.

Homer made expert use of advanced French art from the 1860s onward, whether he acknowledged his sources or not. He felt no particular kinship with French society and culture, however. Having visited once, he never returned. Paris offered no especial sense of freedom and opportunity to him. In that he was unlike American painter Henry Ossawa Tanner (1859–1937) from Philadelphia, who moved to France in 1891 and remained, creating many of his greatest works there, among the first of many African American artists, writers and musicians who found a particularly liberating freedom from racism among the French. As interested as Homer was in recording the Black American experience, it was not an experience this Yankee child of privilege ever shared.

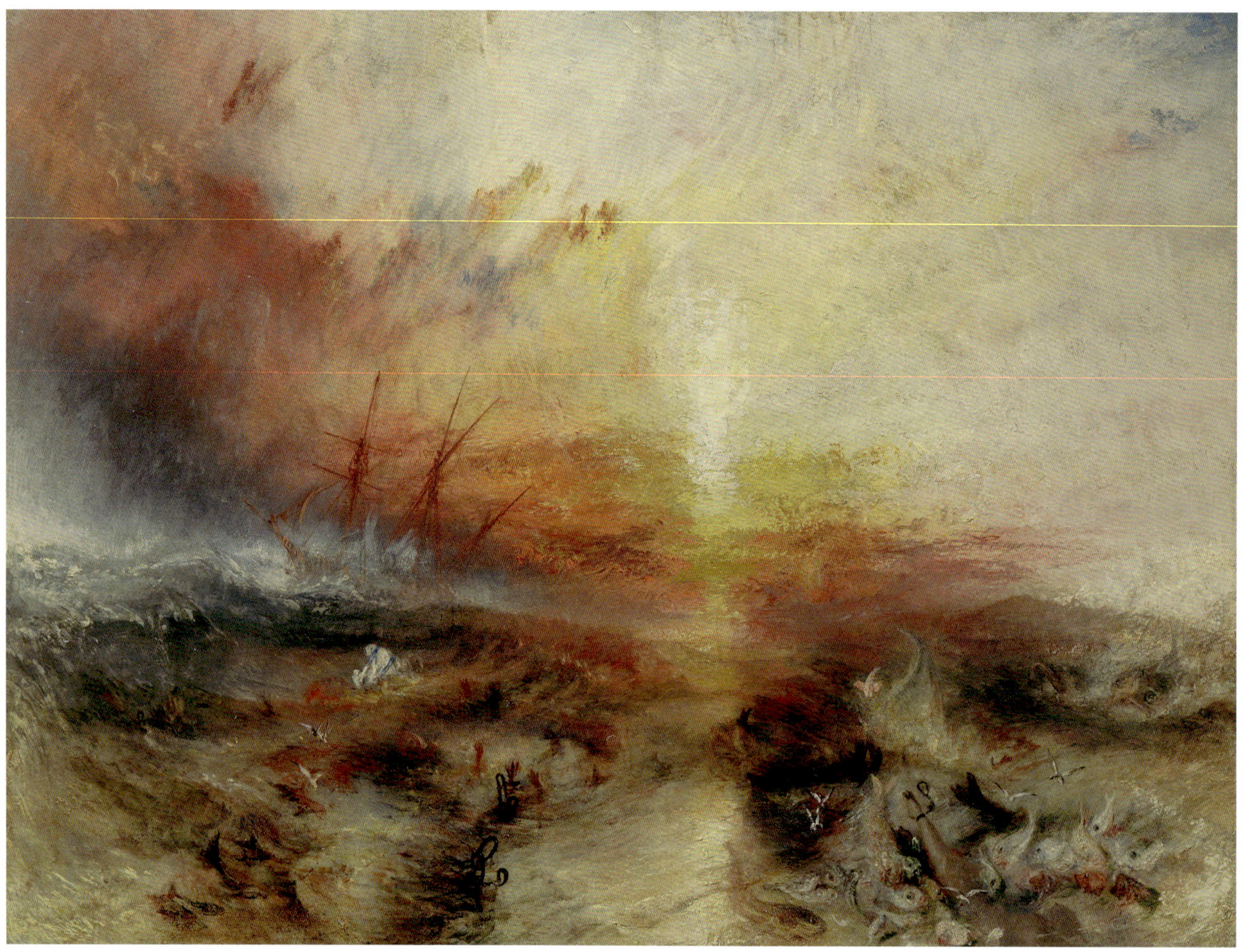

Fig. 17 Joseph Mallord William Turner (1775–1851), *Slave Ship (Slavers Throwing Overboard the Dead and Dying, Typhoon Coming On)*, 1840, oil on canvas, 90.8 × 122.6 cm. Museum of Fine Arts, Boston, Massachusetts. Henry Lillie Pierce Fund (99.22)

Reconstruction, So-called

Homer returned to the USA late in 1867. Primarily based in New York, he played an active role in its burgeoning art world. As reticent as he could be about explaining his motives or defining his place in the increasingly market-oriented American art scene, Homer certainly moved freely among the leading American artists of the day at the Tenth Street Studio, National Academy of Design and elsewhere artists gathered. It is important to see him comporting himself with confidence in these milieus and in those of prominent dealers, critics and collectors as well, rather than as an isolated and self-isolating loner. Like many American artists, from George Bellows (1882–1925) to Jackson Pollock (1912–1956) to Jasper Johns (b. 1930), in later years he retreated to the countryside and storm-wracked coast, but he also always knew the time of the next train to Manhattan.

One collector of his works, John Taylor Johnston, in 1872 acquired Joseph Mallord William Turner's harrowing depiction of the horrors of the slave trade, *Slave Ship* of 1840 (fig. 17), and Homer was a guest in Johnston's home the evening the painting was first displayed. Its subtitle is *Slavers Throwing Overboard the Dead and Dying, Typhoon Coming On*, and it presages Homer's own fascination with the perils Black lives faced and the ways in which nature – that menacing typhoon! – pays attendance on human tragedy. The imperilled ship on a tempest-tossed sea had been a forceful motif in art and literature since the ancient Greeks, of course, but Turner, like Manet and Homer after him with powerful works such as *The Gulf Stream* (1899, reworked by 1906, fig. 84), understood its radical contemporaneity and unaltered allegorical potency.

During the 1870s, as the USA continued to recover from the ravages of the Civil War, expanding its wealth, strength and global reach, Homer persisted in addressing the lives of African Americans, over and again returning to the racial division long at the heart of the American predicament, as to a wound that failed to heal. How had Black lives changed with emancipation? Not much, it seems. The two women in *The Cotton Pickers* (1876, fig. 34) go about their monotonous labours much as before. This monumental painting had been acquired by a British cotton merchant who, returning to London, lent it to the Royal Academy Summer Exhibition of 1878 (it is in fact the first Homer painting ever exhibited in the UK). Not much was known about Homer in the UK at this time, and indeed when you consult the original RA catalogue you find the artist identified as one W. Horner!

In another painting from 1876, Homer addressed race relations directly. *A Visit from the Old Mistress* (fig. 35) shows emancipated slaves receiving a visit from a former enslaver. A year later, in 1877, his *Dressing for the Carnival* (fig. 36) presents Black men, women and children as they prepare for a festival prominent in the West Indies and pre-emancipation America called Jonkonnu. Formerly associated with the Christmas season, it was now observed in the USA on or around the Fourth of July, thus associating a reaffirmation of traditional Black culture with the very notion of independence.

Fig. 18 *The Houses of Parliament*, 1881, watercolour on paper, 32.3 × 50.1 cm. Hirshhorn Museum and Sculpture Garden, Smithsonian Institution, Washington, DC. Gift of Joseph H. Hirshhorn, 1966 (66.2488)

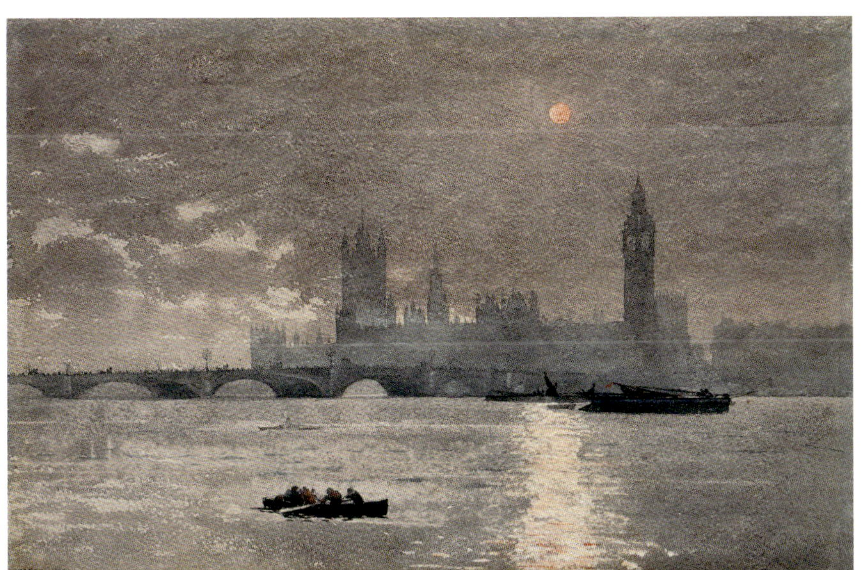

On the Heroism of Modern Life[9]

As the richness and complexity of Homer's painting deepened in the late 1870s, he began to ponder returning to Europe. Perhaps, as he had in Paris, he sought renewed confirmation in the Old World of the direction his art was already taking in the New. From the mid-1870s, for example, he had become increasingly interested in depicting the sea and sailing, as in *Breezing Up (A Fair Wind)* of 1873–6 (fig. 32). It is a benign image of the pleasure young boys might derive from a stiff wind and taut sail on the open water. But he was also aware, not least from Turner, that the sea was a place of danger and of the elemental, ever-repeated, often fatal confrontation of man with the forces of nature. Homer's thoughts turned not this time to France but to England with its tradition of sea painting. Arriving at Liverpool in March 1881, he passed through London, visiting the museums and dealers. The National Gallery would have exposed him to Turner in new depth and complexity, and the British Museum to ancient Greek and Roman sculpture in the original (whereas

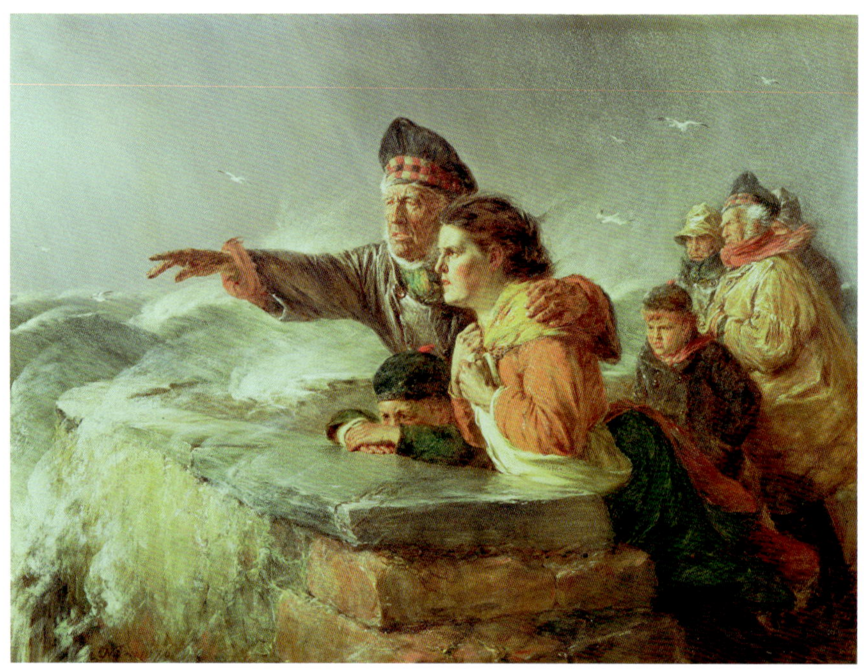

Fig. 19 Erskine Nicol (1825–1904), *The Missing Boat*, 1876, oil on canvas, 86.3 × 116.7 cm. Royal Holloway, University of London (THC0054)

at home primarily he would have known plaster casts). In his only watercolour created in London, he painted the Palace of Westminster overlooking the River Thames (fig. 18), just as another fascinated foreigner, Claude Monet, had done ten years earlier. But as we learn in greater detail elsewhere in this volume (see pp. 54–8), his destination was the small fishing village of Cullercoats on the North Sea above Newcastle upon Tyne. It was already something of an artists' colony, the perils of life on the raging sea a popular theme there, enjoying a ready market. Here was a new range of conflict and contestation for Homer to explore.

A fastidious chronicler of peasant life in Scotland and Ireland, Scottish realist painter Erskine Nicol (1825–1904) was also drawn to the newly popular genre exploring the hazards of life at sea. In *The Missing Boat* (fig. 19) an old man, his daughter-in-law (?) and kin, stare into the storm, distraught, in search of a son and husband whose ship has failed to return.

At Cullercoats in 1881, Homer soon witnessed a foundering ship, the *Iron Crown*, and the courageous efforts of the local Life Saving Brigade to rescue passengers and crew from its deck. From this event emerged one of Homer's most audacious and thrilling watercolours, *The Wreck of the Iron Crown* (1881, fig. 44). Richly detailed but at the same time strikingly simple in its juxtaposition of the two vessels, it is a terrifying distillation of danger and a celebration of the heroism of the Life Savers in their oared boat, tossed on the frothing waves like Jason's imperturbable Argonauts. Other images of the Brigade, its skills and the men's selflessness soon followed. They were primarily drawings and watercolours; when the alarm sounded, day or night, the artist made his way quickly to the shore and began to record what he observed there, his reportorial instincts entirely intact, indeed made acute once more. Homer also soon found equally stark and grand exemplars of local heroism in the proud, resolute women of the fishing village, silhouetted against the raging sea and sky like so many figures from ancient sculpture, their sodden cloaks, shawls and skirts wrapped dramatically around them – comparisons have been made with the Tanagra figurines from Greece of the fourth century BC that he would have seen at the British Museum – as they waited, fearful but unwavering, for their menfolk to return from sea. Or not.

The key painting to emerge from the 18 months Homer spent in Cullercoats, *The Gale* (1883–93, fig. 47), is monumental in scale. It shows a single such woman, baby strapped to her back, mercilessly buffeted by the elements. This is the work Homer exhibited in New York in 1883 to demonstrate the new grandeur and sublimity to which his art now aspired. Within a decade, however, he had repainted the canvas, editing the image down to something simpler and grander than the picture he brought from England, removing what he had come to see as extraneous and merely anecdotal detail.[10] Again, he sought the pith of a powerful visual experience. The months he stayed at Cullercoats – far longer than originally intended – and the visual documents he assembled there provided motifs of conflict and bravery that would last Homer throughout his career. Back in America, almost immediately he executed some 20 works inspired by memories of Cullercoats. Even years later, the recollection of all he witnessed there infused such austere and compelling paintings as *The Life Line* of 1884 (fig. 51) and *Signal of Distress* of 1890–6 (fig. 56).

The completion of Homer's most ambitious figure paintings grew ever further removed in time from the original observation of motifs on which they were based. It is as if he cherished the possibility of reflecting on what he had seen, allowing it to settle in his imagination in a way that he had had little time to do as a Civil War reporter. As with *The Gale*, he now sought to make the motif simpler, more emotionally intense and increasingly metaphorical in its implications. At Atlantic City, New Jersey, in 1883, for example, he witnessed a shocking event: two female bathers caught in the undertow and in danger of drowning. Two brave male bathers appeared on the scene to pull them bodily from the waves. The actual life-saving incident must have been fraught, ugly, noisy with shouting and crashing waves, confusing to observers as it unfolded. Imminent disaster is always arbitrary and incoherent. After three years of distillation in Homer's mind, however, and following numerous preliminary drawings and the use of studio models to recreate the scene – models whom Homer sometimes doused with water; wet drapery continued to fascinate him – a masterpiece took form.[11] *Undertow* (1886, fig. 55) is one of his most timeless, austere, frieze-like compositions, as if a bas-relief on an ancient Greek pediment. It is also a rare example of heroic nudity in his work, and it has an erotic charge. Here was the realisation of William Wordsworth's (1770–1850) 'emotion recollected in tranquillity'. That personal heroism he had observed at Cullercoats and returned to in his imagination ever since; the eternally recurring battle with the elements, which for him epitomised the human condition; the moment tensely suspended between life and death: here he had found his greatest, most stirring, in some ways most deeply personal theme.

At Peril on the Sea

The Gulf Stream of 1899 (fig. 84) seems to have begun percolating in Homer's imagination in the mid-1880s. From that time, he frequently visited Florida, Cuba, The Bahamas, Bermuda and the Caribbean, especially during the winter months. There, the Gulf Stream carried warm waters north and east, uniting both shores of the Atlantic. Homer's watercolours and paintings often show the colourful, sweet-smelling vegetation and elegant white bungalows that made life pleasant amid the balmy sea breezes (see figs 68 and 69). There, however, he was made aware of the significant presence in the population of Black people, some formerly enslaved – as slavery was not abolished in Cuba until 1886, some most likely were still enslaved – and it carried his mind back to old concerns in the 1860s with the Civil War and the fight for emancipation in the USA, and in the 1870s with the role that African Americans would play as free citizens in the life of the Republic. Or rather as citizens struggling for freedom where the vaunted Reconstruction did little to improve their standing. More often quite the contrary occurred, as the forces of reaction held sway and the notorious Jim Crow laws enacted in those years actively enforced racial segregation.

Early on in his visits to the Caribbean, Homer sketched small sailing boats whose masts had snapped off and were

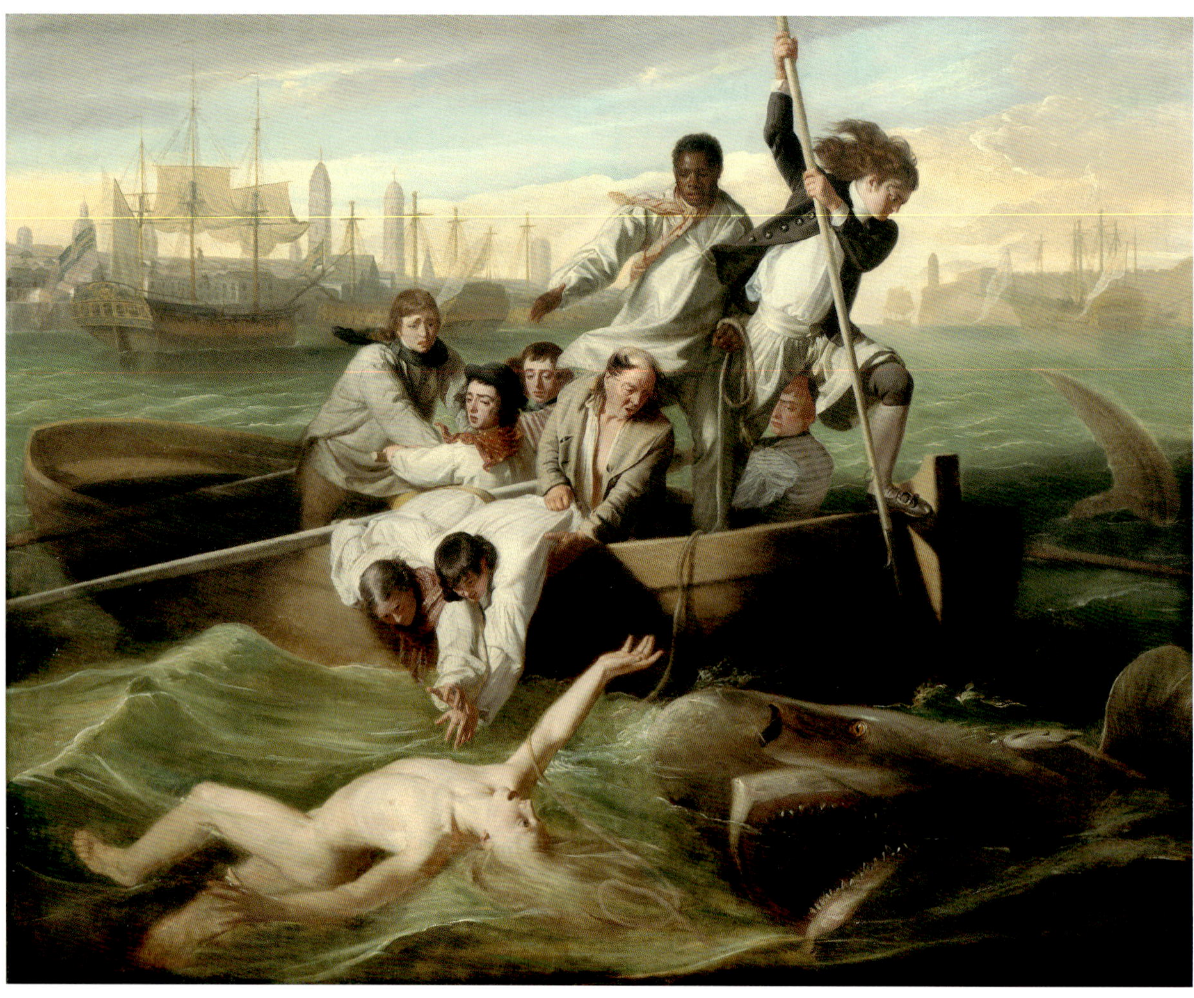

Fig. 20 John Singleton Copley (1738–1815), *Watson and the Shark*, 1778, oil on canvas, 182.1 × 229.7 cm. National Gallery of Art, Washington, DC. Ferdinand Lammot Belin Fund (1963.6.1)

powerless on the sea (see figs 81–3). As well, he sketched encircling sharks; the motif had been a fearsome symbol in American art of the dangers lurking at sea since John Singleton Copley painted *Watson and the Shark* in 1778 (fig. 20). Homer, clearly, was assembling a repertoire of menacing motifs. Watson's attack by a shark famously took place in Havana harbour, which might have recalled the motif and its metaphorical power to Homer's mind when America and Spain fought a war over Cuba in 1898. Homer was on hand, observing, sketching and later painting austere, symbolic representations of the conflict such as *Searchlight on Harbor Entrance, Santiago de Cuba* of 1902 (fig. 75).

A year after the war, Homer completed the monumental canvas on which sharks feature so prominently. A Black man, exhausted and helpless, now occupies the de-masted boat rocking so precariously on the waves. Homer gave the boat a name, *Anna – Key West*; it, and its occupant, are American. A menacing waterspout approaches from the distant right. A three-masted schooner with the promise of rescue appears in the distance to the left, but the man does not see it. He confronts his fate, alone at the moment of potential – perhaps all but inevitable – annihilation. Here, Homer has created his greatest and most resonant image of fate and eternal conflict with nature. But it is also and specifically – he wants us to know – about the USA and its travails, the Atlantic world of which it formed a part, and the wider interplay of power and powerlessness in the modern world order. Perhaps the pertinent contemporary comparison is with Polish-born writer Joseph Conrad (1857–1924) and his coruscating analysis of globalisation and its myriad discontents.[12]

Force of Nature

The depiction of conflict and the exercise of force in Homer's art – whether human or natural – long revolved around the human figure. Men might engage in physical confrontation with one another; powerless women might be rescued by stalwart men in whose arms they swoon; powerful women might confront the elements, indomitable in their isolation; solitary men might feel the full force of nature unleashed on their puny selves. The human body *in extremis*, with life and death in the balance, was the vehicle through which Homer explored the theatre of existence, honoured the primordial struggle, analysed issues of race, blind force and the raw power nations exerted against one another. In the final decades of his life, however, as Homer retreated further from cities to Prouts Neck on the rocks facing the Atlantic on the rugged coast of Maine, as he interacted with fewer and fewer friends and family, and as he entered an austere final phase of his long career, the human form largely, although not entirely, disappeared from his art. Rather, he turned to 'pure' landscape and seascape painting.

Northeaster (fig. 90) dates to 1895; Homer repainted the canvas in 1901. Such reconsiderations after a painting had been exhibited, sometimes even sold to a collector, had become, as we have seen, a frequent recourse in Homer's later years. In the original version, two men in raingear, buffeted by relentless wind and rain, crouched on the rocks. In the version six years later, the men had disappeared, replaced by rock, cloud, waves alone. Now, nature holds dominion. Its brutal force needs no human antagonist. Or rather we, the viewers, assume that role. We become the imperilled object of nature's wrath. With such late works Homer reached a final, thrillingly concise metaphorical evocation of the ceaseless play of power that had challenged and provoked him since his days reporting on the brutal Civil War, its essential issues still unresolved almost a half century later.

1 Jamestown was the first permanent British settlement in North America.
2 *Le peintre de la vie moderne: Constantin Guys* is the title of the work that Charles Baudelaire probably wrote in 1859 or 1860 and published in 1863.
3 On American art at the Exposition Universelle of 1867, see Troyen 1984, pp. 3–29.
4 Thomas Eakins to his father, Benjamin Eakins, 31 May 1867, in T. Eakins, *The Paris Letters of Thomas Eakins,* W.I. Homer (ed.), Princeton, New Jersey, 2009, p. 112.
5 P. Ndiaye and L. Madinier, 'Chronologie 1848–1870', in *Le modèle noir de Géricault à Matisse*, exh. cat., musée d'Orsay, Paris, 2019, p. 125 (under year 1867).
6 'Paris International Exhibition, no. VI: National Schools of Painting; Pictures from America', *Art Journal* (London), new series 6 (1 November 1867), p. 248.
7 The works likely painted in France in 1867 are shown in Gerdts and Goodrich 2005–14, vol. 2, cat. nos. 295–317, pp. 38–63.
8 See most recently J. Elderfield, *Manet and the Execution of Maximilian*, exh. cat., Museum of Modern Art, New York, 2006.
9 'De l'héroïsme de la vie moderne' is the eighteenth and final chapter of Baudelaire's 'Salon de 1846'. See C. Baudelaire, *Critique d'art*, C. Pichois (ed.), Paris, 1965, vol. 1, pp. 173–6.
10 E. Athens, 'The Gale' in Worcester and Milwaukee 2017–18, pp. 34–9.
11 On *Undertow*, see Simpson 2013, pp. 86–93.
12 On Conrad in an increasingly international world, see M. Jasanoff, *The Dawn Watch: Joseph Conrad in a Global World*, London, 2017.

Overleaf Detail of fig. 47

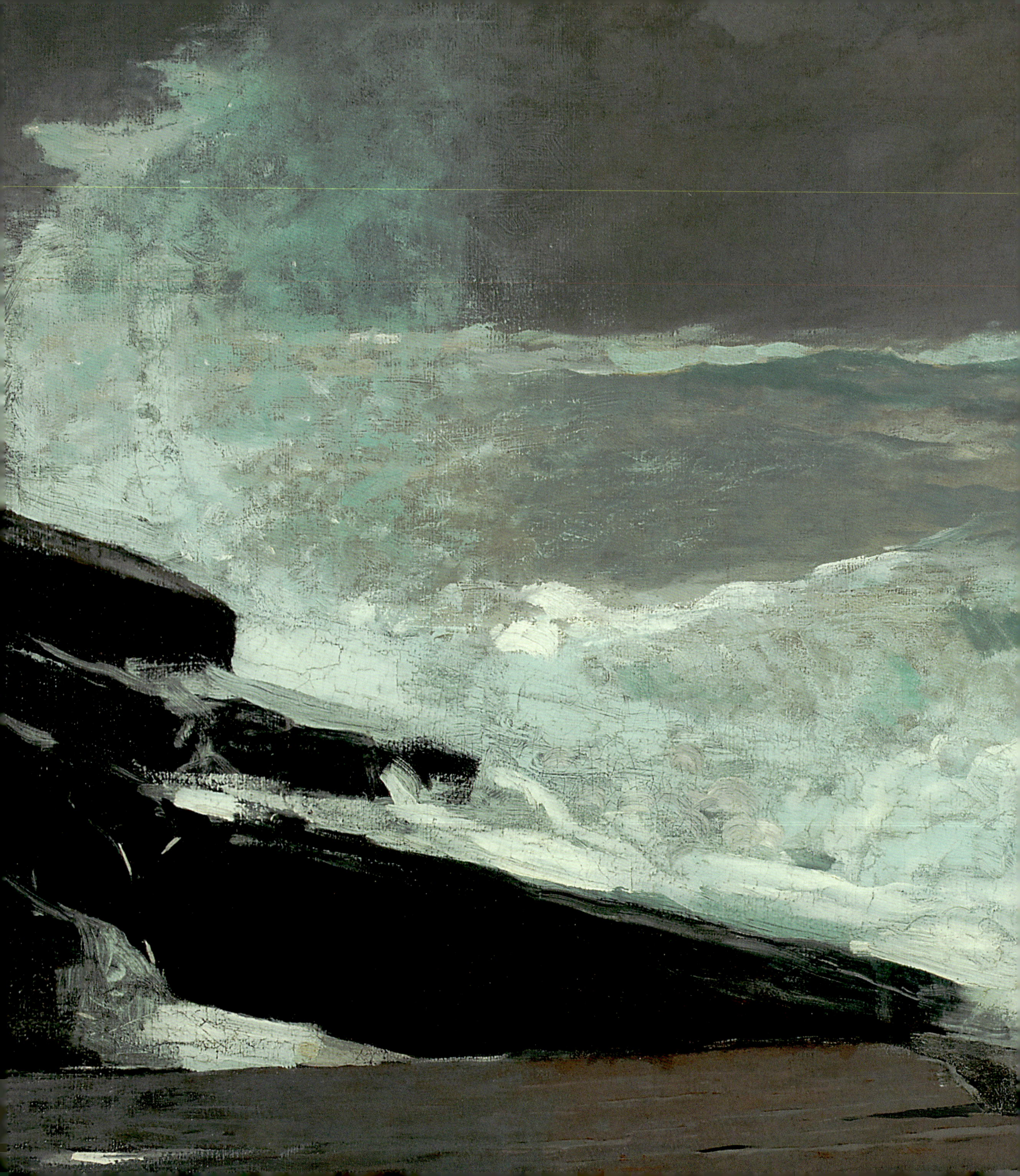

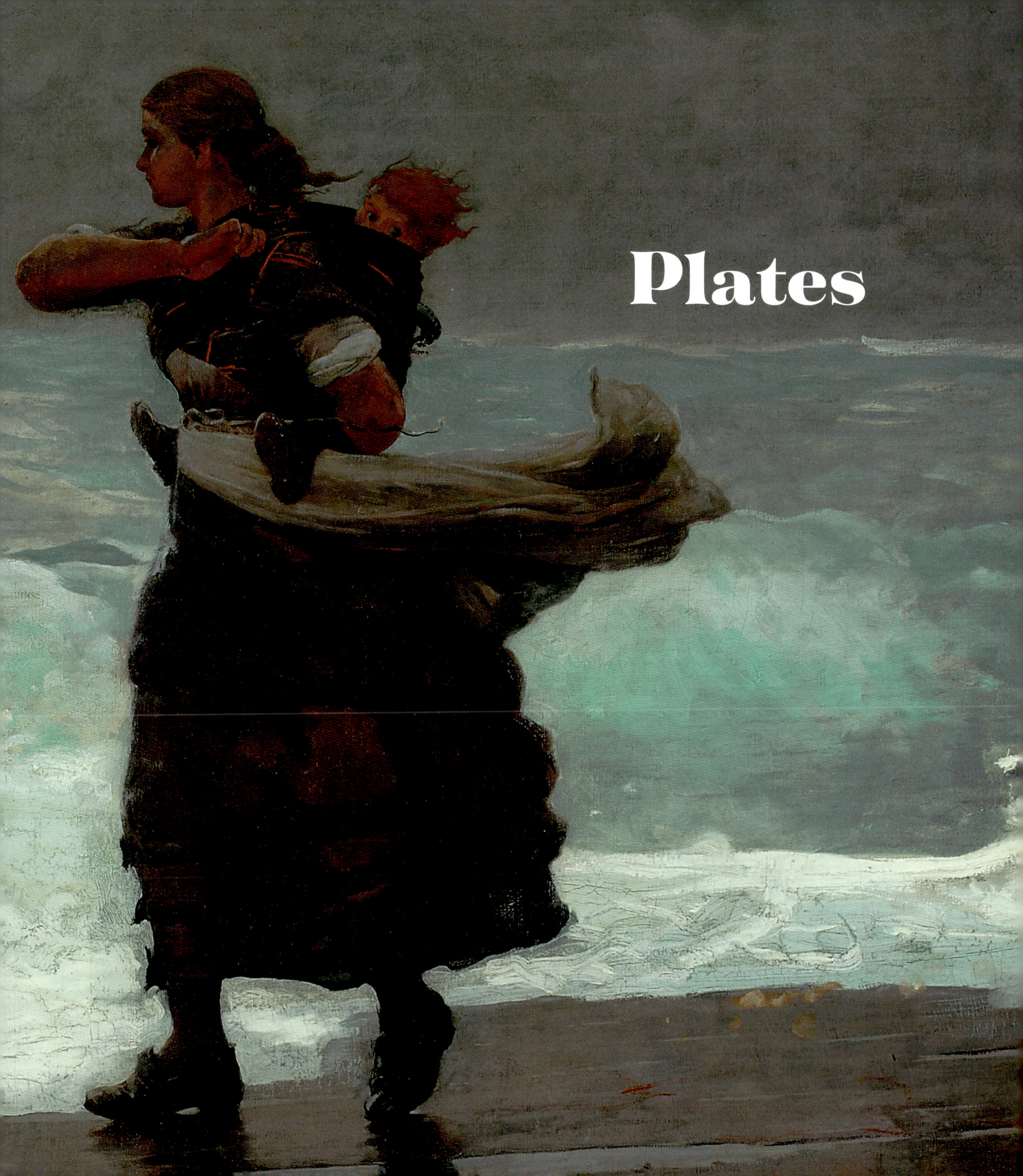

Plates

Civil War and Reconstruction

Christopher Riopelle

Harper's Weekly was a popular American magazine published in New York from 1857. Subtitled *A Journal of Civilization*, it covered an international range of social, political and cultural topics. With the outbreak of the American Civil War on 12 April 1861, pitting the Union in the North against the Confederacy in the South, *Harper's* shifted editorial direction to focus on what would become the bloodiest conflict in American history. It now unreservedly supported President Abraham Lincoln (1809–1865) and the Union cause, a prime objective being the abolition of slavery across the USA.

To report on the progress of the war, the magazine increasingly used wood engravings: produced rapidly, they were photographic in detail and immediacy. Both photography and wood engraving served the public thirst for visually accurate reportage from the front. However, publications printed on relatively cheap newsprint did not yet have the technical means to use photographic reproduction, although the Civil War was extensively 'covered' by photographers and the resulting imagery is one of the first examples of what is now known as documentary photography.[1] Hence the demand for skilled, fast-working wood engravers. One of the artists *Harper's* employed to turn out a steady stream of such topical, photo-like images was Winslow Homer, just 25 when the war began. He had studied print-making techniques since 1855 (see pp. 9–10).

On 15 November 1862, *Harper's* published a Homer print entitled *The Army of the Potomac—A Sharp-Shooter on Picket Duty* (fig. 21). Encamped with the Union Army at Yorktown, Virginia, Homer had witnessed the scene. A rifleman has climbed a tree where, seated precariously on a branch, he aims his weapon, eye to scope, as he prepares to pick off the enemy. One distant Confederate soldier is in his sights, although not in ours. The almost horizontal cant of the rifle barrel is supported by a tree branch that establishes the exact angle of fire the picket needs. It is a stark and violent image. Homer on the battlefield has quickly taught himself to edit out extraneous visual detail, carrying us to the brutal heart of the matter.

In 1863 Homer completed what may well have been his first painting in oils. It is this very image, in vivid colour now but of almost the same dimensions as a contemporary wood engraving (fig. 24). It is as if the print, widely

Fig. 21 *The Army of the Potomac—A Sharp-Shooter on Picket Duty* (detail), 15 November 1862, wood engraving on newsprint, 23.5 × 35 cm. Sterling and Francine Clark Art Institute, Williamstown, Massachusetts (1955.1473)

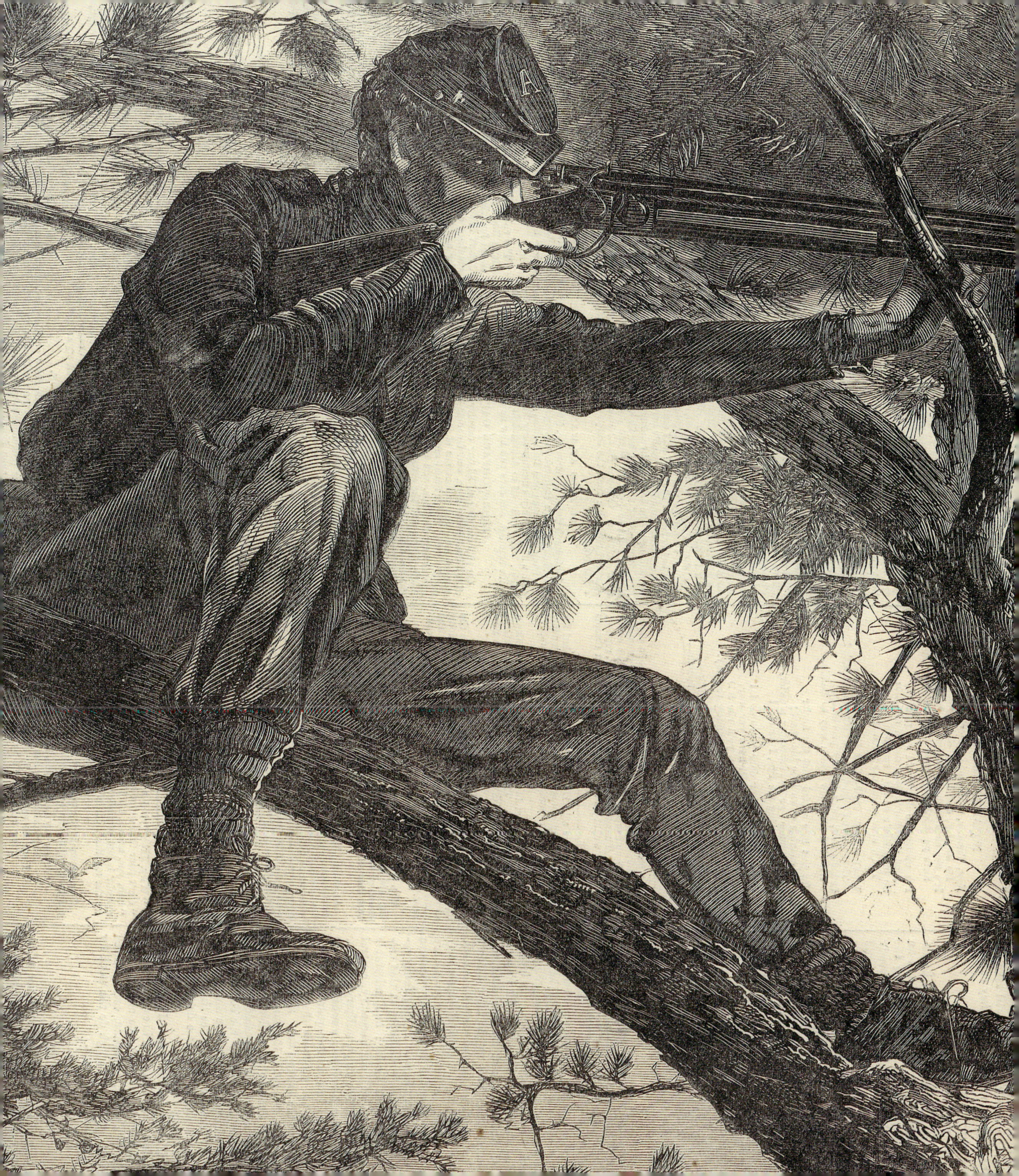

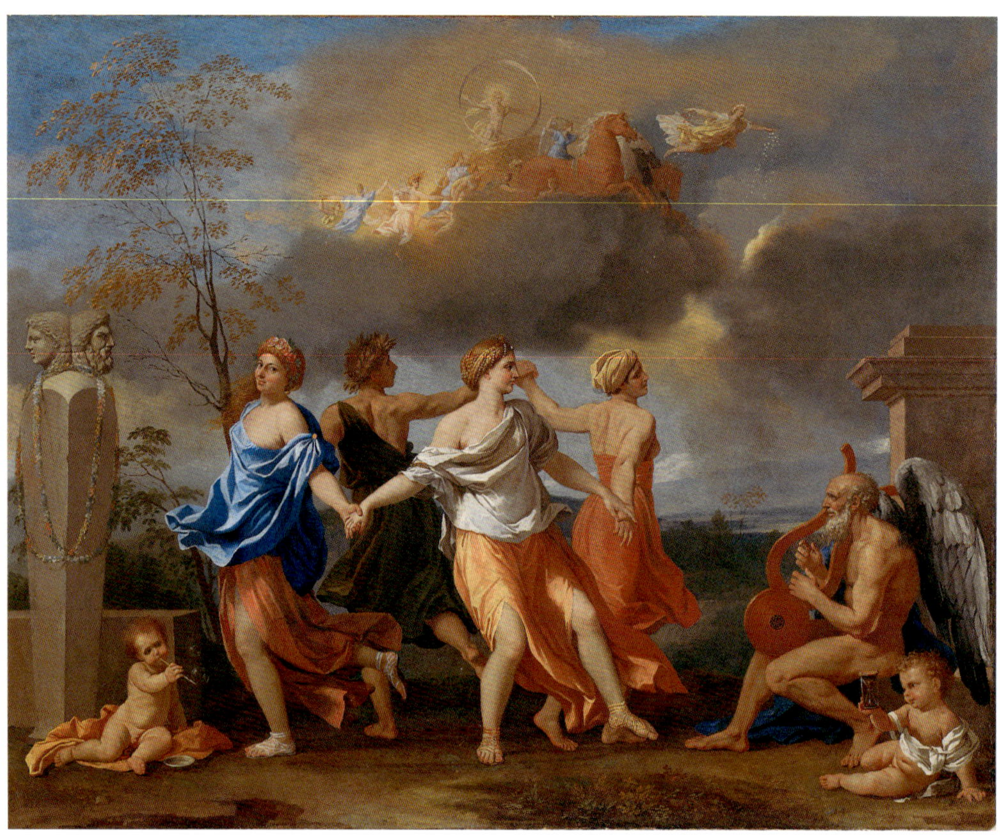

Fig. 22 Nicolas Poussin (1594–1665), *A Dance to the Music of Time*, about 1634–6, oil on canvas, 82.5 × 104 cm. The Wallace Collection, London (P108)

distributed, serves to confirm the veracity of the painting. Details have changed little from one medium to the other. More foliage surrounds the picket, to be sure, but pose and terrible concentration on the fatal line of fire remain. At the same time, Homer is feeling his way to an understanding of what he can achieve uniquely with colour. That single, bright red dot, a badge on the soldier's cap like a bullseye, establishes with brilliant economy of means that the picket may well be a target in turn. Homer knew of course that a painting is a distinct object. The print's highly descriptive and specific title, itself reportage, becomes *Sharpshooter* in the painting, which is a chilling universal symbol of the anonymity of modern warfare.

As the war drew to a close with Union victory in April 1865, Homer increasingly staked his future on a career as a professional painter in oils and watercolours. Scenes of urban and rural sociability followed, helping to establish Homer's painterly reputation as an unsurpassed chronicler of American leisure and informal conviviality. *Snap the Whip* of 1872 (fig. 28) is the masterpiece in a long line of such jolly scenes. Here, heedless farm lads pull one another's arms in a merry round as they try to throw their pals off balance. In the formal intricacy of its intertwined figures, the painting recalls Nicolas Poussin's (1594–1665) *A Dance to the Music of Time* of about 1634–6 (fig. 22), a modern evocation of an ancient bacchanal. Almost instinctively, as he explored the return of American life to peace and plenty, Homer seems to have found its innocent equivalent on a Virginia farmstead.

Yet he also continued to produce paintings, like *Sharpshooter*, based on his war experiences. *Defiance: Inviting a Shot before Petersburg* of 1864 (fig. 25) shows a foolhardy Confederate soldier climbing onto a hillock daring a Union sharpshooter to pick him off. (Homer the reporter seems to have been able to move back and forth across enemy lines.) Beneath the bluff, however, a Black banjo player as if from a minstrel show strums away, seemingly oblivious to danger. Such early works often employed caricature and racial stereotyping – art historian Gwendolyn DuBois Shaw has remarked on Homer's use of 'racist ideas about Black workers'[2] – sanctioned by decades of white American genre painters and music-hall performers in their depictions of African Americans. Such tropes would linger long.

The masterpiece of Homer's Civil War imagery is *Prisoners from the Front* (1866, fig. 27). The Union officer confronts his Confederate captives, including a handsome golden-haired officer like a Wagnerian hero. The two officers in particular exchange frank and sustained gazes. Both are heroic: one a victor, the other vanquished, to be sure, but standing face to face, gentleman to gentleman. War may have driven them apart but now it is time to rebuild the nation on the bases of equality and fellow feeling. Here, in an image of conflict and confrontation, Homer discerns faint signs of potential reconciliation. Compositionally, the painting may owe a debt to the radical refusal of hierarchy in multi-figure compositions by Frenchman Gustave Courbet, such as *A Burial at Ornans* (fig. 23).[3]

Reconstruction

Perhaps to a greater extent than any other USA-based contemporary painter, Homer knew – was even at home with – the works of the most daring French artists of the day, including the Barbizon painters and Gustave Courbet. His interest in advanced contemporary art had begun early as naturalist works by Jean-François Millet and contemporaries started to appear in Boston and New York in the 1850s. Claude Monet and a new generation of radical French artists were even beginning to be seen there in the 1860s. Homer intended to make a living from his brush and kept a sharp eye on the burgeoning art market as well. It was well worth noting, for example, that an academic master of historical genre like Jean-Léon Gérôme – meticulous, anecdotal and detailed in execution – found increasing favour among the USA's plutocrat collectors.[4] Homer's 10-month stay in Paris, starting in December 1866, increased his exposure to such novel and rapidly changing currents. He also knew the work of John Constable (1776–1837), Joseph Mallord William Turner and the more overtly sentimental British painters. He was aware in the decade following the Civil War of debates swirling in the American art world as to whether French or British models of art-making served American interests best, but saw little point in choosing sides.[5]

Fig. 23 Gustave Courbet (1819–1877), *A Burial at Ornans*, 1849–50, oil on canvas, 315 × 660 cm. Musée d'Orsay, Paris (RF 325)

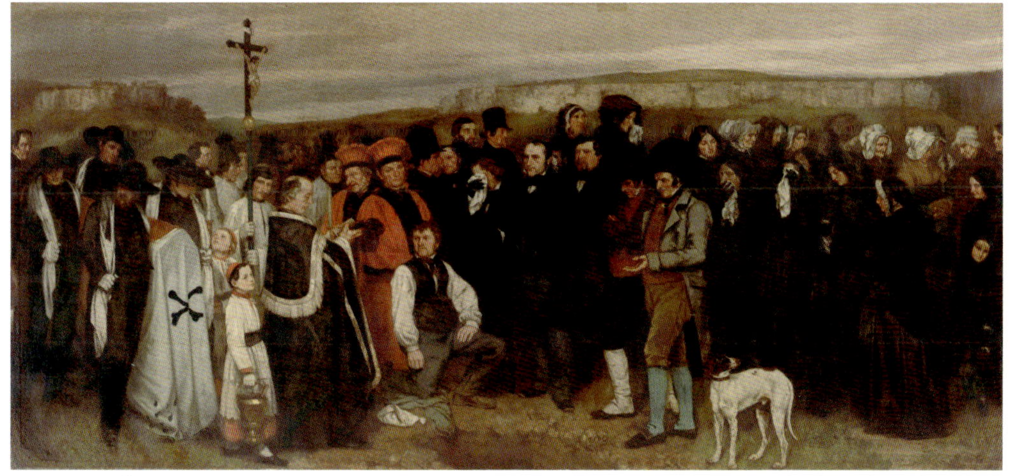

Still, in the decade or more following the end of the Civil War, Homer kept finding himself drawn back to an investigation of the lives of African Americans, now emancipated. How had their lives changed? The period after the war was given the noble and optimistic name of 'Reconstruction', yet was anything but for the majority of African Americans as Jim Crow laws, among many other indignities, were enacted to ensure the maintenance and reinforcement of a vicious system of racial segregation. Homer addressed the issues over and again in such masterpieces as *The Cotton Pickers* of 1876 (fig. 34). Two African American women continue their repetitive labours. Now they are paid subsistence wages, but much remains as it was before the war. Yet these women are somehow grand, heroic, stoic and determined. It is a monumental depiction of endurance and the first painting by Homer ever to be seen in the UK when it was shown at the Royal Academy, London, in 1878.

Also in 1876, Homer addressed a cognate issue in *A Visit from the Old Mistress* (fig. 35). The scene is set in (formerly Confederate) Virginia. The composition is already familiar to us – an updating of the anti-hierarchical linear disposition of figures in *Prisoners from the Front* – with a row of women and an infant distributed across a single plane. The former enslaver confronts the formerly enslaved; the two tallest women are of the same height, however, and the gazes they exchange are frank. Inequality of rank, opportunity and wealth are implicated here, not least in the clothing, with the old mistress wearing swathes of expensive lace. Such divisions had not changed.

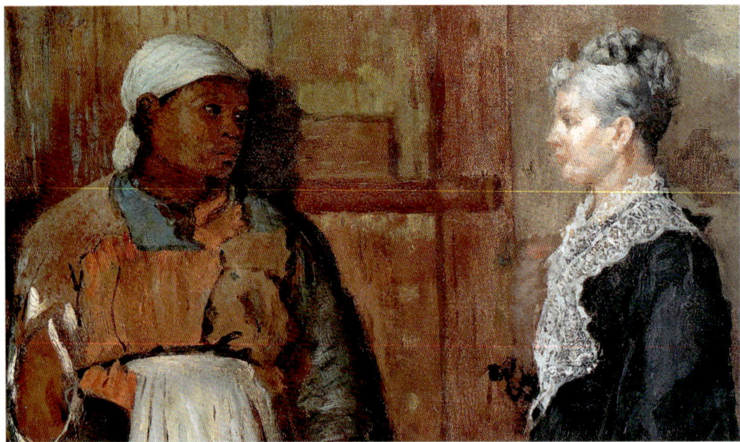

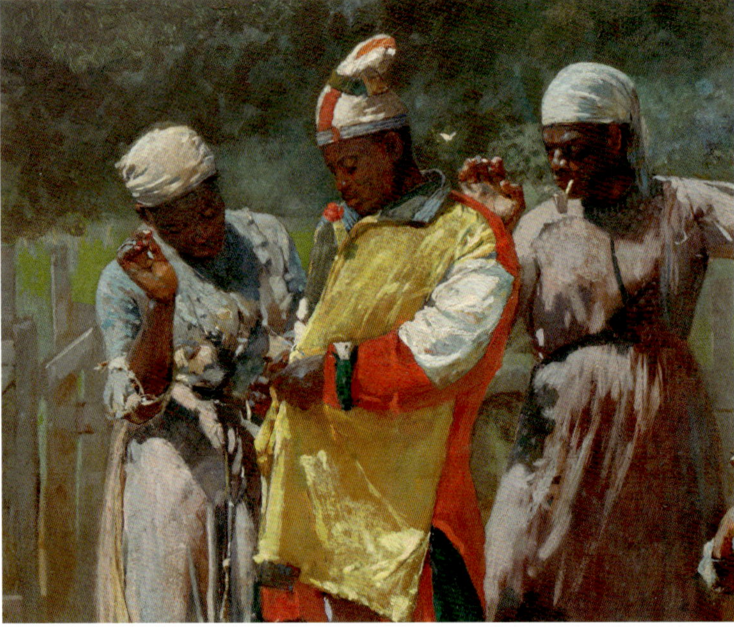

Top Detail of fig. 35
Bottom Detail of fig. 36

But as with *Prisoners*, Homer establishes a kind of visual equivalency between opposites, however tentative.

A year later, in 1877, Homer's *Dressing for the Carnival* (fig. 36) shows African American men, women and wide-eyed children preparing for Jonkonnu, a celebration of traditional Black culture. Two women sew the young man into his shimmering costume as the Lord of Misrule, the fabric moving sinuously around their bodies as in a graceful dance. The three are complexly intertwined, as if figures from an ancient Greek or Roman frieze: the Three Fates perhaps – incarnations of destiny in ancient myth – who oversee human life. Sewing and the snipping of a thread are implicated in both motifs,[6] and the young man's future in so-called Reconstruction America is not clear. Homer was beginning to endow even his most genre-like depictions of rural pleasures with a similar classical resonance.

During the 1860s and 1870s Homer fashioned a daring career as a fine art painter. He balanced reportorial image making, chronicling the Civil War and its aftermath, with increasingly symbolic interpretations. He brought to bear a rare and discerning knowledge of international artistic currents, but still focused his work primarily on the USA. He turned a scrupulous eye to the realities of war and peace, often finding the latter falling below its promise.

1 On the imagery of the American Civil War, including prints and photographs, see D. Immerwahr, 'Frontier, Ocean, Empire: Vistas of Expansion in Winslow Homer's United States', in New York 2022, pp. 20–6.
2 See G. DuBois Shaw, '"The Various Colors and Types of Negroes": Winslow Homer Learns to Paint Race', in New York 2022, pp. 44–52.
3 The argument for the influence of Courbet is made in greater depth in my essay '"These Works Are Real": Winslow Homer and Europe', in New York 2022, pp. 84–92.
4 Ibid., p. 85. Some 12 paintings by Gérôme were already owned by American collectors in 1867, five of which were loaned to the Exposition Universelle. See Troyen 1984, p. 19.
5 The increasing amount of British art coming to America in the 1870s, and the assertion by some critics that American art's natural affinity lay with its British counterpart, is discussed by E. Athens, 'Turning to England', in Worcester and Milwaukee 2017–18, pp. 15–21.
6 The Three Fates (Moirai in ancient Greek mythology; Parcae in ancient Roman) are Clotho, the spinner, Lachesis, the allotter, and Atropos, the inflexible one, who in the end cuts the thread of life. Homer here would seem to evoke the myth in the complicated interweaving of three principal figures, the leftmost one of whom, arm extended, holds the thread.

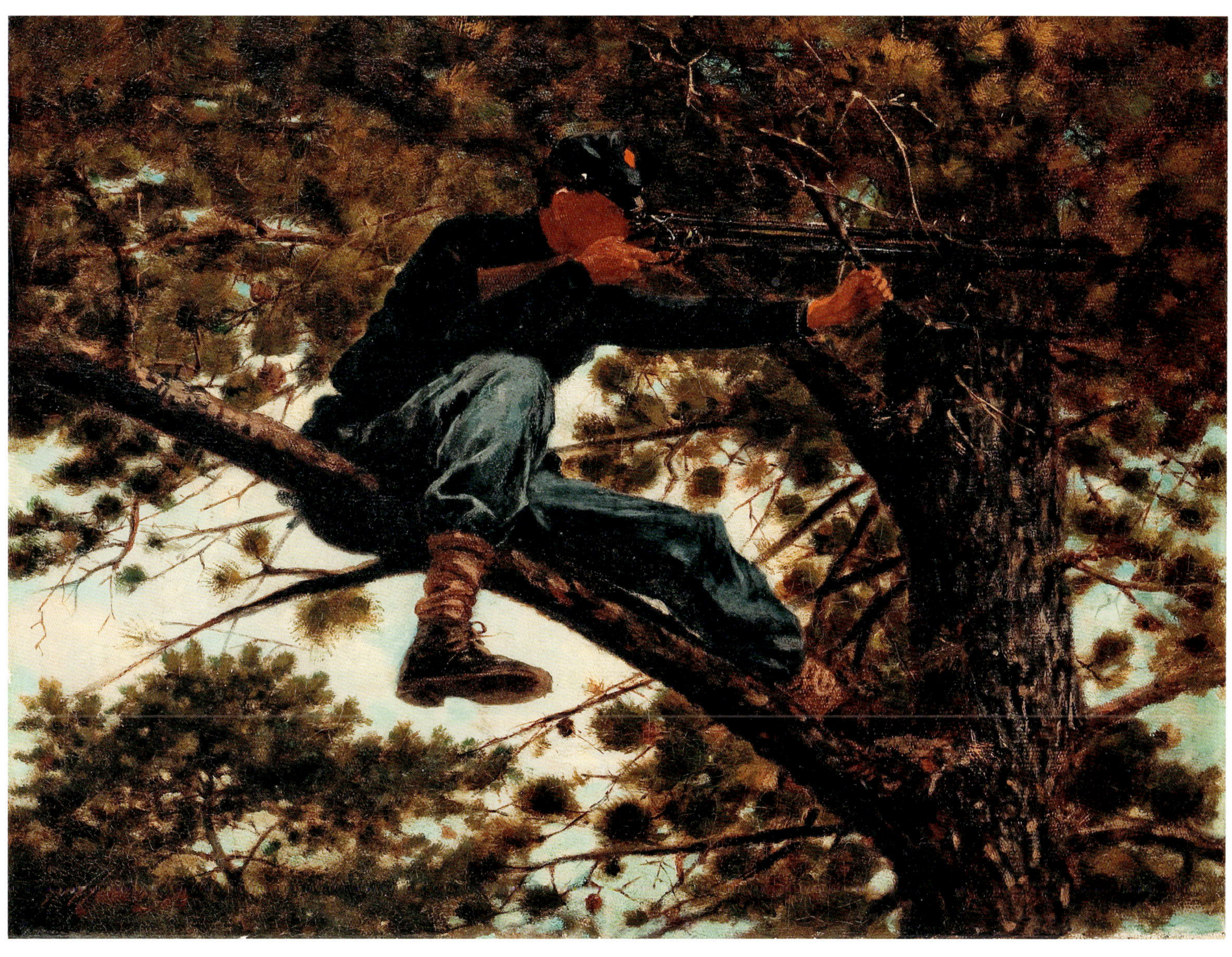

Fig. 24 *Sharpshooter*, 1863

Oil on canvas, 31.1 × 41.9 cm
Portland Museum of Art, Maine. Gift of Barbro and Bernard Osher (1992.41)

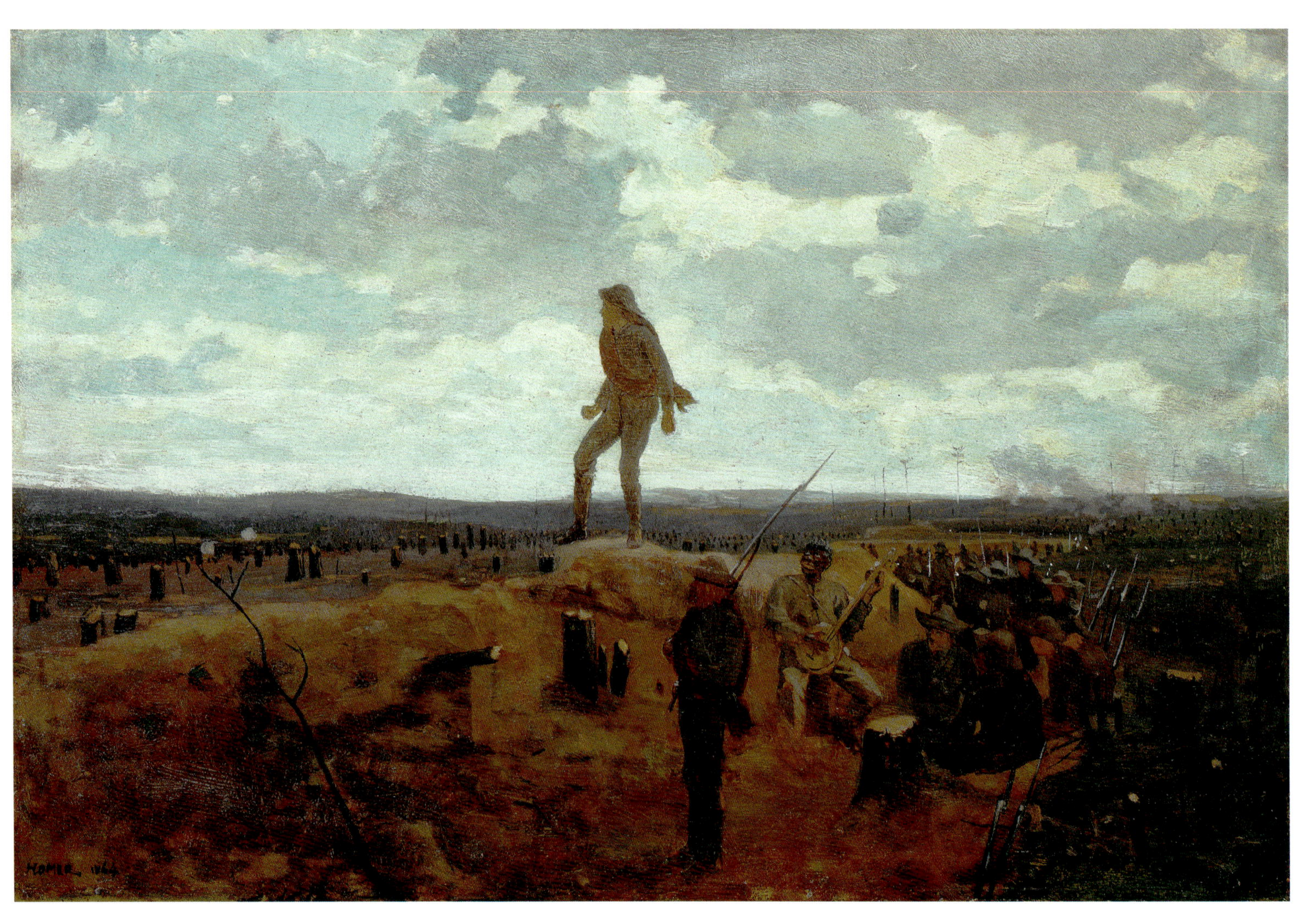

Fig. 25 *Defiance: Inviting a Shot before Petersburg*, 1864

Oil on panel, 30.5 × 45.7 cm
Detroit Institute of Arts, Michigan. Founders Society Purchase with funds from Dexter M. Ferry, Jr (51.66)

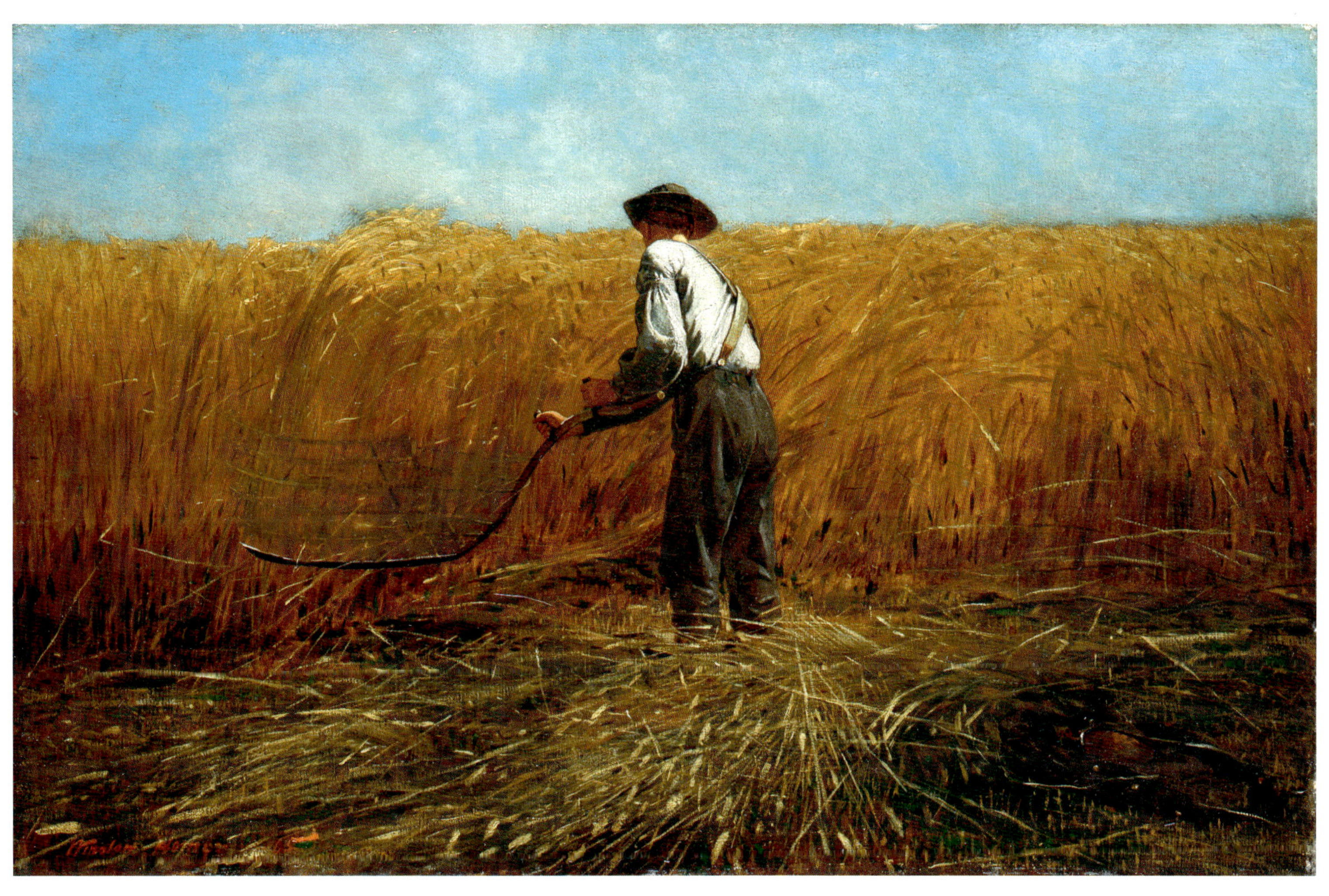

Fig. 26 *The Veteran in a New Field*, 1865

Oil on canvas, 61.3 × 96.8 cm
The Metropolitan Museum of Art, New York. Bequest of Miss Adelaide Milton de Groot (1876–1967), 1967 (67.187.131)

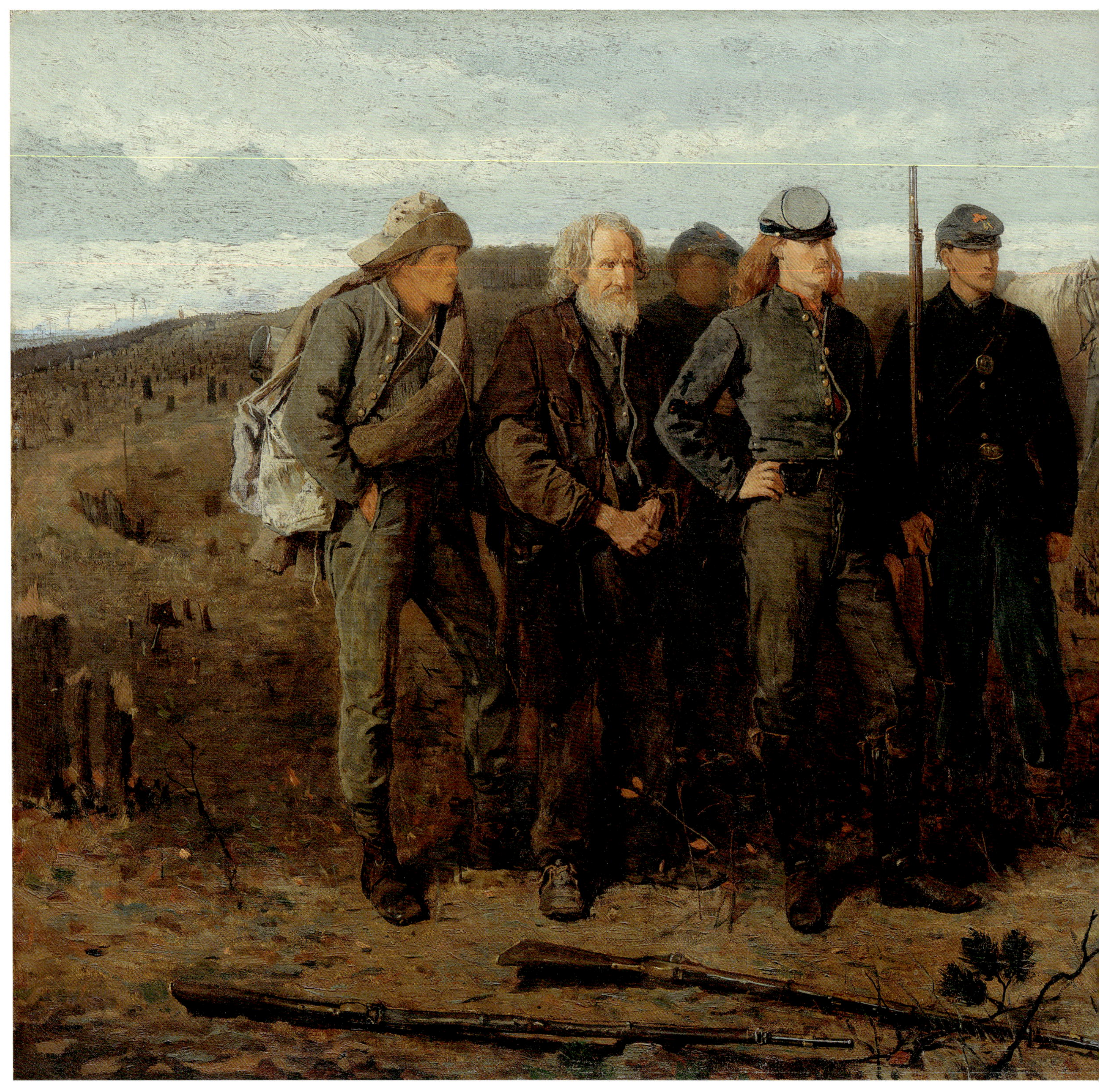

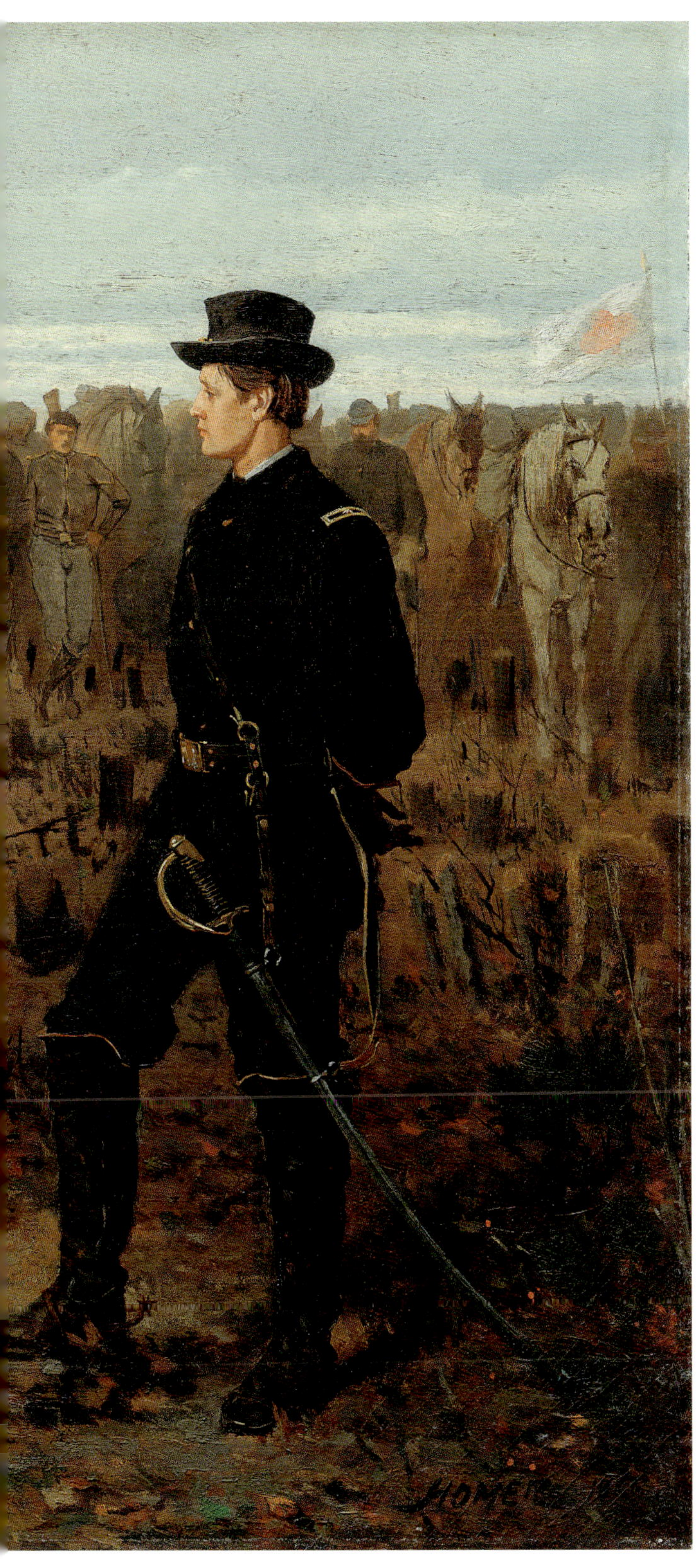

Fig. 27 *Prisoners from the Front*, 1866

Oil on canvas, 61 × 96.5 cm
The Metropolitan Museum of Art, New York. Gift of Mrs Frank B. Porter, 1922 (22.207)

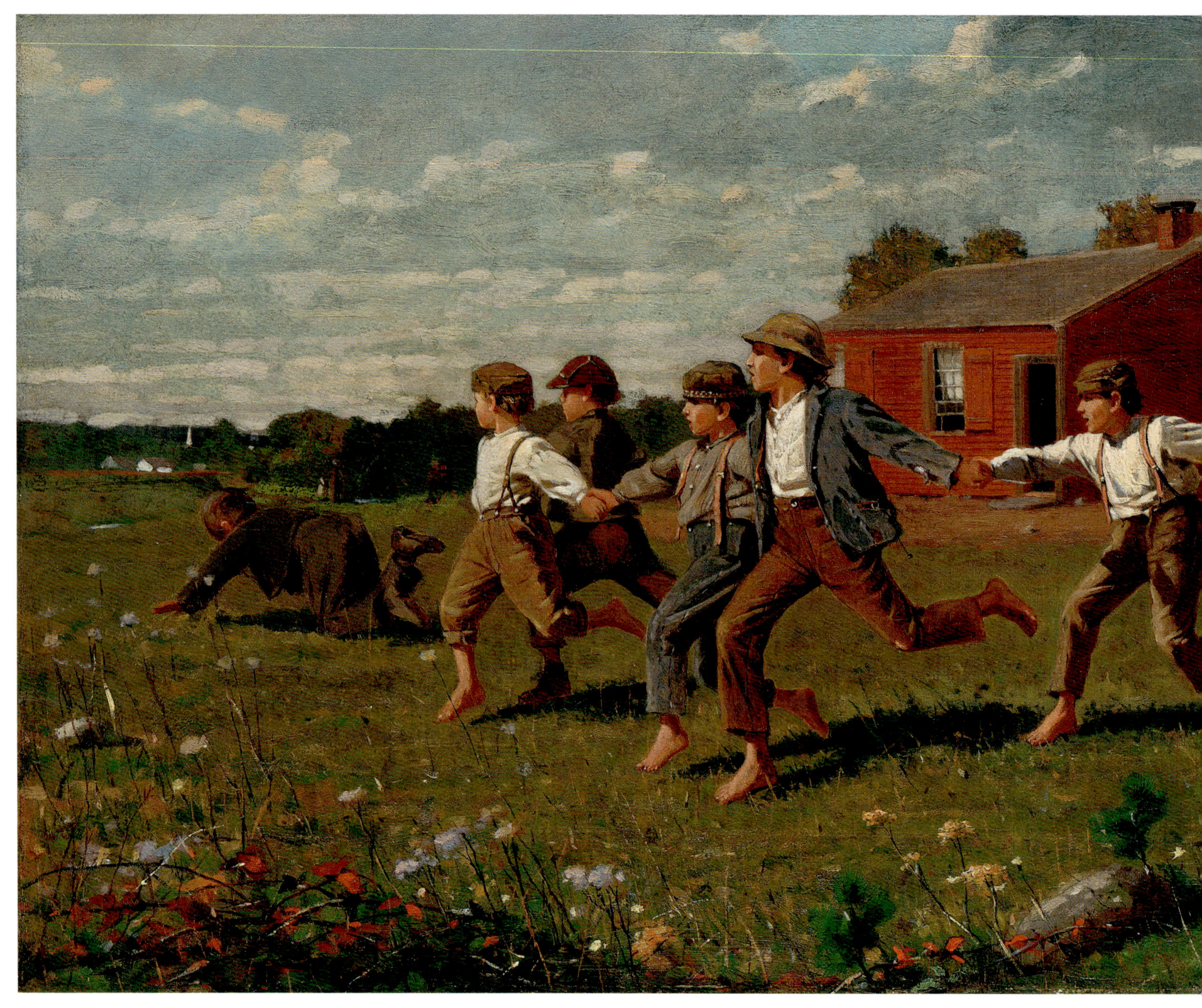

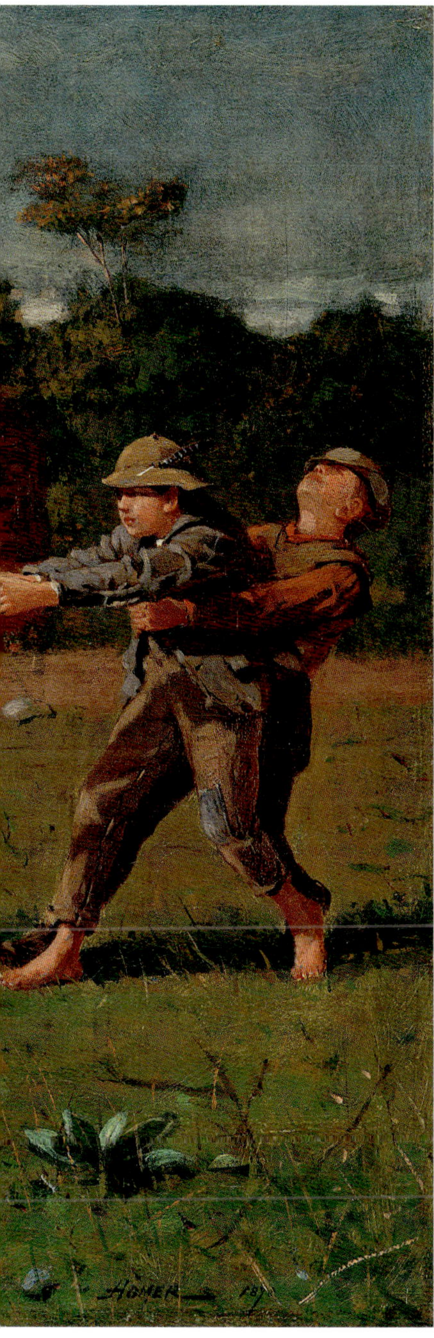

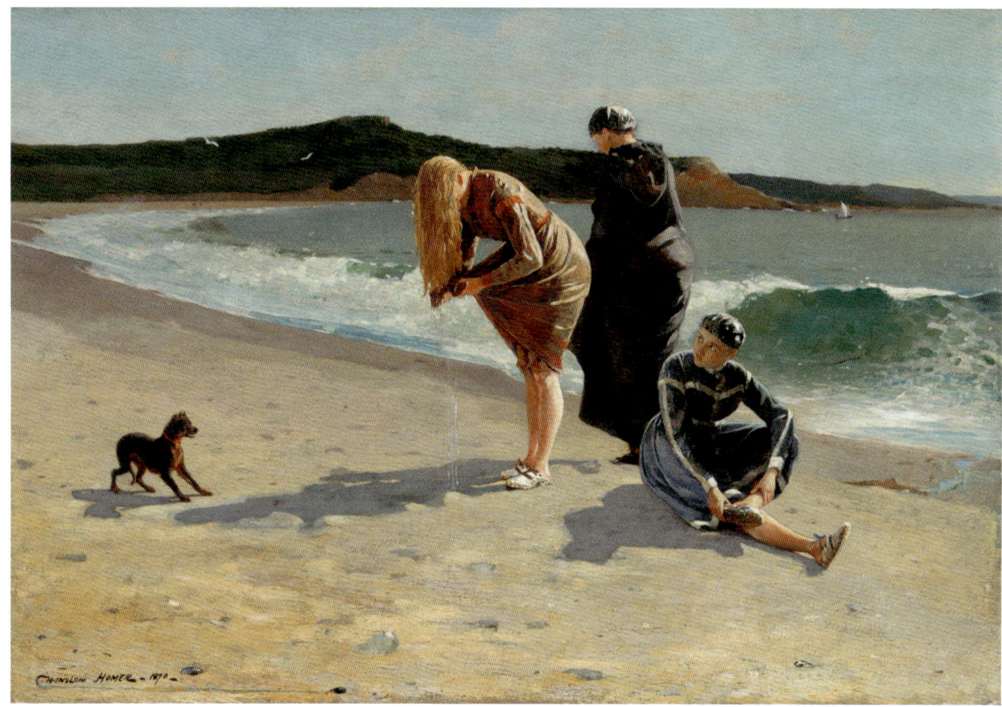

Fig. 28 *Snap the Whip*, 1872

Oil on canvas, 30.5 × 50.8 cm
The Metropolitan Museum of Art, New York. Gift of Christian A. Zabriskie, 1950 (50.41)

Fig. 29 *Eagle Head, Manchester, Massachusetts (High Tide)*, 1870

Oil on canvas, 66 × 96.5 cm
The Metropolitan Museum of Art, New York. Gift of Mrs William F. Milton, 1923 (23.77.2)

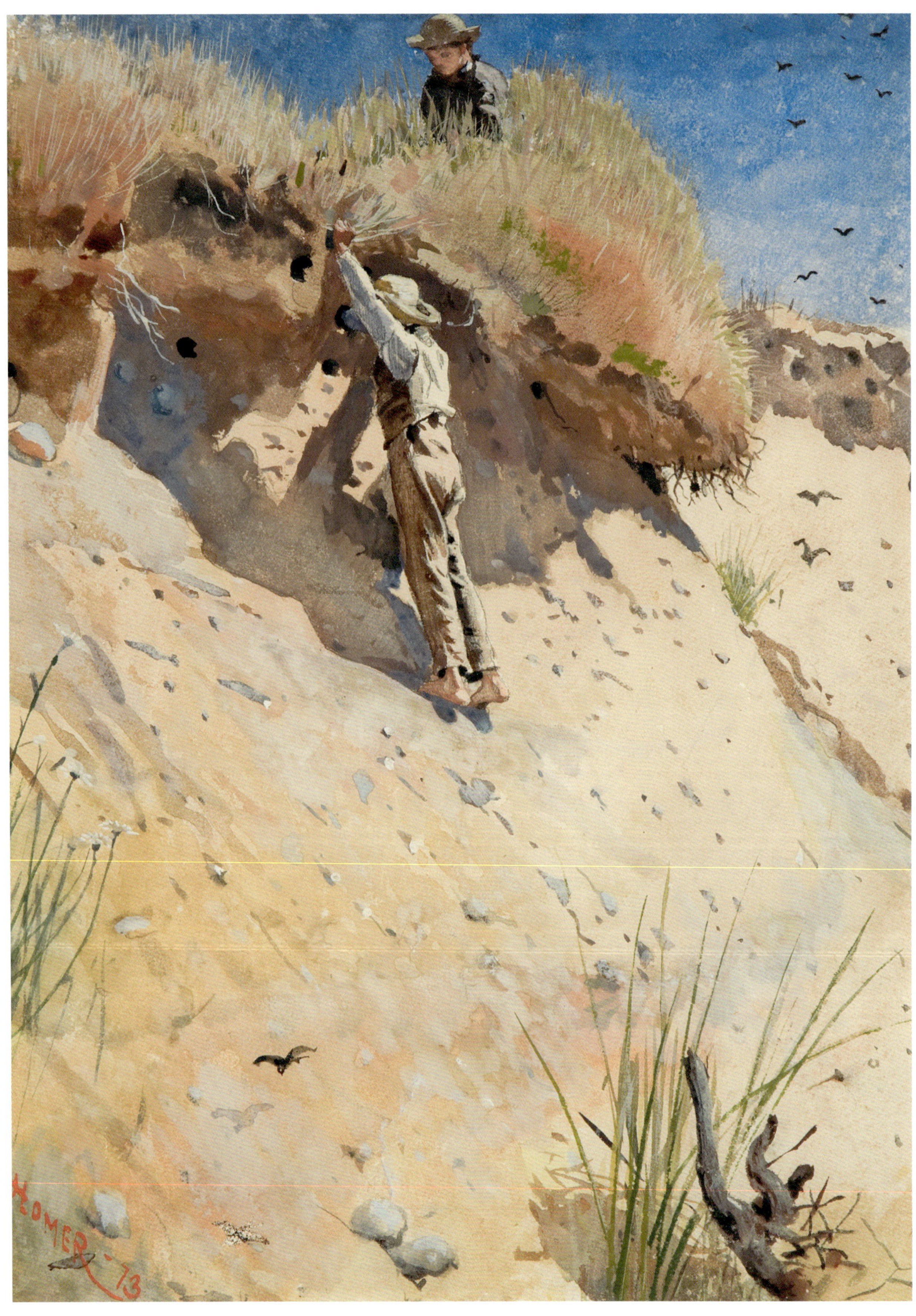
HOMER - 73

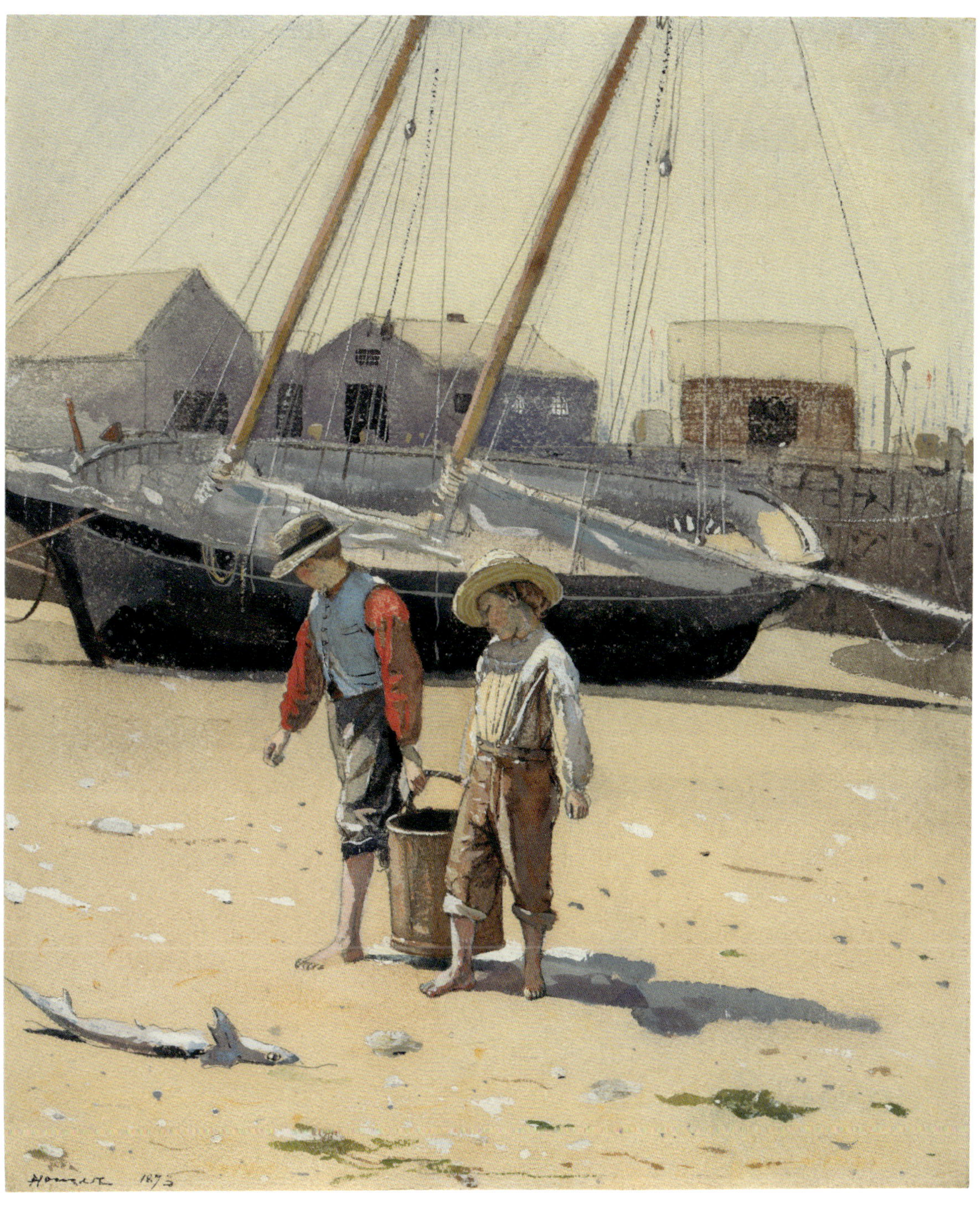

Fig. 31 *A Basket of Clams*, 1873

Watercolour on wove paper, 29.2 × 24.8 cm
The Metropolitan Museum of Art, New York. Gift of Arthur G. Altschul, 1995 (1995.378)

Opposite
Fig. 30 *How Many Eggs?*, 1873

Watercolour on paper, 32.4 × 23.8 cm
Karen and Kevin Kennedy

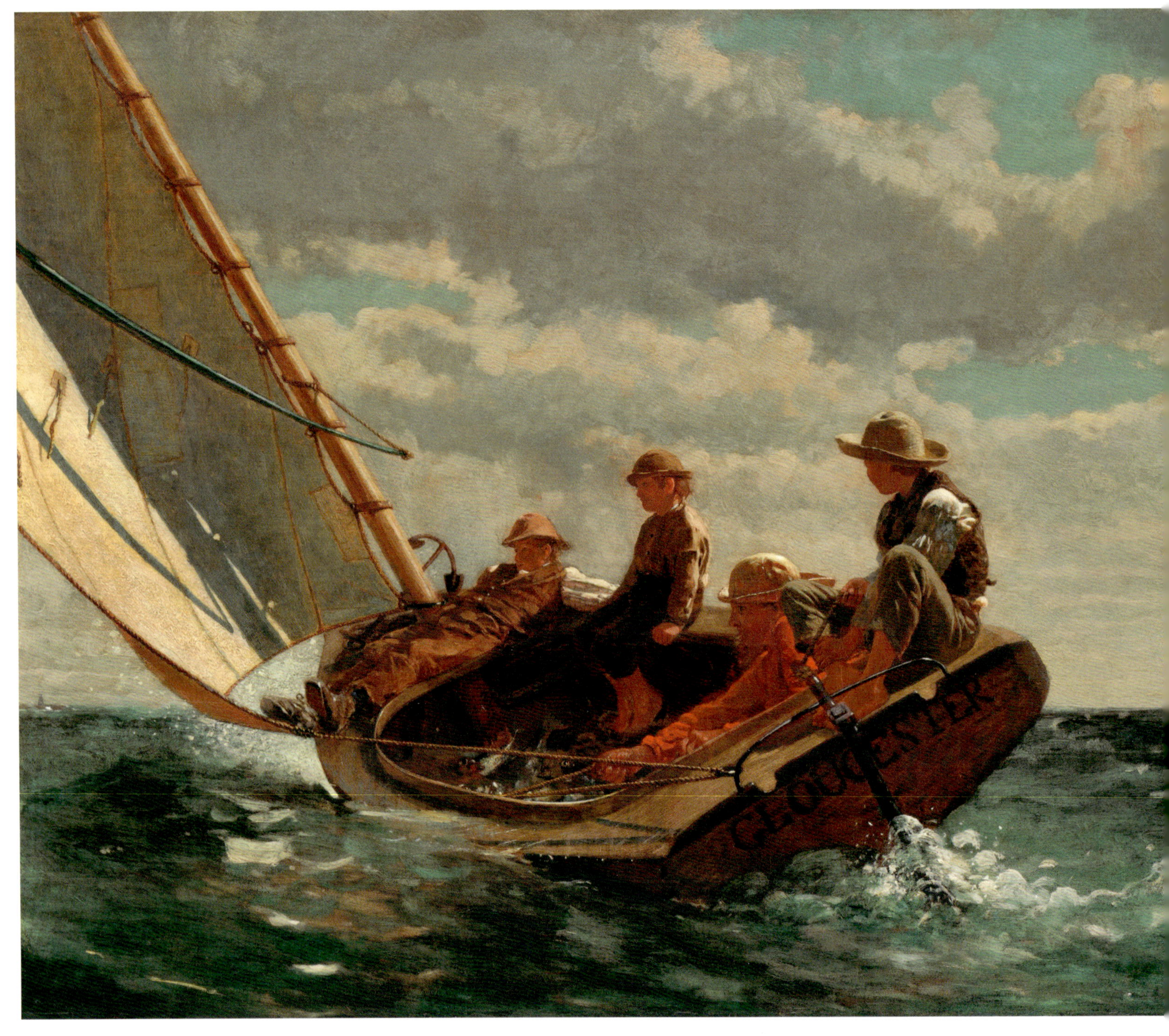

Fig. 32 *Breezing Up (A Fair Wind)*, 1873–6

Oil on canvas, 61.5 × 97 cm
National Gallery of Art, Washington, DC.
Gift of the W.L. and May T. Mellon Foundation (1943.13.1)

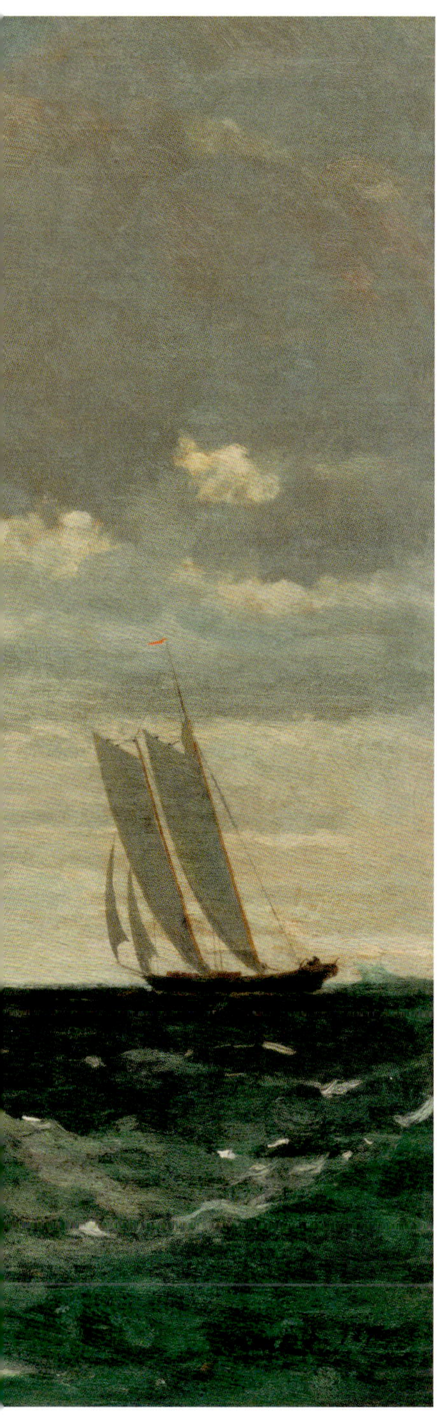

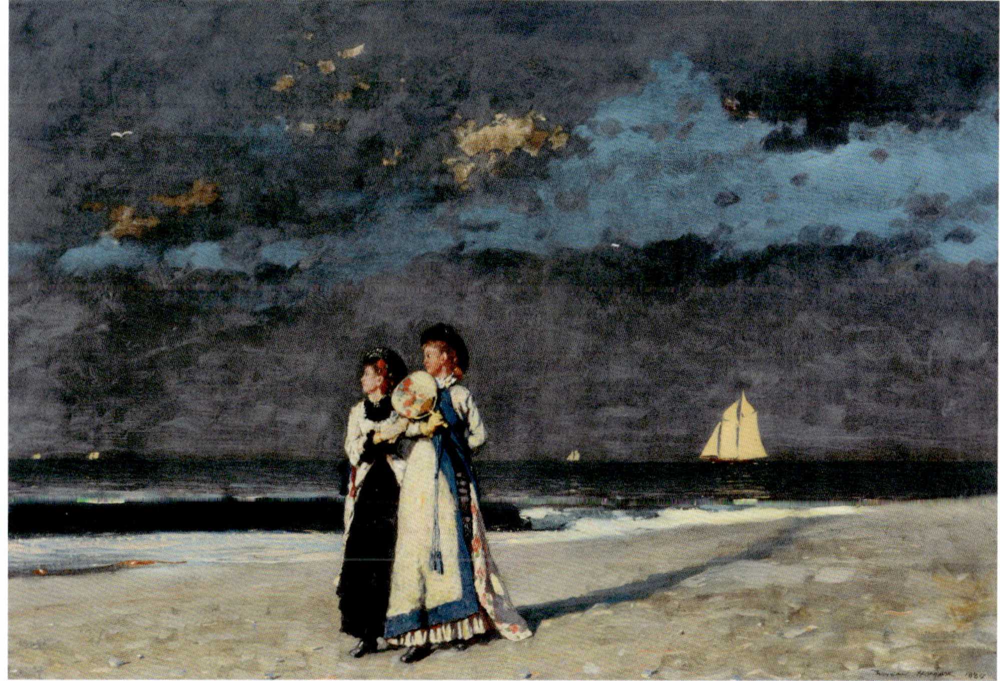

Fig. 33 *Promenade on the Beach*, 1880

Oil on canvas, 50.8 × 76.2 cm
Michele and Donald D'Amour Museum of Fine Arts, Springfield, Massachusetts. Gift of the Misses Emily and Elizabeth Mills in memory of their parents, Mr & Mrs Isaac Mills (36.06)

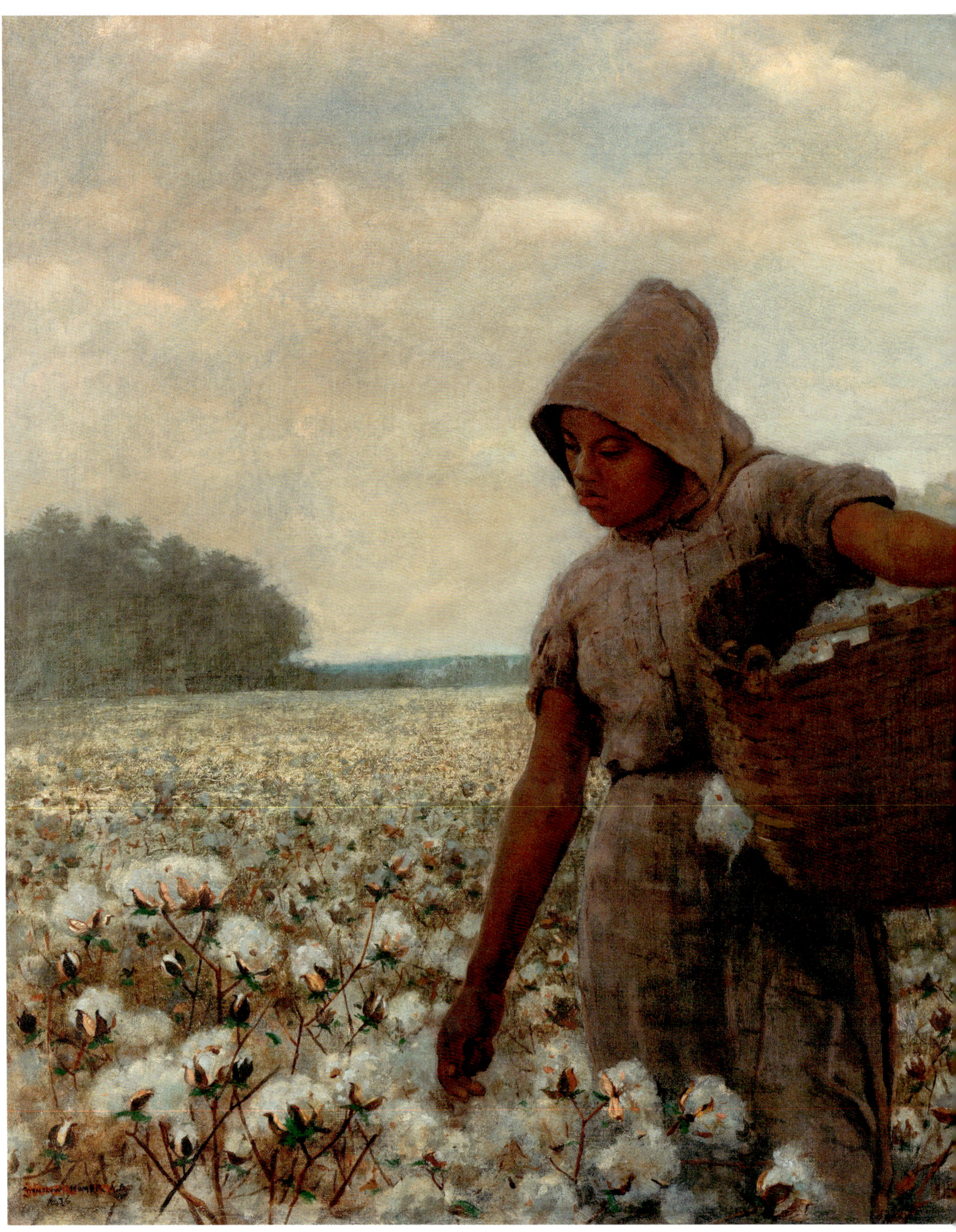

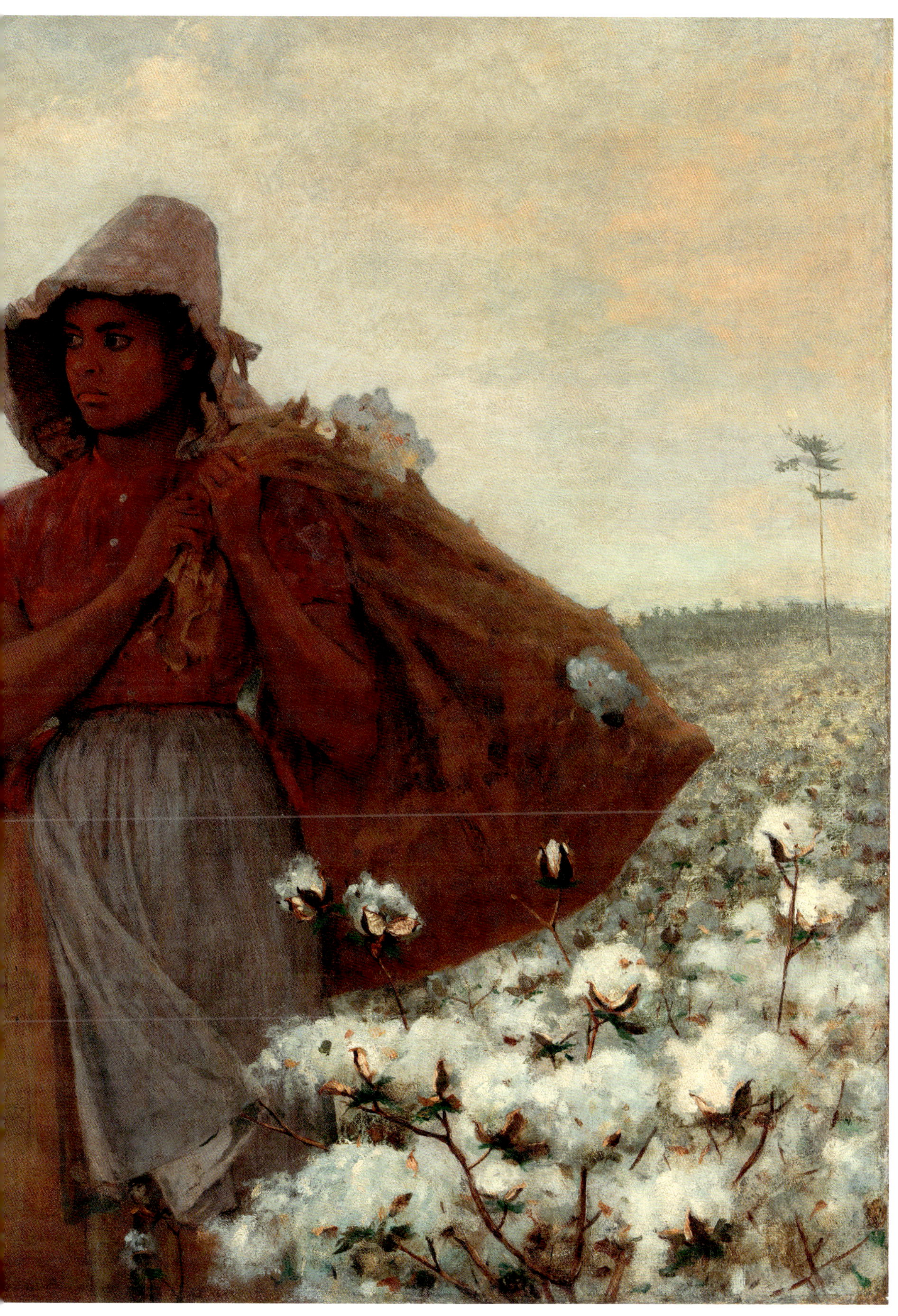

Fig. 34 *The Cotton Pickers*, 1876

Oil on canvas, 61.1 × 96.8 cm
Los Angeles County Museum of Art, California. Acquisition made possible through Museum Trustees: Robert O. Anderson, R. Stanton Avery, B. Gerald Cantor, Edward W. Carter, Justin Dart, Charles E. Ducommun, Camilla Chandler Frost, Julian Ganz, Jr, Dr Armand Hammer, Harry Lenart, Dr Franklin D. Murphy, Mrs Joan Palevsky, Richard E. Sherwood, Maynard J. Toll, and Hal B. Wallis (M.77.68)

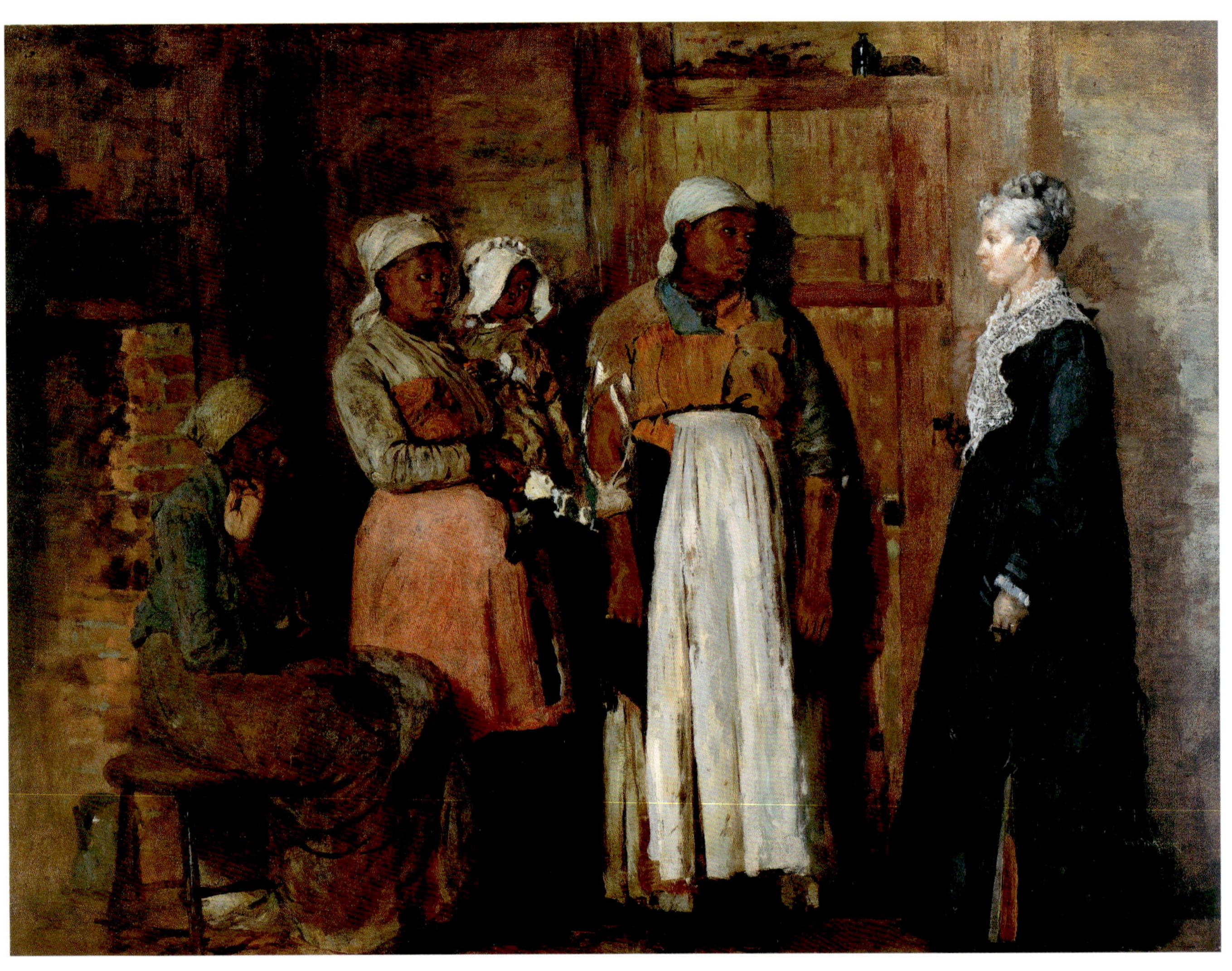

Fig. 35 *A Visit from the Old Mistress*, 1876

Oil on canvas, 45.7 × 61 cm
Smithsonian American Art Museum, Washington, DC. Gift of William T. Evans (1909.7.28)

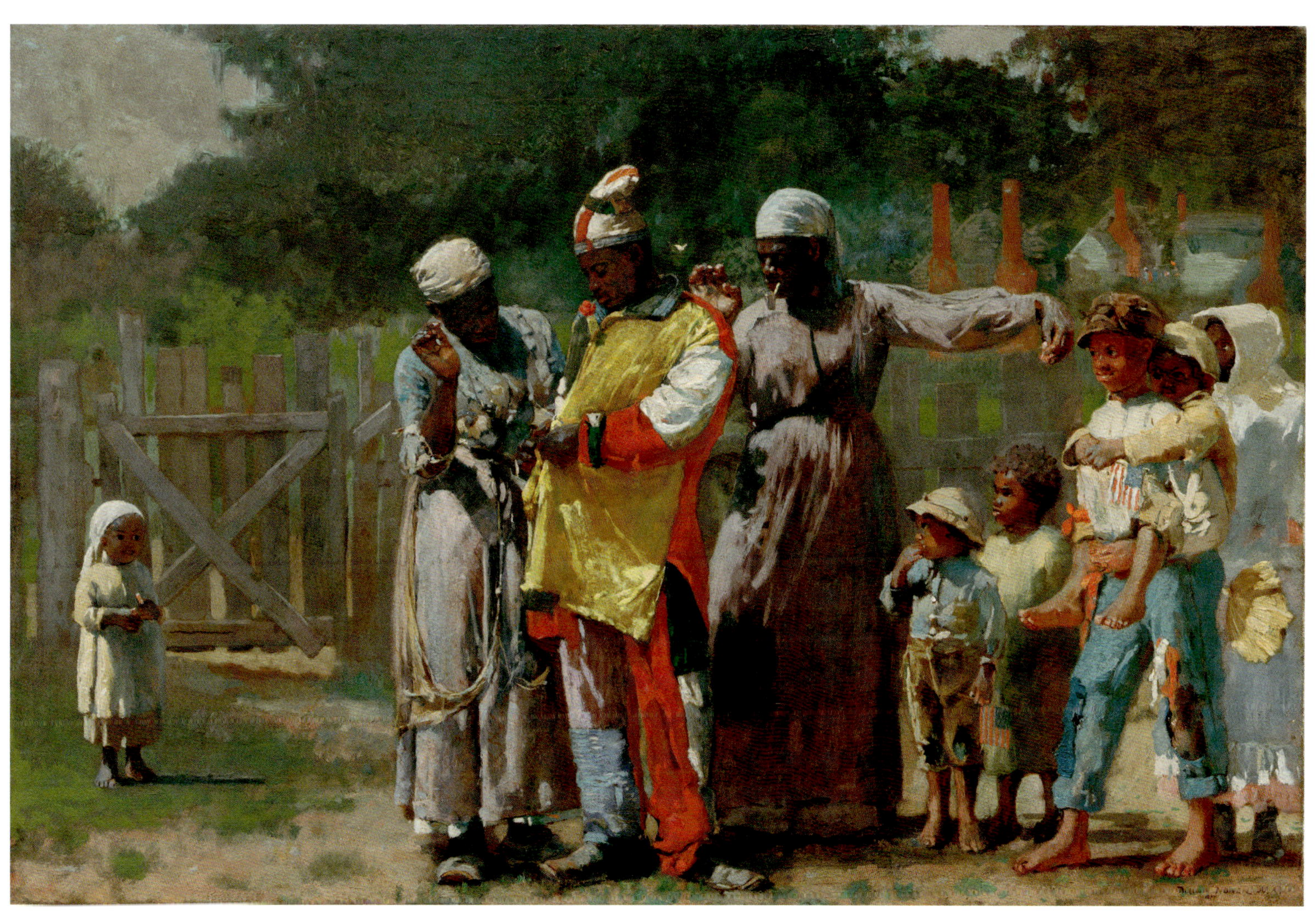

Fig. 36 *Dressing for the Carnival*, 1877

Oil on canvas, 50.8 × 76.2 cm
The Metropolitan Museum of Art, New York. Amelia B. Lazarus Fund, 1922 (22.220)

Homer and England

Christine Riding

In the spring of 1881, Winslow Homer made his second and last trip to Europe. It was also his first to the UK. After arriving in Liverpool in late March, he went directly to London. Beyond a visit in April to the national library and British Museum (both then occupying the same site in Bloomsbury, and the former now the British Library), little is known of his itinerary, although it can be assumed that he took the opportunity to visit the National Gallery, the Royal Academy and other galleries, exhibitions, artist studios and cultural sites. The following month he travelled, via Scarborough and Newcastle upon Tyne, to the North Sea fishing village of Cullercoats in Northumberland (now Tyne and Wear), where he remained for some 18 months. There, he took lodgings, and rented rooms for a studio, most likely located on Bank Top adjacent to the Watch House and, importantly for Homer, overlooking the bay (fig. 37).[1]

Many of Homer's paintings at Cullercoats and nearby Tynemouth took as their subjects working men and women, their daily activities and challenges, the images characterised by a solidity and sombreness that was new to his art. Equally, they evoke a strong sense of community, of common purpose and interdependence. Homer responded above all to the young women he encountered, portraying them going about their business: chatting, striding, carrying, sorting the catch, mending nets and bait lines, setting off to sell fish in local towns and villages, and many other tasks. But he also showed them pausing to listen or gazing out to sea from clifftops and shorelines (fig. 43). While his output in England was mainly sketches and watercolours – including relatively finished works such as *The Wreck of the Iron Crown* (1881, fig. 44), which was based on an event that Homer had witnessed in October 1881[2] – he also began at least seven

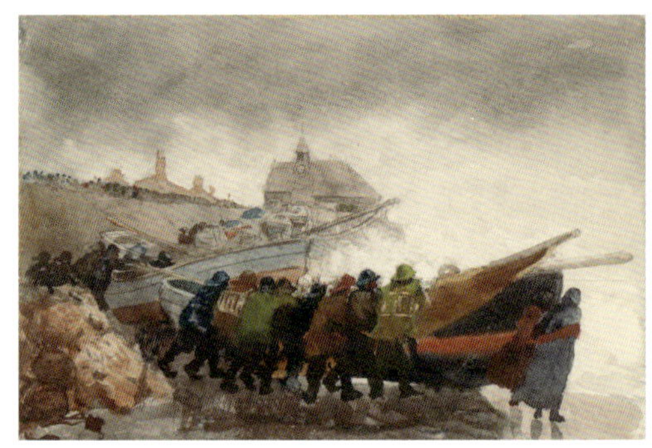

Fig. 37 *Watching the Tempest*, 1881, watercolour over graphite on off-white wove paper, 35.6 × 50.4 cm. Harvard Art Museums/Fogg Museum, Cambridge, Massachusetts. Bequest of Grenville L. Winthrop (1943.296)

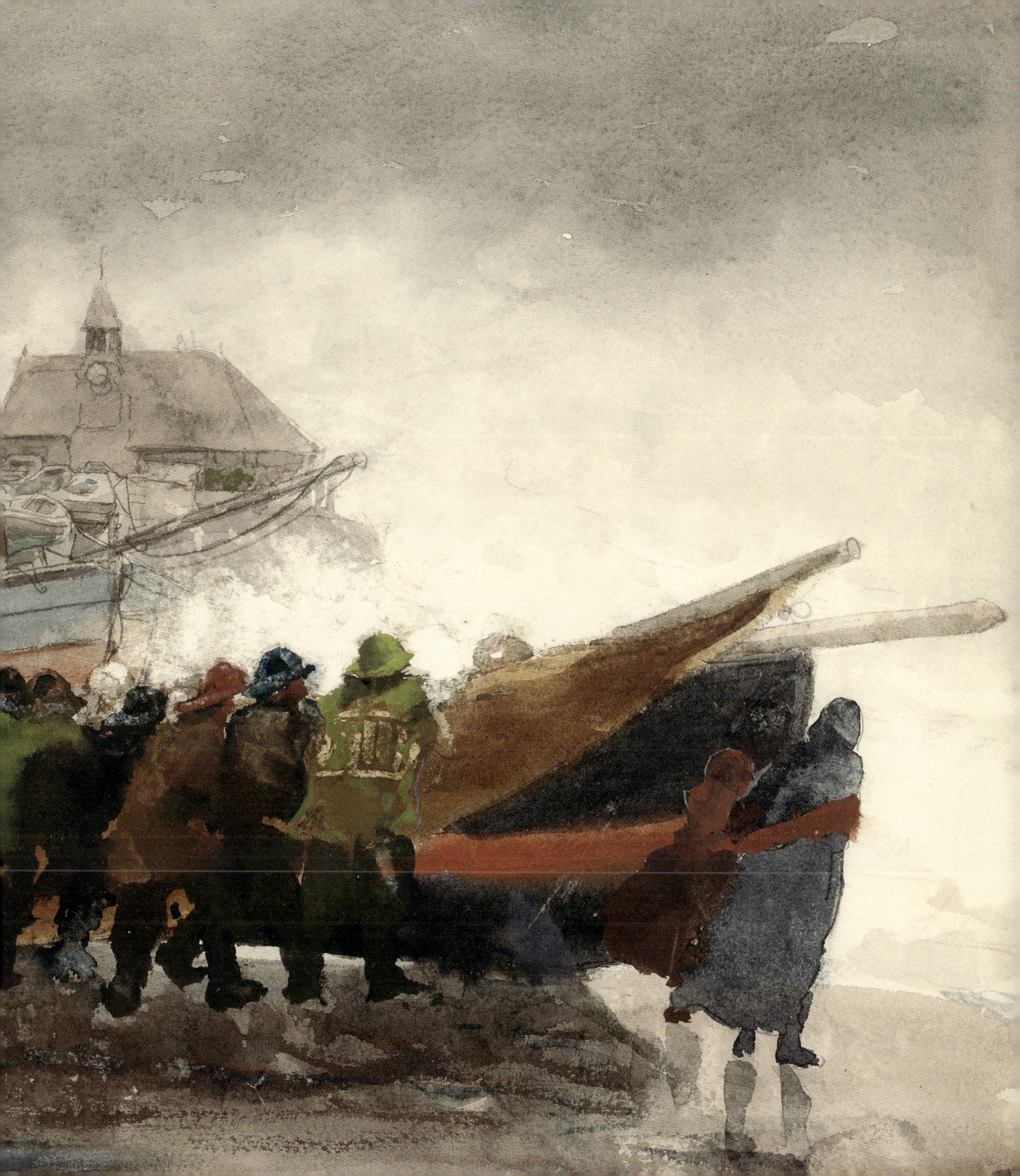

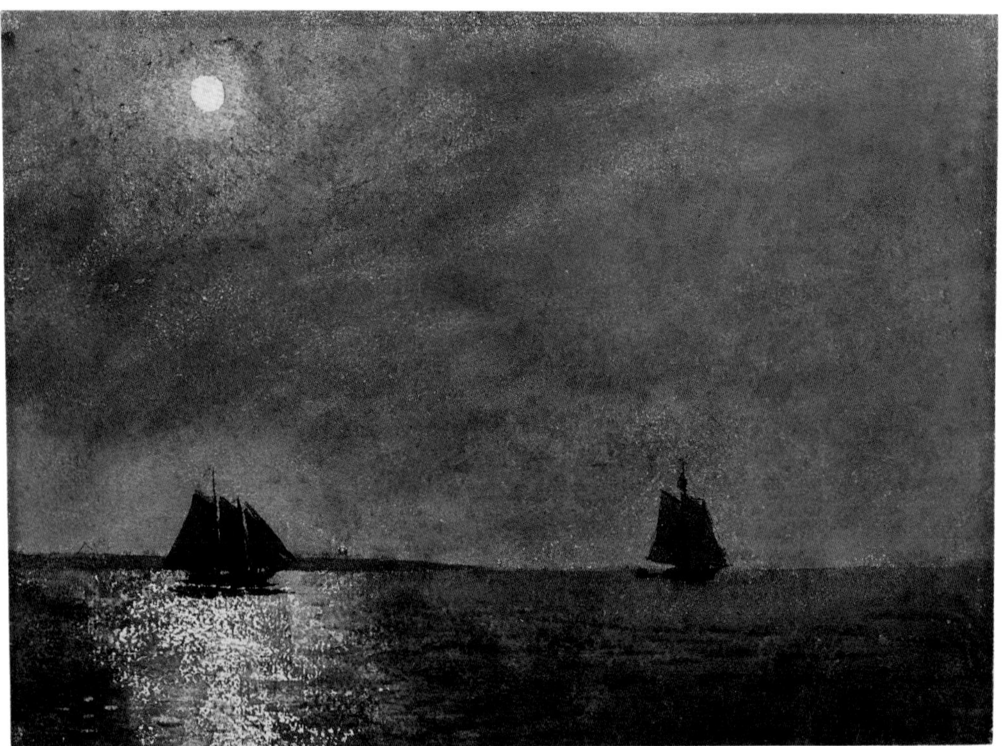

Fig. 38 *Eastern Point Light*, 1880, watercolour over graphite, 24.6 × 34.1 cm. Princeton University Art Museum, Princeton, New Jersey. Gift of Alastair B. Martin, Class of 1938

ambitious oil paintings, some larger in scale than he had hitherto attempted, and some of which were completed after his return to the USA.[3] Preeminent among these is the painting now known as *The Gale* (1883–93, fig. 47).

It has long been held that Homer's extended visit to England profoundly shaped his practice, further exposing him to the work of past and present artists and to new subject matter that he would refer to long after he had departed for home. Following his first trip to Europe from 1866 to 1867, Homer had continued to develop a warmer palette, looser brushwork and a greater focus on painting outdoor subjects, which paralleled the approach of contemporary French artists, such as Gustave Courbet (figs 23 and 86) and Edouard Manet (figs 12 and 16). Furthermore, his spirited, sun-lit scenes of coastal leisure and pursuits, such as the now celebrated *Breezing Up (A Fair Wind)* (1873–6, fig. 32), promoted a simpler, brighter, more positive vision of the USA in the post-Civil War period, and specifically in the years leading up to the nation's centennial in 1876.[4] At the same time, Homer had witnessed the challenging lives of fishing communities on his visits to Gloucester, Massachusetts, between 1873 and 1880. His experiences in New England undoubtedly revived his interest in the sea, offering a rich source of themes through his close observation of the fishermen, the harbour and the coastline, alongside the dynamics of marine weather and climate. These visits may also have provided the impetus for him to travel to Europe once again, this time to immerse himself in British maritime culture and traditions, and equally the art associated with them, not least the work of Joseph Mallord William Turner, whose stature as the foremost painter of the sea, in the Western landscape tradition, was gaining traction in the USA (see p. 15 and figs 7 and 17). Painted during the summer of 1880, the moonlit scene *Eastern Point Light* (fig. 38) already demonstrates that the bold expressiveness of Homer's experiments in watercolour chimed with those by Turner, created a generation before. Soon afterwards, Homer embarked for England where he spent almost his entire time observing and depicting the sea.

In fact, Homer was among a group of American painters in the 1870s and 1880s who sought rural and coastal subjects, as well as heroic models in French and British fishing villages. For example, in Brittany, France, Robert Wylie (1839–1877) was working at Pont-Aven, John Singer Sargent at Cancale[5] and Edward Moran around the region, the latter painting the local fisherwomen between 1878 and 1879. Within the UK, Cullercoats, already famous for its vibrant fishing industry and the 'picturesque' dress, dwellings and activities of its fisherfolk, was but one location that attracted artists and tourists alike. Another was the fishing port of Newlyn in southwest Cornwall, where a community of painters developed maritime subjects with an eye on French contemporary art influences. Furthermore, the female type that Homer came to admire in England, and the tragic subject of waiting and grieving fisherwomen as

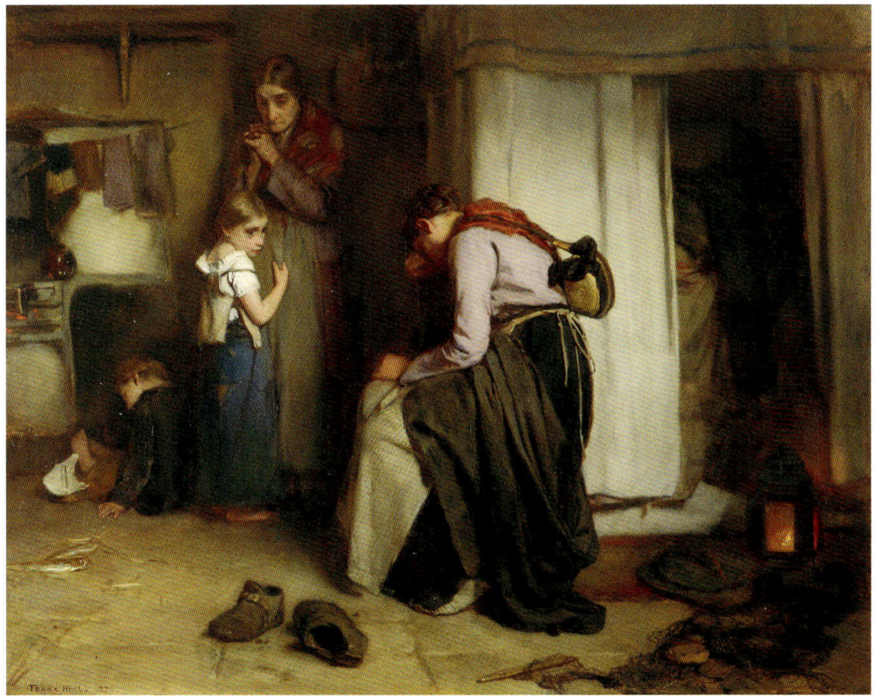

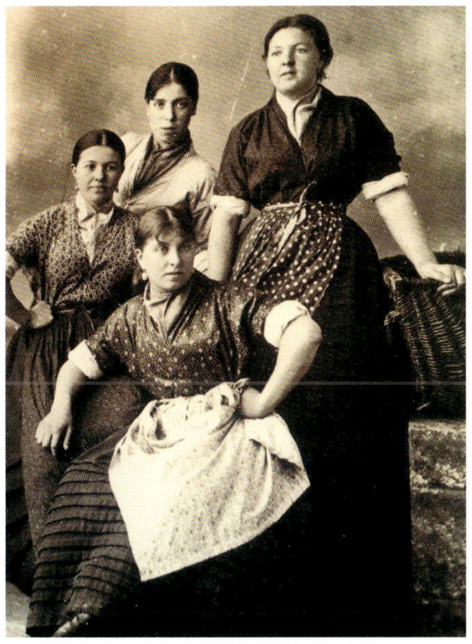

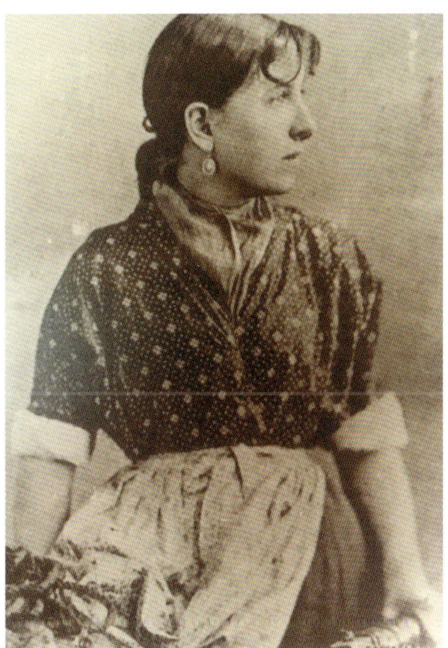

Top
Fig. 39 Frank Holl (1845–1888), *No Tidings from the Sea*, 1870, oil on canvas, 71.4 × 91.4 cm. Royal Collection/Her Majesty Queen Elizabeth II (RCIN 405161)

Left
Fig. 40 Maggie Jefferson with her cousins, 1880s, photograph. Susan Johnson, Cullercoats

Right
Fig. 41 Maggie Jefferson, 1880s, photograph. Susan Johnson, Cullercoats

exemplified in *The Gale* (fig. 47), were already present in the work of Jozef Israëls (1824–1911), a leading figure in the Hague School of Dutch landscape painters,[6] whose paintings were exhibited to great acclaim in London from the 1860s. And this was equally true of contemporary British art, particularly by such artists as Frank Holl (1845–1888) and Stanhope Forbes (1857–1947). To give one example, Holl's *No Tidings from the Sea* (fig. 39), commissioned by Queen Victoria and shown at the Royal Academy in 1871, was painted following a family holiday in Cullercoats.[7]

After 1880, Homer rarely featured genteel ladies at leisure, focusing instead on images of working women. While resident in Cullercoats, he not only sketched and observed figures outdoors, but also utilised photographs and employed models, his favourite among whom was the teenager Maggie Jefferson (figs 40 and 41).[8] That he and others were drawn to the everyday lives of coastal communities, their resilience and stoicism in the face of the relentless power of the sea, represents another chapter in the ongoing story in Western art of the natural sublime.[9] As the century progressed, this focus drew fresh impetus from the desire to capture and affirm the essence of a community and an environment that struck Homer and others as the very antithesis of the industrial and the urban, but whose way of life was consequently in danger of disappearing altogether. In melding and adapting the painterly conventions of the natural sublime and monumental human forms, Homer was also seeking to reinvigorate the concept of the pictorial epic in a thoroughly contemporary way. The Renaissance drawings and Greek and Roman sculpture he saw at the British Museum, particularly the Parthenon sculptures, and his exposure to the statuesque, classicised representations of Albert Moore (1841–1893), Lawrence Alma-Tadema (1836–1912) and other contemporary artists in the UK, contributed to a significant development in the artist's figuration.[10] At the same time, his palette moved away from the spontaneity and brighter colours of his earlier paintings to embrace the more sombre tones and other pictorial devices long associated with landscapes and figurative subjects of the Romantic period, particularly those by Turner and Théodore Géricault (1791–1824) respectively.[11] Having made his name previously as a quintessential 'American' and thus national artist, Homer often portrayed his English subjects in a manner that was more universal and timeless, more heroic, perhaps, by virtue of his unsentimental approach. Such a shift underscored Homer's purpose in exploring both traditional and modern modes of picture making, and how he ultimately sought and found a new direction for his artistic vision.

After his return to the USA in November 1882, Homer exhibited a group of his English watercolours in New York. Critics immediately recognised a significant change in his style and approach. 'He is a very different Homer from the one we knew in days gone by,' noted one: his pictures now 'touch a far higher plane ... They are works of High Art.'[12] Another extolled his focus on the inhabitants of the 'oceans and fields', who were 'of simple and noble beauty' and 'equal to those which inspired the old Greek masters when they gave to the world treasures of hewn marble'.[13] The inference here seems to be that in transforming living beings, via the example of Renaissance and classical art, Homer had created archetypes rather than individuals to draw out their universal significance and appeal (as mentioned above). Interestingly, the critical reception of *The Gale* was much less straightforward. First begun in Tynemouth, it was exhibited in 1883 as *The Coming Away of the Gale* at the National Academy of Design in New York, where it garnered lukewarm reviews. Homer kept it for nearly a decade at his studio in Prouts Neck, Maine, before reducing and reworking the canvas, removing the boat and brigade house that dominated one side of the composition, leaving the woman and child alone, battered by the forces of nature. Thus altered, *The Gale* was exhibited at the World's Fair in Chicago in 1893, where this time round it was greatly admired.[14]

As more recent commentators have suggested, Homer may have made a deliberate calculation to move from his depictions of African American women in the 1870s, as represented by *The Cotton Pickers* (1876, fig. 34), to his focus on the female inhabitants of Cullercoats and Tynemouth, as seen in *The Gale*. Powerful in build, far from fashionable society and lowly in their respective social hierarchies, they were 'the most natural and least threatening of women'.[15] However, the advantage to Homer of white working women on the other side of the Atlantic was that they 'were unencumbered by the problematic racial questions of black fieldworkers'.[16] Given the context of the Civil War and Reconstruction period (see pp. 34–8), the move to the UK may have offered Homer an artistic direction that avoided (with his female subjects at least) the continuing social, political and racial tensions and injustices in the USA (see pp. 100–4).

1 See Harrison 1983, p. 20.
2 The *Iron Crown* was a bark driven onto the shoals near Tynemouth during a storm on 20 and 21 October 1881. Hundreds of villagers rushed to the Life Brigade House to launch rescue operations.
3 See B.K. Rudd, 'Hark! The Lark' in Worcester and Milwaukee 2017–18, p. 64.
4 See London and Giverny 2006, p. 15.
5 See S. Cash, 'Testing the Waters: Sargent and Cancale', in S. Cash (ed.), *Sargent and the Sea*, exh. cat., Corcoran Gallery of Art, New Haven and London 2009, pp. 89–117.
6 The Hague School is a group of artists who lived and worked in The Hague between 1860 and 1890. They were influenced by the realist painters of the French Barbizon School.
7 See www.rct.uk/collection/405161/no-tidings-from-the-sea (accessed 4 February 2022).
8 See Harrison 1983, pp. 26–7.
9 For Winslow Homer's seascapes and rescue scenes in the context of the pictorial epic and the natural sublime, see Christine Riding, 'The Nature of Our Looking', in Christine Riding (ed.), *Kehinde Wiley: The Prelude*, exh. cat., National Gallery, London, 2021, pp. 42–63.
10 See E. Athens, 'Turning to England' in Worcester and Milwaukee 2017–18, pp. 21–3.
11 See Philadelphia 2012, pp. 41–3.
12 Worcester and Milwaukee 2017–18, p. 42.
13 Ibid, p. 52.
14 Ibid, pp. 36–7.
15 S. Burns, 'Winslow Homer and the Natural Woman', in T.J. Jackson Lears (ed.), *American Victorians and Virgin Nature*, Boston 2002, p. 35.
16 Ibid.

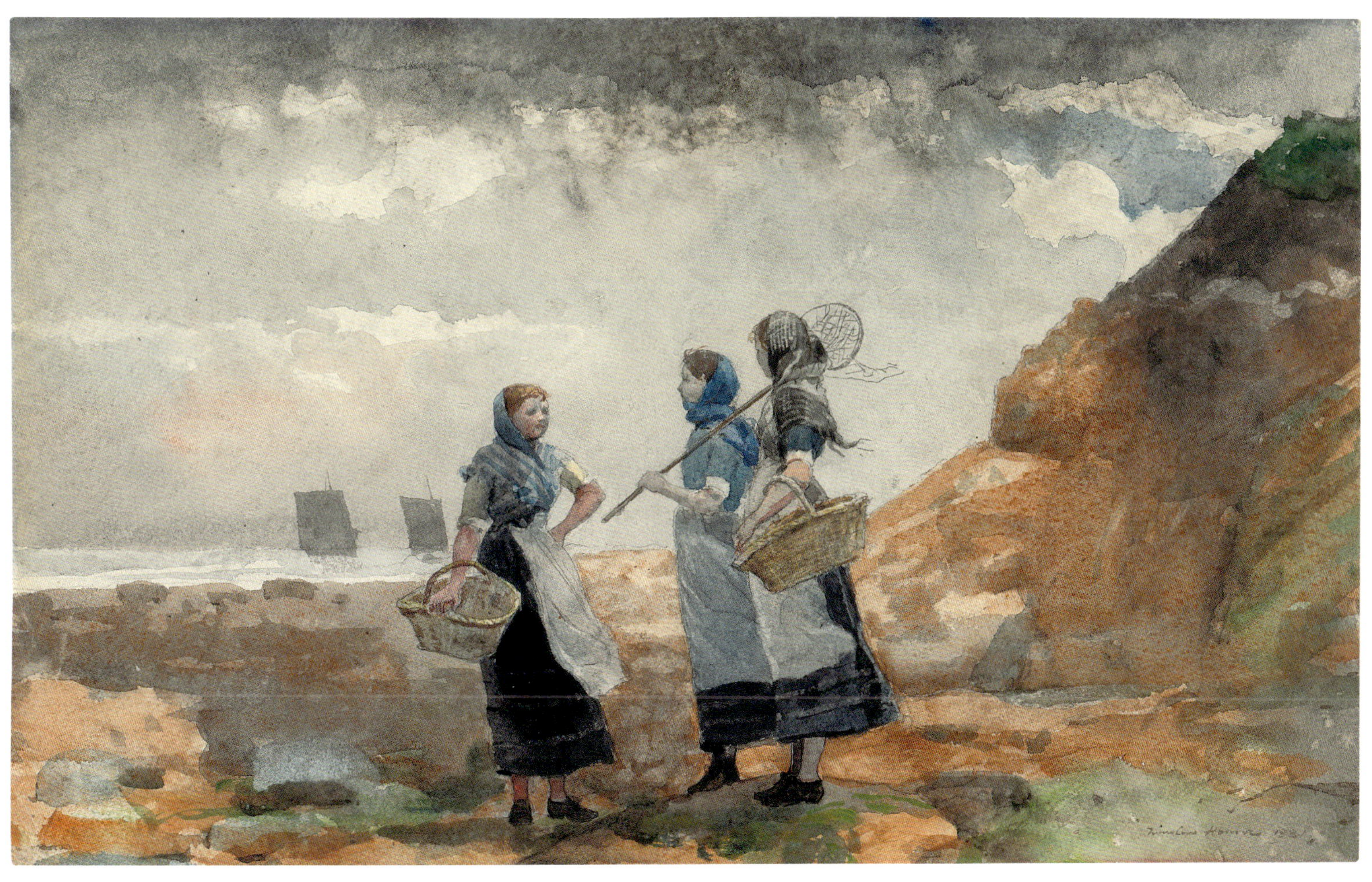

Fig. 42 *Three Fisher Girls, Tynemouth*, 1881

Watercolour over graphite on wove paper, 29.85 × 48.9 cm
National Gallery of Art, Washington, DC. Collection of Mr and Mrs Paul Mellon (2012.89.4)

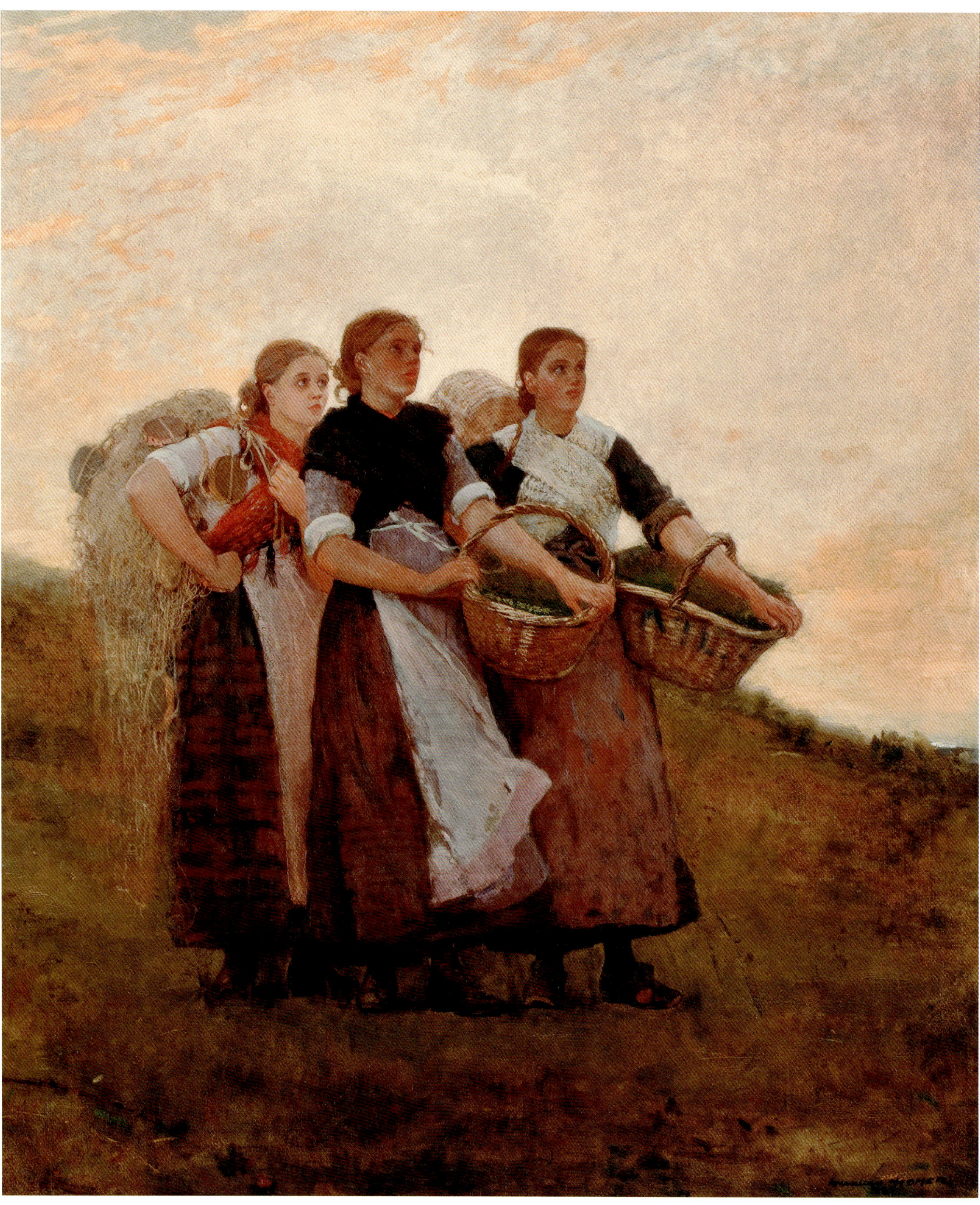

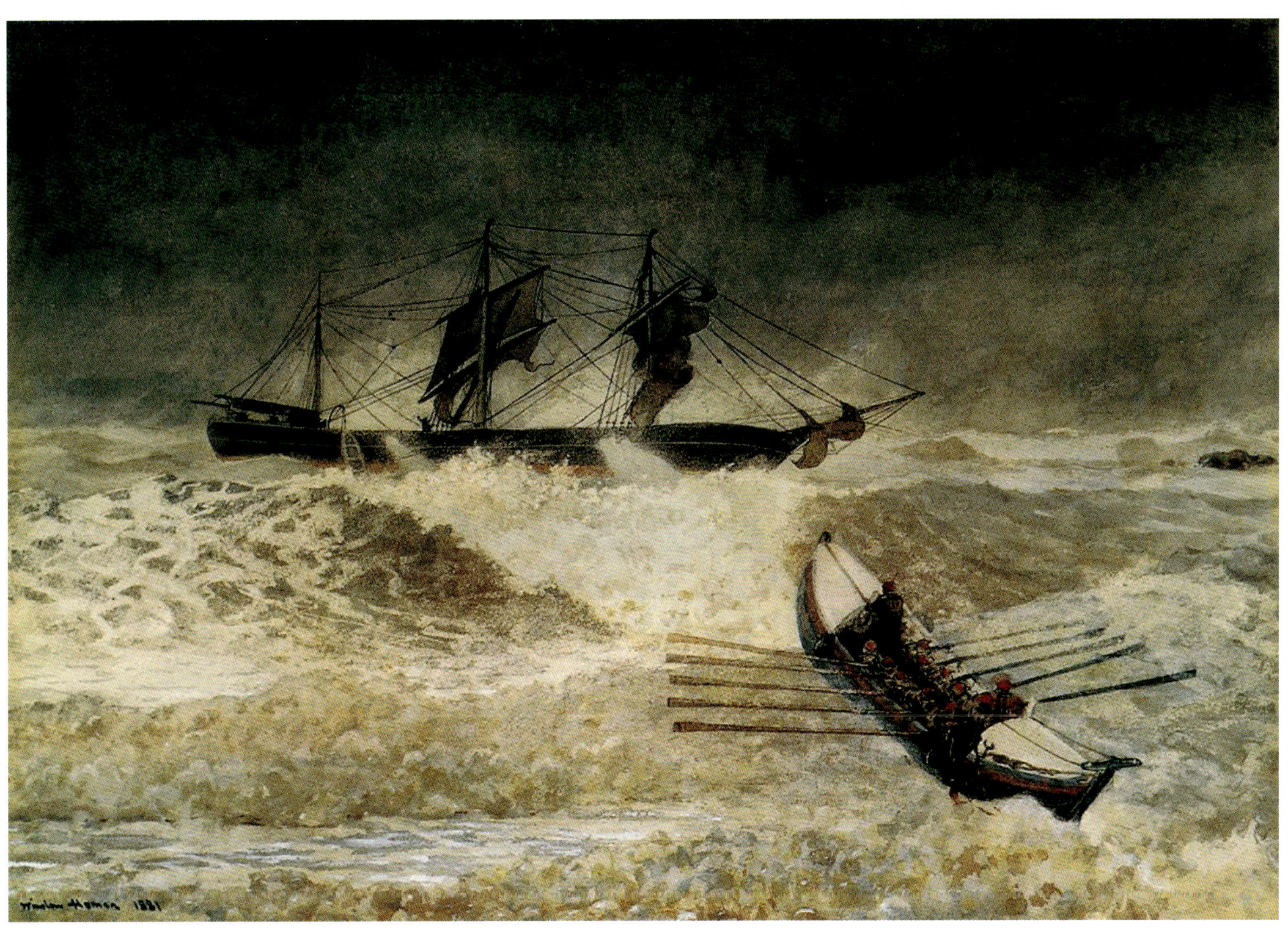

Opposite
Fig. 43 *Hark! The Lark*, 1882

Oil on canvas, 92.4 × 79.7 cm
Milwaukee Art Museum, Milwaukee, Wisconsin. Layton Art Collection Inc. Gift of Frederick Layton (L99)

Fig. 44 *The Wreck of the Iron Crown*, 1881

Watercolour, graphite and charcoal on paper, 51.4 × 74.6 cm
Private collection, on extended loan to The Baltimore Museum of Art, Baltimore, Maryland (BMA R.8613.2)

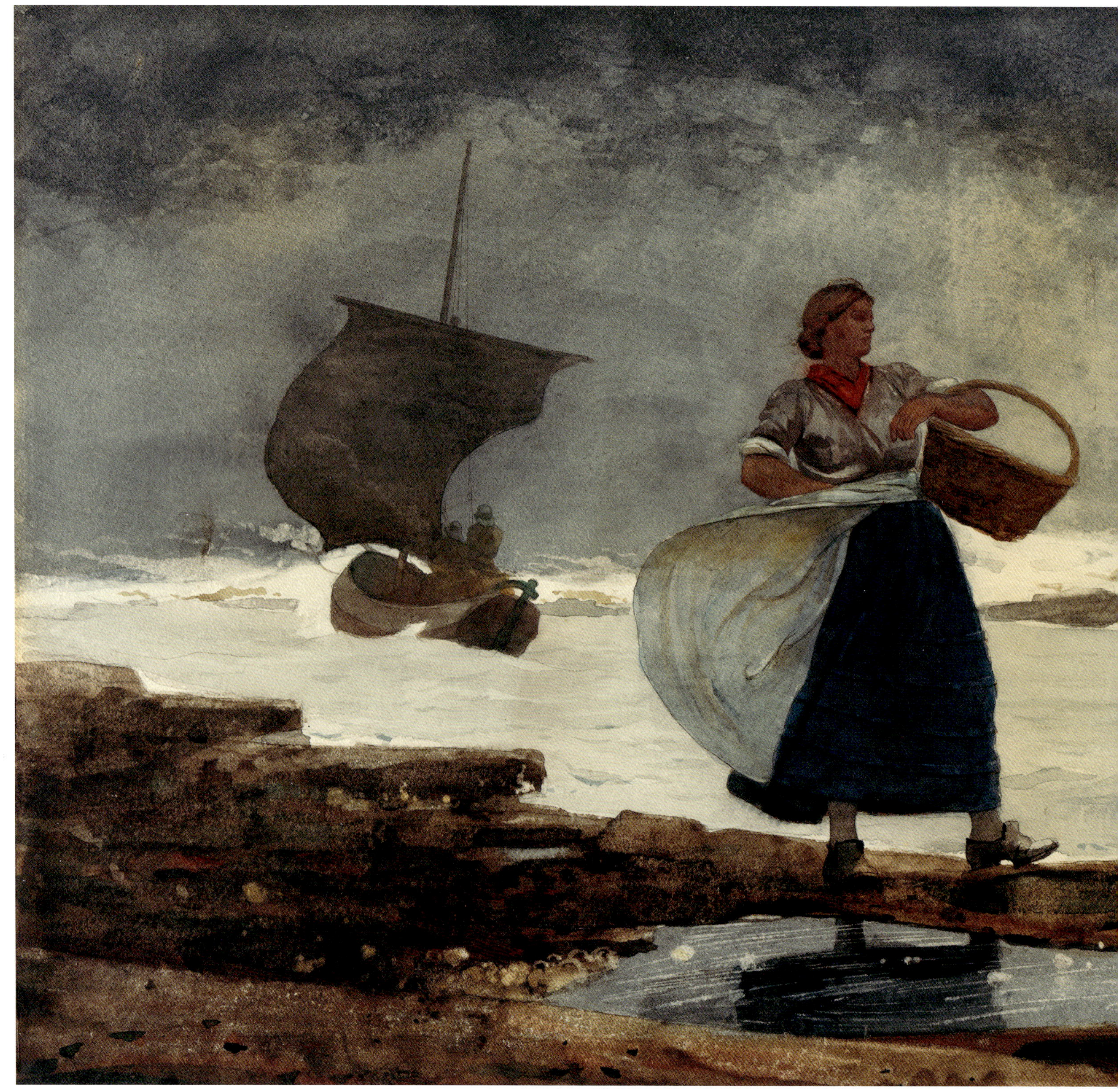

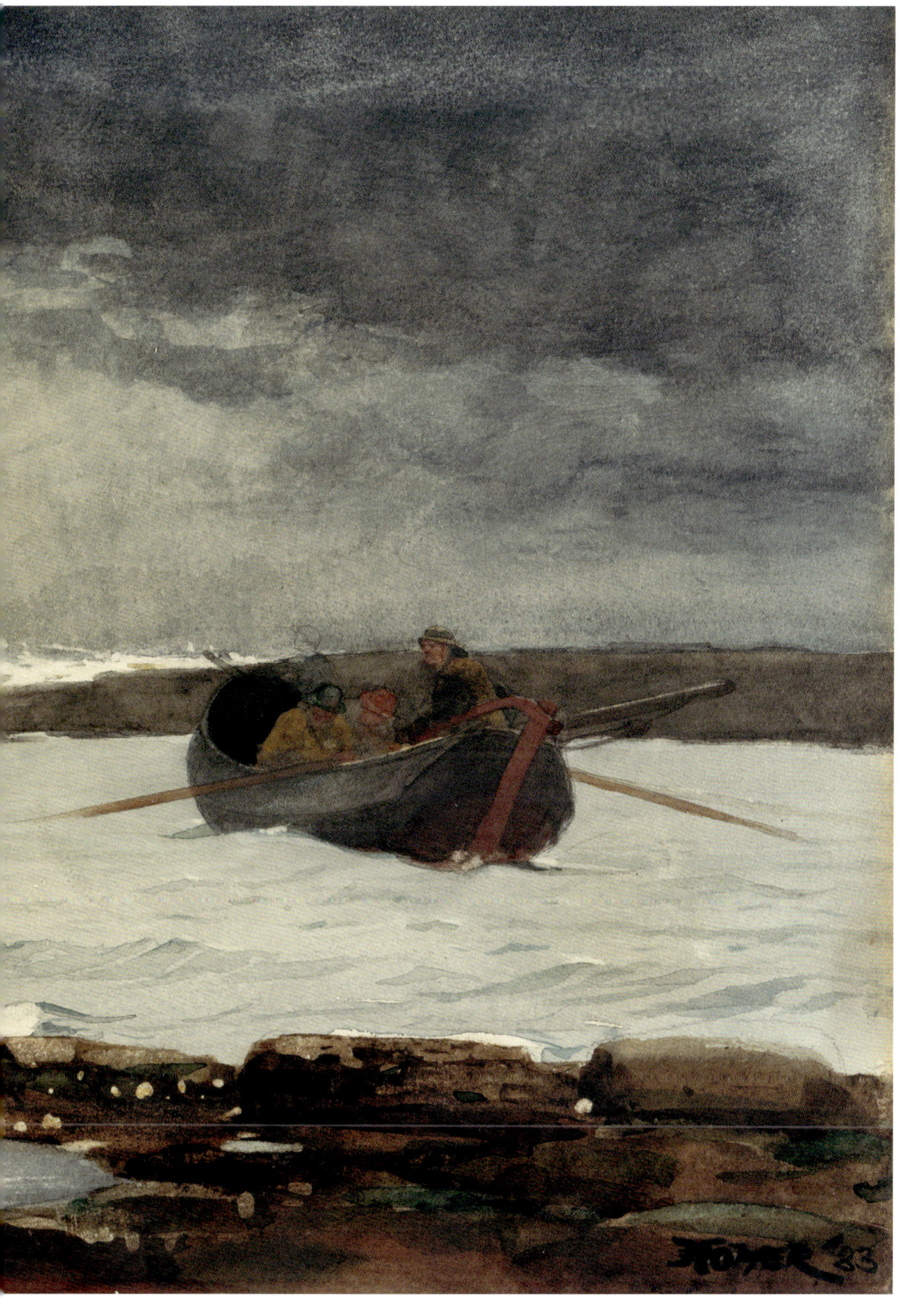

Fig. 45 *Inside the Bar*, 1883

Watercolour and graphite on wove paper, 40.6 × 73.7 cm
The Metropolitan Museum of Art, New York. Gift of Louise Ryals Arkell, in memory of Bartlett Arkell, 1954 (54.183)

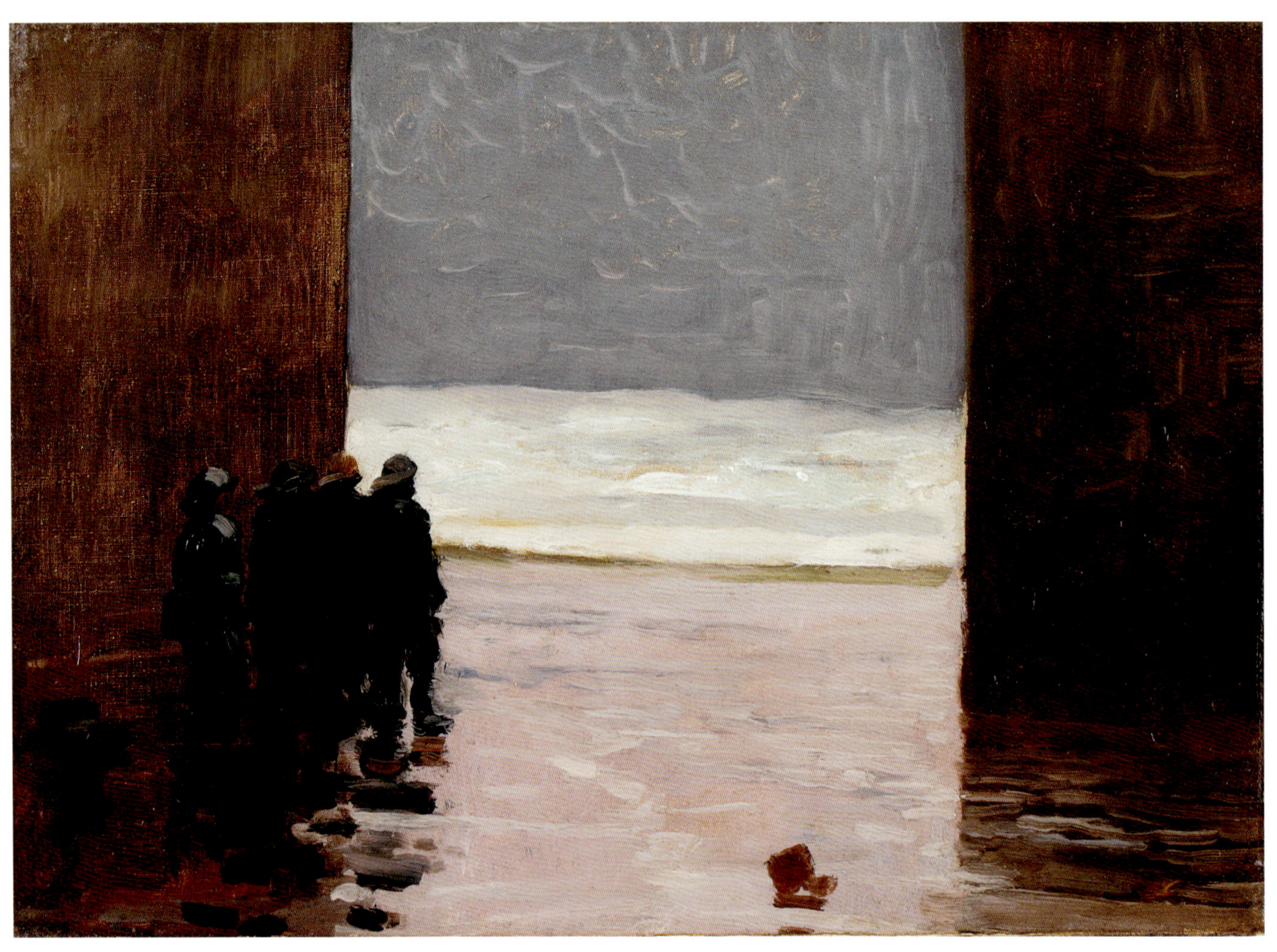

Fig. 46 *The Life Brigade*, about 1882

Oil on canvas, 30 × 44.1 cm
Myron Kunin Collection of American Art, Minneapolis, Minnesota (1997.12.04.1)

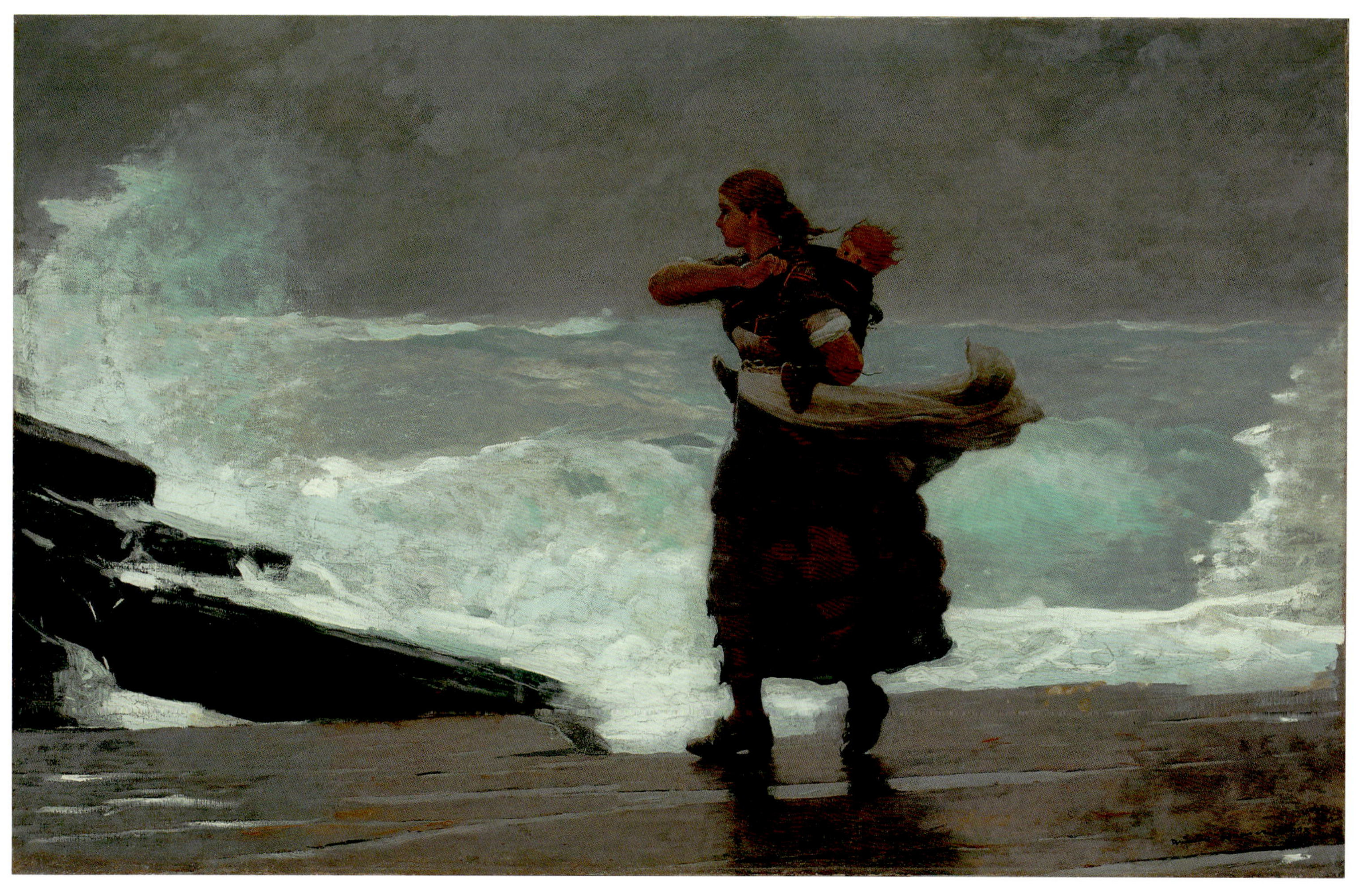

Fig. 47 *The Gale*, 1883–93

Oil on canvas, 76.8 × 122.7 cm
Worcester Art Museum, Worcester, Massachusetts. Museum Purchase (1916.48)

Between Life and Death

Christine Riding

Homer's time in Cullercoats, England – with its thriving fishing industry that attracted artists and tourists alike – provided him with profound, timeless themes inspired by the arduous lives of the local community (see pp. 54–65). After returning to the USA in late 1882, he settled the following year in the coastal peninsula of Prouts Neck, Maine, also a maritime centre and popular summer resort, and equally cold and inhospitable during the winter. There, he would continue to develop imagery based on his experiences in England, above all featuring the fisherwomen of Cullercoats and Tynemouth (fig. 48).[1] At the same time, Homer studied and painted the fishermen and local population in Prouts Neck and its environs. His first-hand observations in England, of storms at sea, shipwreck and rescue, had resulted in such works as *The Wreck of the Iron Crown* (1881, fig. 44). Building on these experiences but in an American context, Homer created some of his most critically acclaimed works, beginning with *The Life Line* of 1884 (fig. 51).

The dramatic rescue from a foundering ship was a long-standing and enduringly popular subject in Western art, but for *The Life Line* Homer focused on a method of lifesaving that was made possible only through a recent technological innovation: the breeches buoy. Secured to both the ship and the shore (or ship to ship), it permitted stranded passengers to traverse the sea to safety by means of a pulley, heaved back and forth by the crews positioned at either end. Homer removes almost all evidence of the vessel, shoreline and rescuers within his composition, concentrating instead on two unidentified figures: an unconscious woman and her deliverer.[2] Homer was by no means the first to create a viewpoint within a shipwreck scene that is 'suspended' above the waves and directly confronting the action, and an earlier example is Turner's celebrated *The Shipwreck* exhibited in 1805 (Tate).[3] However, the exaggerated close crop Homer deployed, which amplifies the intimacy between the struggling protagonists and the viewer standing before the canvas, was unprecedented in his career to date and a novelty in American art. Indeed, *The Life Line* was admired by critics and first viewers as much for its formal innovation and painterly virtuosity as for the pleasingly heroic modernity of its subject.[4]

Fig. 48 *The Fisher Girl* (detail), 1894, oil on canvas, 71.8 × 71.8 cm. Five Colleges and Historic Deerfield Museum Consortium, Massachusetts. Gift of George D. Pratt (Class of 1893) (AC P.1933.7)

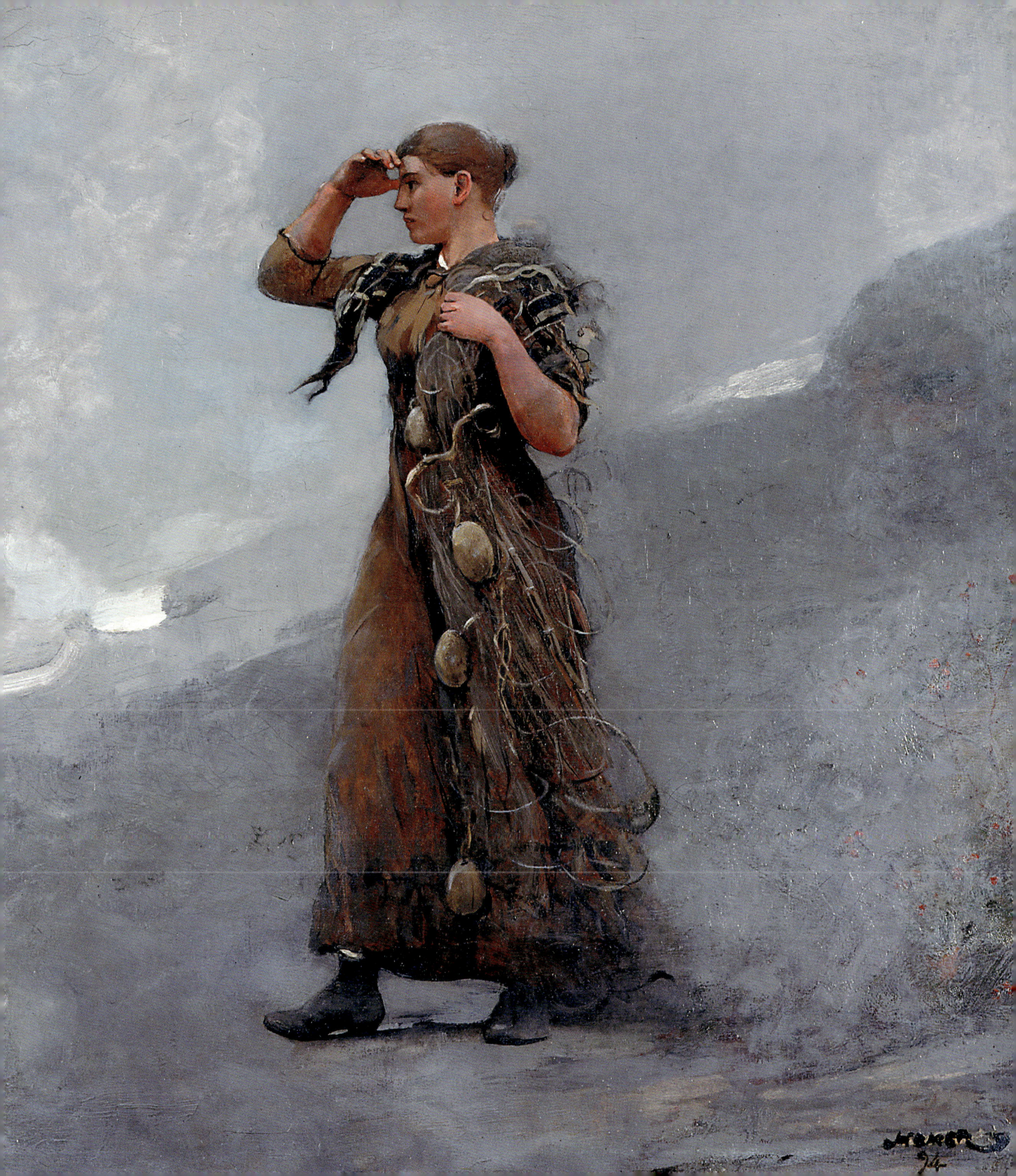

Two years later, Homer followed the success of *The Life Line* with another ambitious, large-scale painting on the theme of rescue, entitled *Undertow* (1886, fig. 55). This dramatic work is thought to have been inspired by an event Homer witnessed in 1883 near Atlantic City, New Jersey. In Homer's painting, rescuers attempt to drag two women to safety, who, exhausted and hampered by their waterlogged bathing costumes, are being pulled downwards by an undertow (a strong cross-current beneath the waterline).[5] Despite the contemporary subject, Homer's solid, monumental figures clearly refer to the sculptural forms in Greek and Roman statues and bas-reliefs, even forming a frieze-like chain of bodies that recalls such renowned artworks as the Parthenon sculptures.

Taken together, *The Life Line* and *Undertow* demonstrate how Homer was seeking to reinvigorate the concept of the pictorial epic for his own time, with images that stand as a testament to the strength, courage and selflessness of the human beings portrayed but, equally, show their fragility when confronted by the overwhelming power of the sea. While these paintings focused on men saving women, a popular theme at the time, Homer also produced a series of major works during the 1880s that dramatised the gruelling lives of the North Atlantic fishermen. Three of these – *The Fog Warning* (fig. 52), *The Herring Net* (fig. 49) and *Lost on the Grand Banks* (fig. 50), all dated 1885 – to a greater or lesser degree grapple with the habitual risks, and often fatal circumstances, that the men experienced.[6] Each painting concentrates on a single figure or pair of figures

Fig. 49 *The Herring Net*, 1885, oil on canvas, 76.5 × 122.9 cm. The Art Institute of Chicago, Illinois. Mr and Mrs Martin A. Ryerson Collection (1937.1039)

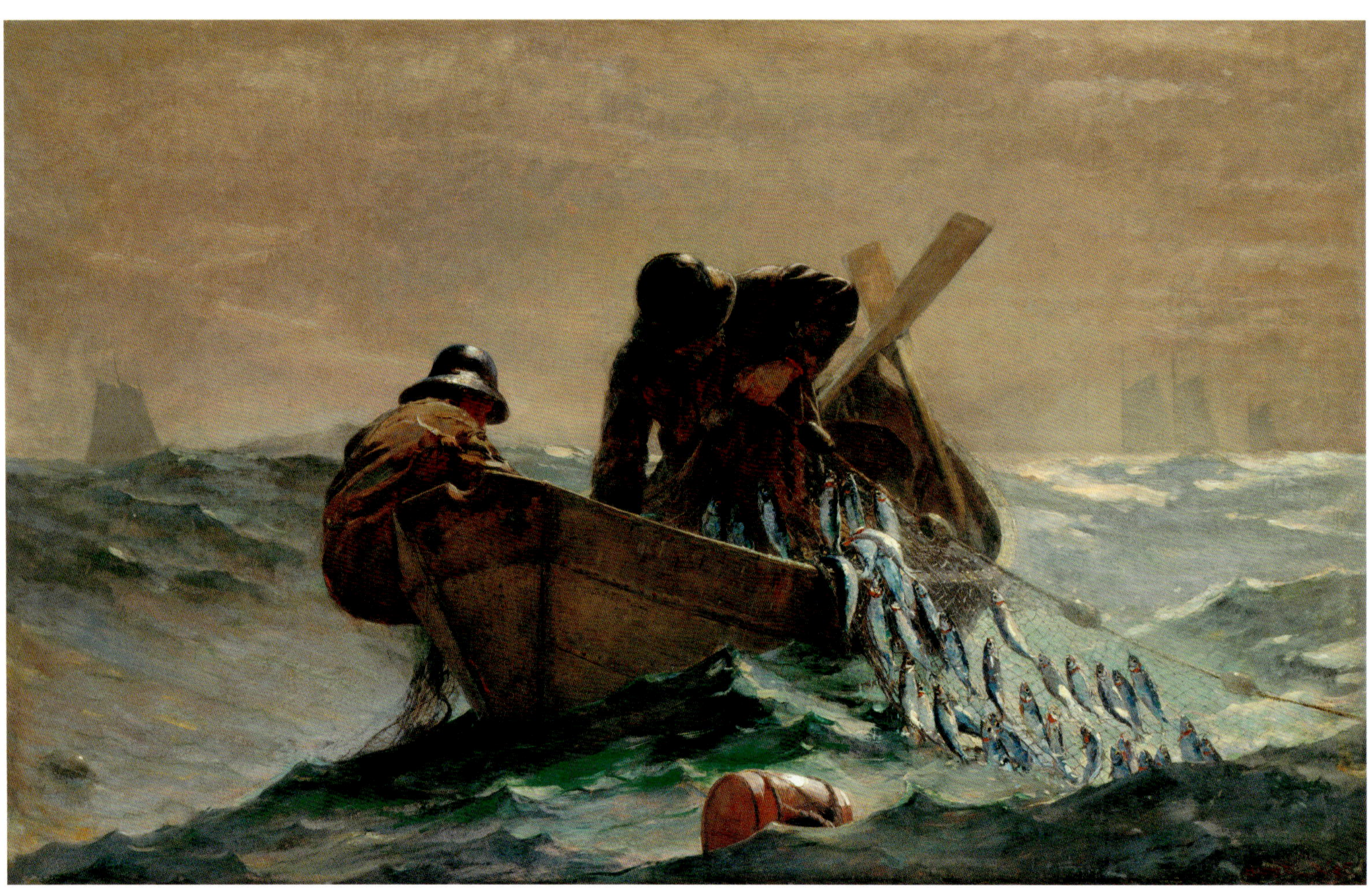

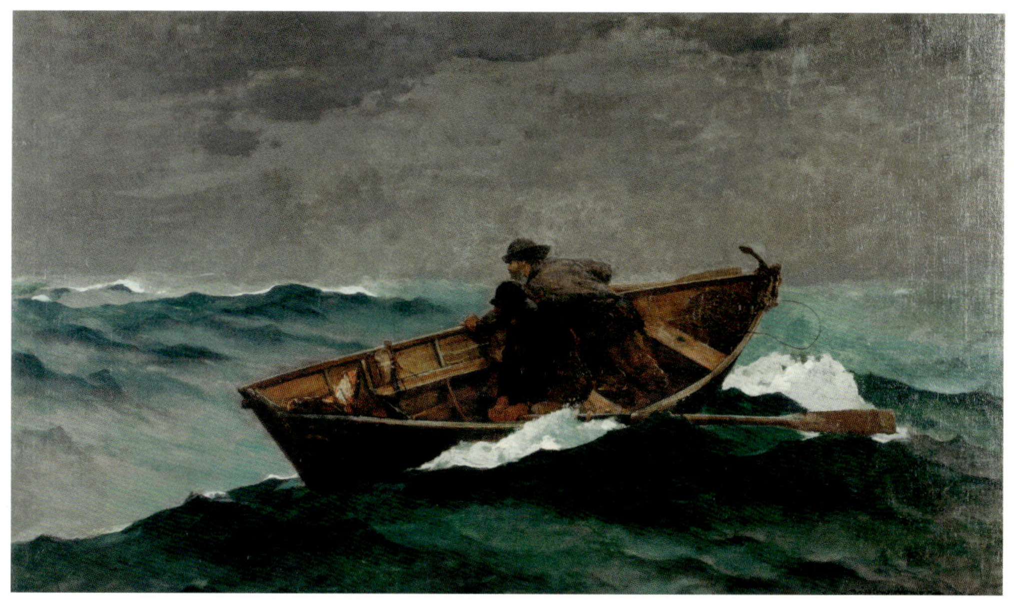

Fig. 50 *Lost on the Grand Banks*, 1885, oil on canvas, 80 × 125.4 cm. Private collection, Seattle

on the open sea, thus playing with the sense of isolation amplified by the perilous conditions that surround them. The fate of the fisherman in *The Fog Warning* is left open-ended. After a successful day catching halibut, he is alerted to the approaching fog that threatens to cut him off as he rows back to the ship in the distance. The pitch of the dory (a flat-bottomed boat) on the heaving waves indicates the sheer physical effort required. The situation for the two fishermen in *Lost on the Grand Banks*, however, seems hopeless as they appear to have lost control of their craft in rough seas. Reflecting the vicissitudes of life at sea, Homer painted *Eight Bells* (fig. 54) the following year, in 1886. Offering a more optimistic conclusion for his protagonists, he shows two oilskin-clad sailors standing on the deck of a ship in order to take their bearing as a tempest subsides. They have weathered the storm, their sou'westers glinting as the sun breaks through the clouds.[7]

During the nineteenth century, the greater understanding of the Earth's history by geologists and palaeontologists made the slow erosion of civilisation by time and the elements a major theme in Western art and culture.[8] This new vision of a dynamic, prehistoric Earth, constantly shifting and evolving, was not only a spur to the artistic imagination, but may also explain why Homer and others were drawn to the rural and coastal communities whose everyday lives had come to define (at least for those observing them) the primordial contest between humankind and the sea. At the same time, the impact of Darwinian theories of evolution and natural selection was so profound and far-reaching that it fundamentally challenged near universal perceptions of the natural world and the dramatic life cycles of the species that inhabited it. Throughout the 1890s, Homer continued to produce impressive forest and river scenes, including images of hunting and fishing inspired by his trips to the Adirondacks. But in some of these, the subject's tone is perceptively darker and more ambiguous than those from earlier in his career and, consequently, they have been appreciated as deliberate reflections on survival and mortality, in a similar vein to the coastal imagery and seascapes inspired by Cullercoats and Maine.

One such painting is *Hound and Hunter* of 1892 (fig. 57), which Homer considered to be among his 'great works'. Deer were hunted in the Adirondacks by dogs driving them into lakes where they could be shot, clubbed or drowned by hunters in boats. Responding to *Hound and Hunter*, critics assumed the deer was still alive because in the version first exhibited its head was only partially submerged in the water. Homer was adamant that the deer was already dead (which was more acceptable to his critics and potential clients) and even noted with palpable irritation that he could 'shut the deer's eyes, & put pennies on them if that will make it better understood'.[9] The painting remained in Homer's possession until 1907 or 1908, during which time (possibly in the early 1900s) he reworked the head, lowering it still further, until the deer's eye was barely visible above water. While *Hound and Hunter* continues and develops in pictorial terms the relationship between

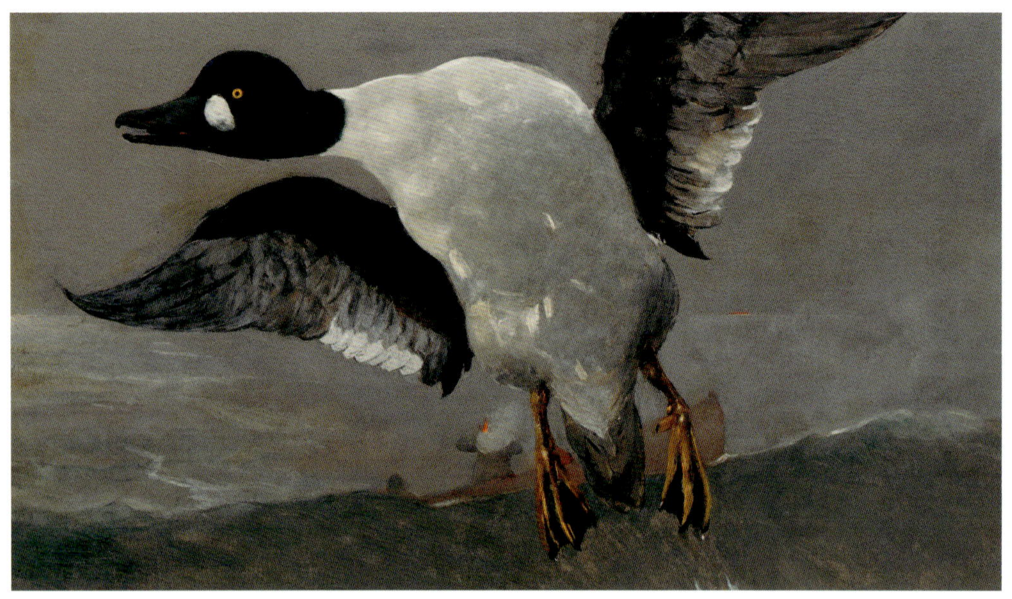

Detail of fig. 59

humankind and nature, several of Homer's paintings from the 1890s and early 1900s are unusual within his oeuvre because the theme of struggle and survival focuses on the wildlife, with the human presence either inferred, reduced or entirely absent. *Fox Hunt* of 1893 (fig. 58), Homer's largest painting at that date, seems to encapsulate the idea, as Alfred Tennyson (1809–1892) famously phrased it, of 'Nature, red in tooth and claw'.[10] This is evoked through the dramatic representation of a stark winter on the Maine coast, with the coastline and ocean in the distance, and the image of a fox running in deep snow, menaced by a flock of half-starved crows. The brutality of the weather has elicited a reversal of roles, with the birds driven to predation and the fox, their natural hunter, as the quarry.[11] The low viewpoint and flattened perspective – often cited as showing the influence of Japanese prints – allows the spectator to witness the unfolding drama from the fox's perspective, with the crows forming a deadly black canopy as they descend (we are left to imagine) for the kill. The redness of the fox's fur and the berries, just visible to the left, perhaps foreshadow the blood about to be spilled.

The unusual use of perspective, to heighten the dramatic effect as well as to provoke sympathy with the subject, is central to one of Homer's last major works, *Right and Left* (fig. 59), painted in 1909, a year before his death. The title refers to the act of shooting birds successively with separate barrels of a shotgun. It is not entirely clear which of the ducks has been shot; the slack, diving pose of the one on the right suggests that it has been mortally wounded, with the other bird possibly attempting to escape the second shot (the hunter, seen to the left of the latter's feet, has just fired his gun).[12] Doubtless the uncertainty and precariousness of the scene is deliberate, accentuated by the elevated vantage point. As with *Fox Hunt*, we are left to ponder how random the transition from life to death can be, as well as the fragility of existence itself.

1 See Worcester and Milwaukee 2017–18, p. 80.
2 See Philadelphia 2012, p. 63.
3 For the evolution of shipwreck imagery in Western art, see C. Riding, 'Shipwreck in French and British Visual Art, 1700–1842', in C. Thompson (ed.), *Shipwreck in Art and Literature: Images and Interpretations from Antiquity to the Present Day*, New York and London 2013, pp. 112–30.
4 Ibid, pp. 73–5.
5 See Simpson 2013, pp. 86–9.
6 See Philadelphia 2012, pp. 77–9; London and Giverny 2006, p. 18.
7 See Philadelphia 2012, p. 81.
8 See A. Staley and C. Newall, *Pre-Raphaelite Vision: Truth to Nature*, exh. cat., Tate Britain, London 2004, pp. 133–4.
9 Quoted in Kelly et al. 1996, p. 340.
10 A. Tennyson, *In Memoriam, A. H. H.*, Canto 56, 1850 poets.org/poem/memoriam-h-h (accessed 6 January 2022).
11 See New York 2022, p. 153.
12 See Washington, DC, Boston and New York 1995–6, pp. 374–5.

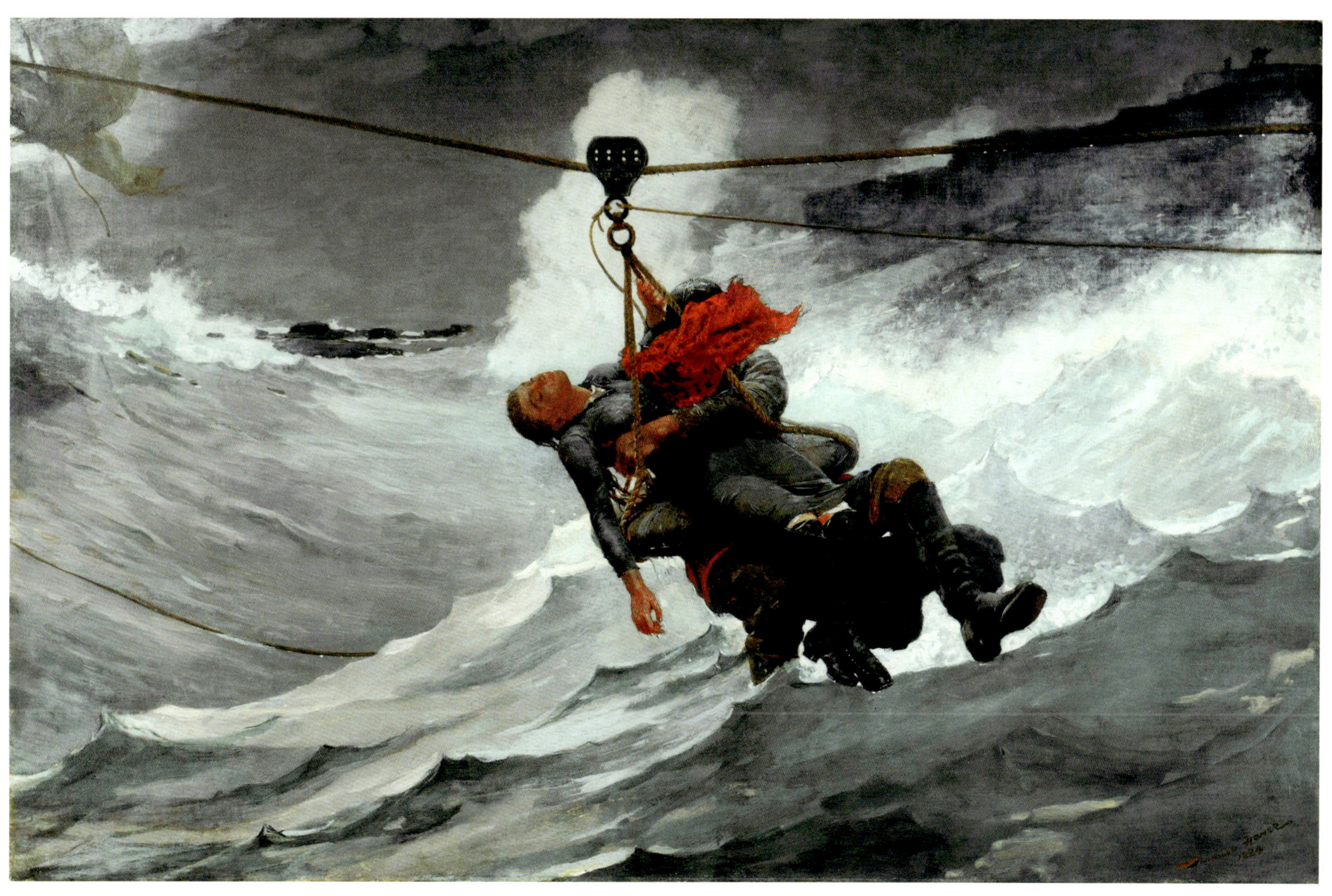

Fig. 51 *The Life Line*, 1884

Oil on canvas, 72.7 × 113.7 cm
Philadelphia Museum of Art, Philadelphia, Pennsylvania. The George W. Elkins Collection, 1924 (E1924-4-15)

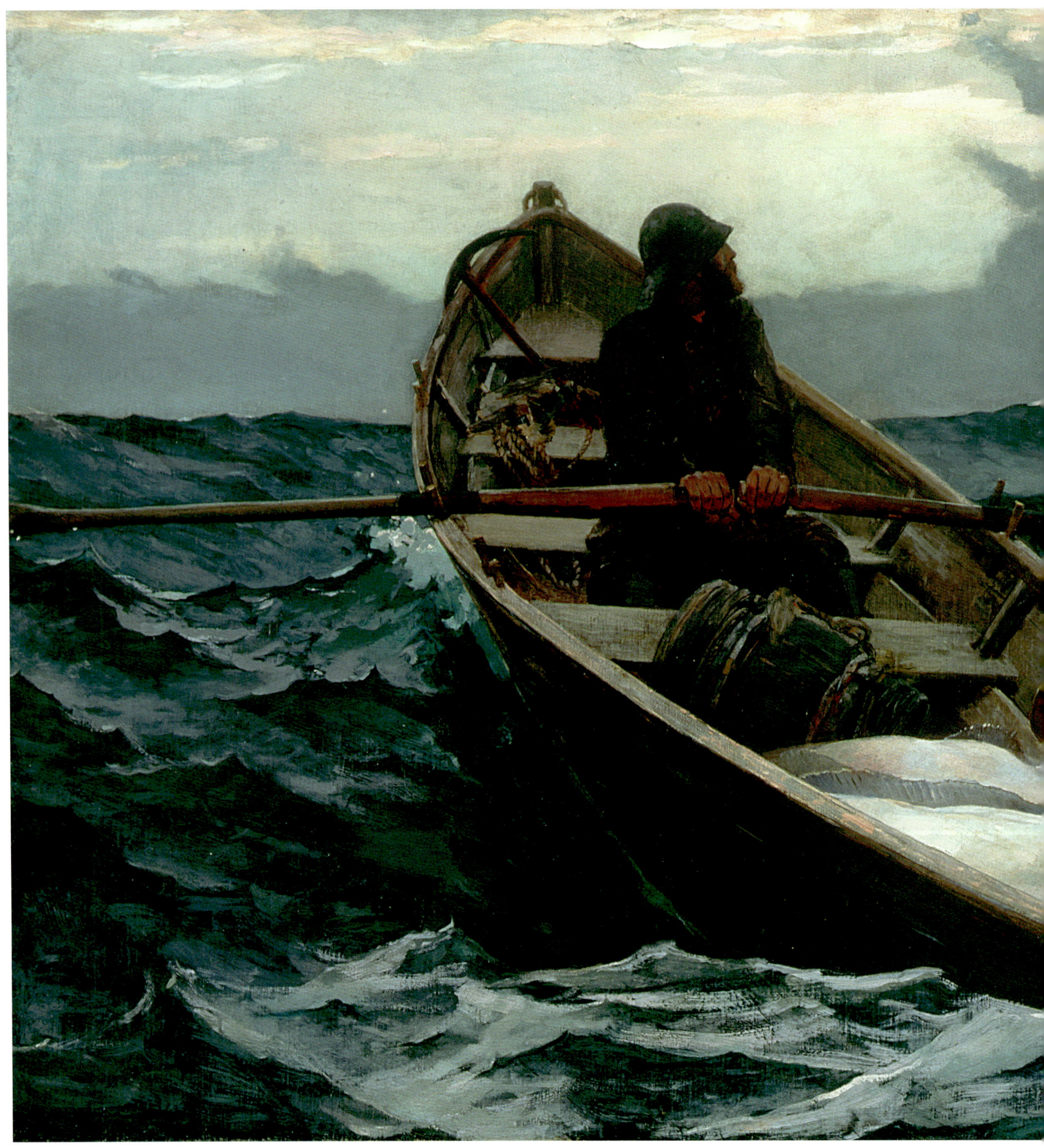

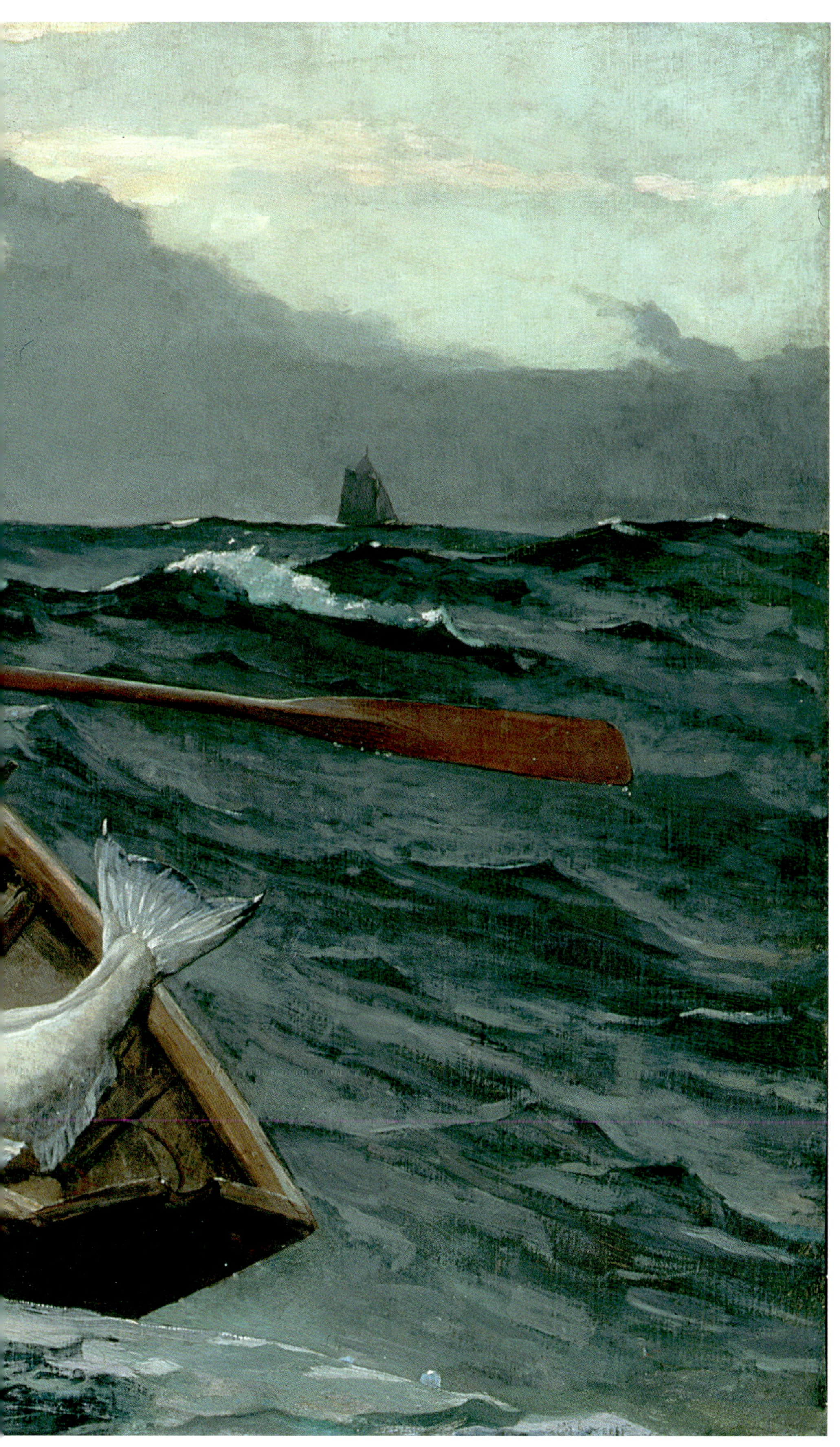

Fig. 52 *The Fog Warning*, 1885

Oil on canvas, 76.8 × 123.2 cm
Museum of Fine Arts, Boston, Massachusetts. Anonymous gift with credit to the Otis Norcross Fund (94.72)

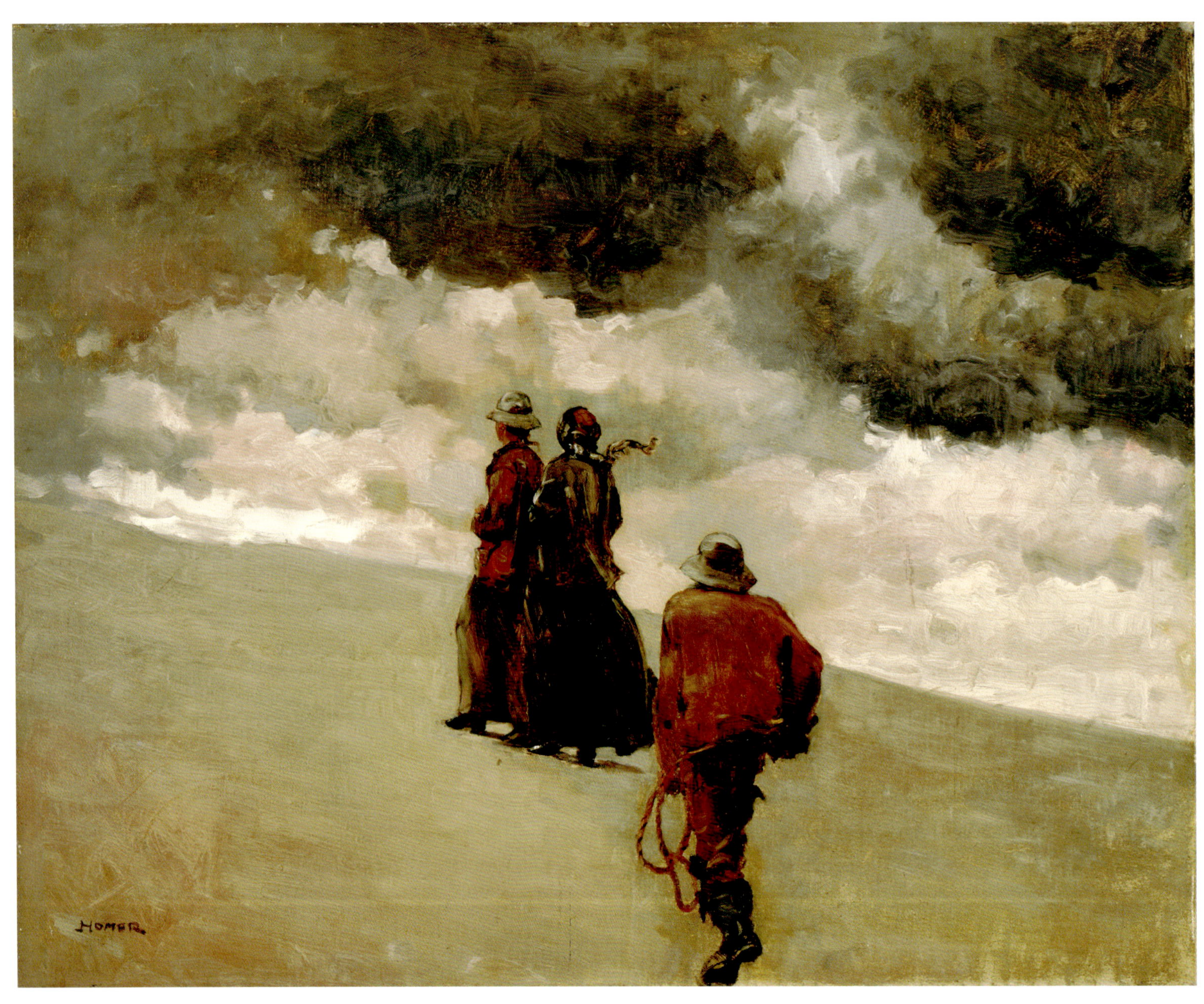

Fig. 53 *To the Rescue*, 1886

Oil on canvas, 61 × 76.2 cm
The Phillips Collection, Washington, DC.
Acquired 1926 (0922)

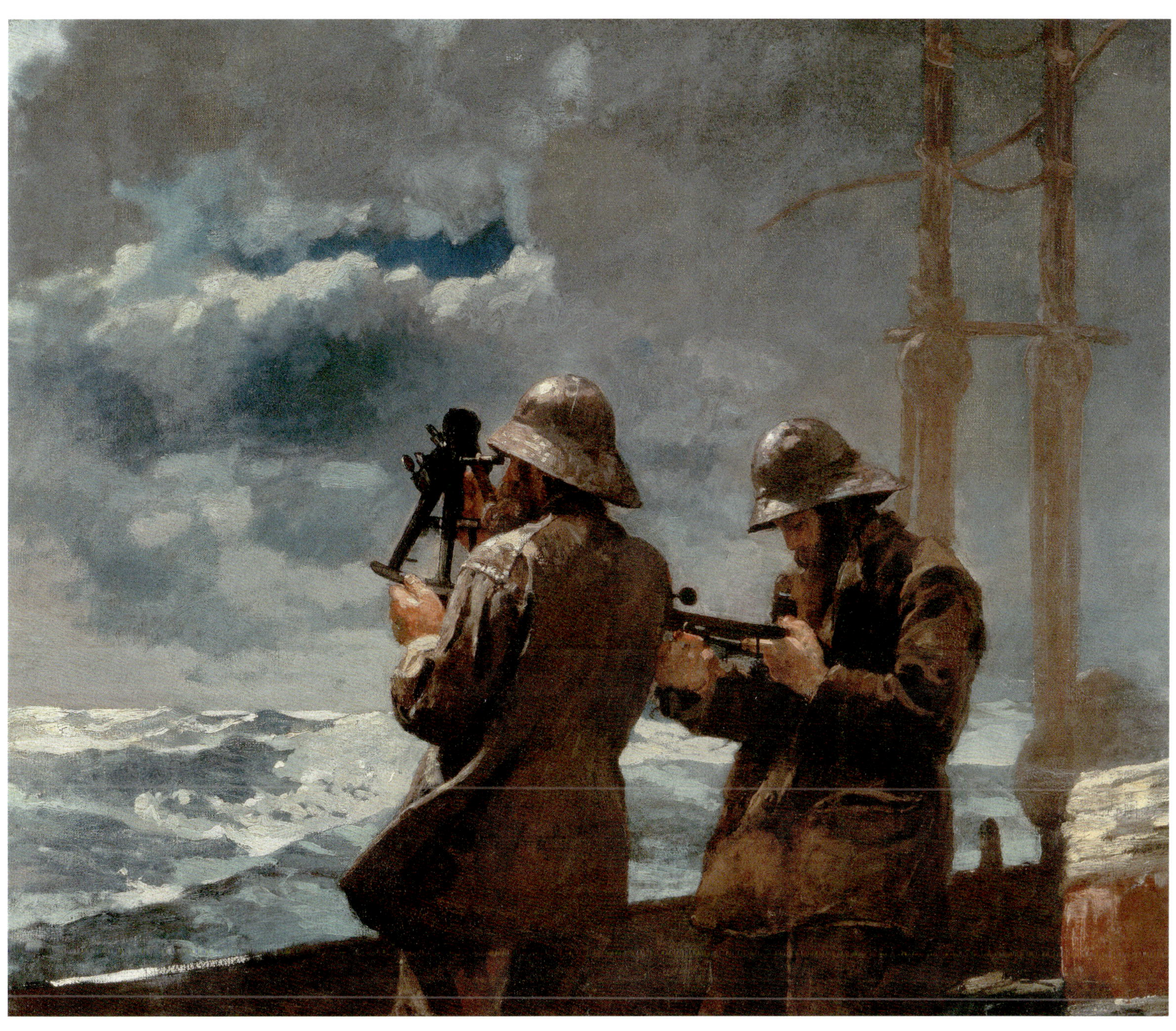

Fig. 54 *Eight Bells*, 1886

Oil on canvas, 64 × 76.7 cm
Addison Gallery of American Art, Phillips Academy, Andover, Massachusetts. Gift of anonymous donor (1930.379)

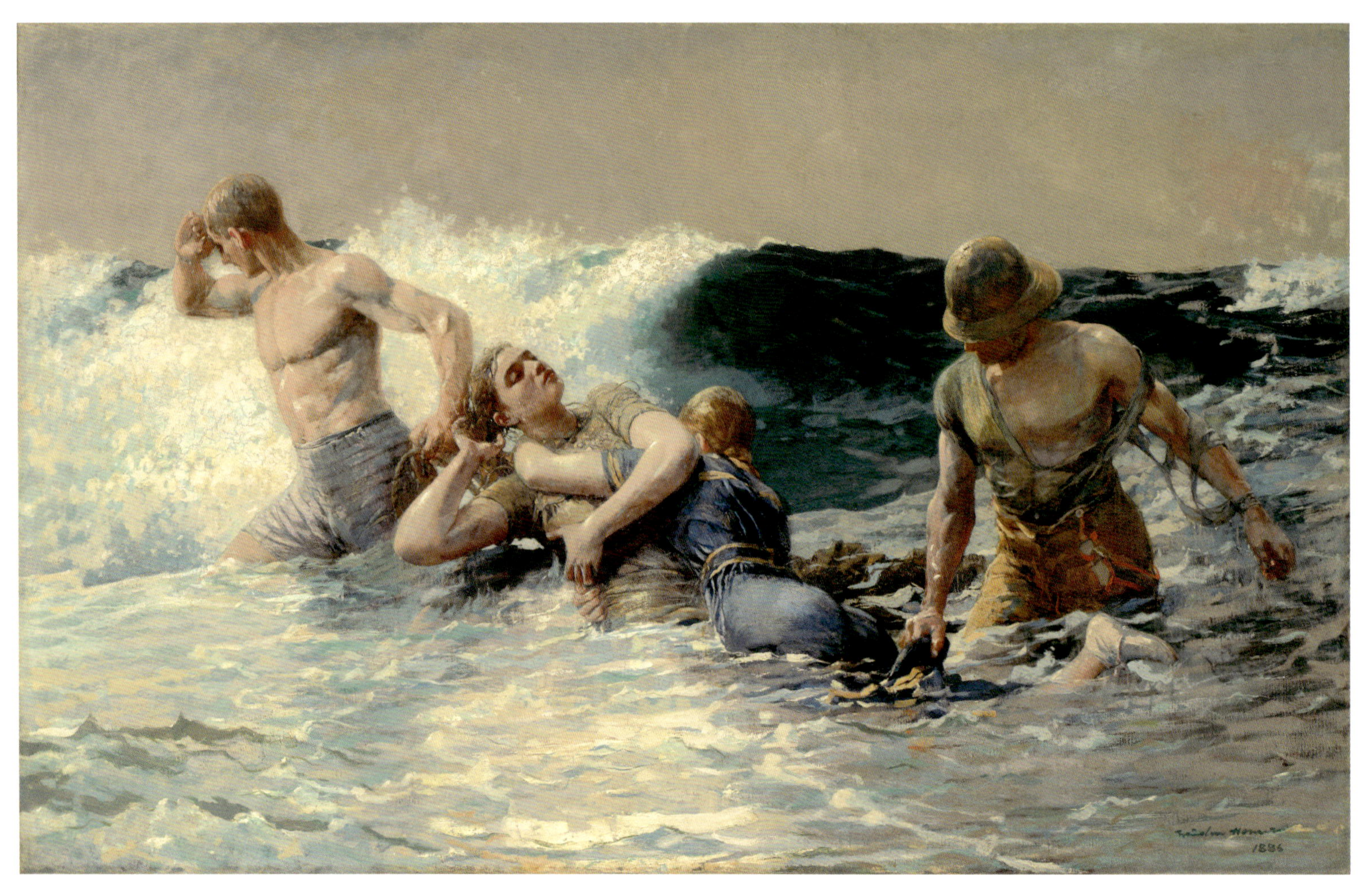

Fig. 55 *Undertow*, 1886

Oil on canvas, 75.7 × 121 cm
Sterling and Francine Clark Art Institute, Williamstown, Massachusetts. Acquired by Sterling and Francine Clark, 1924 (1955.4)

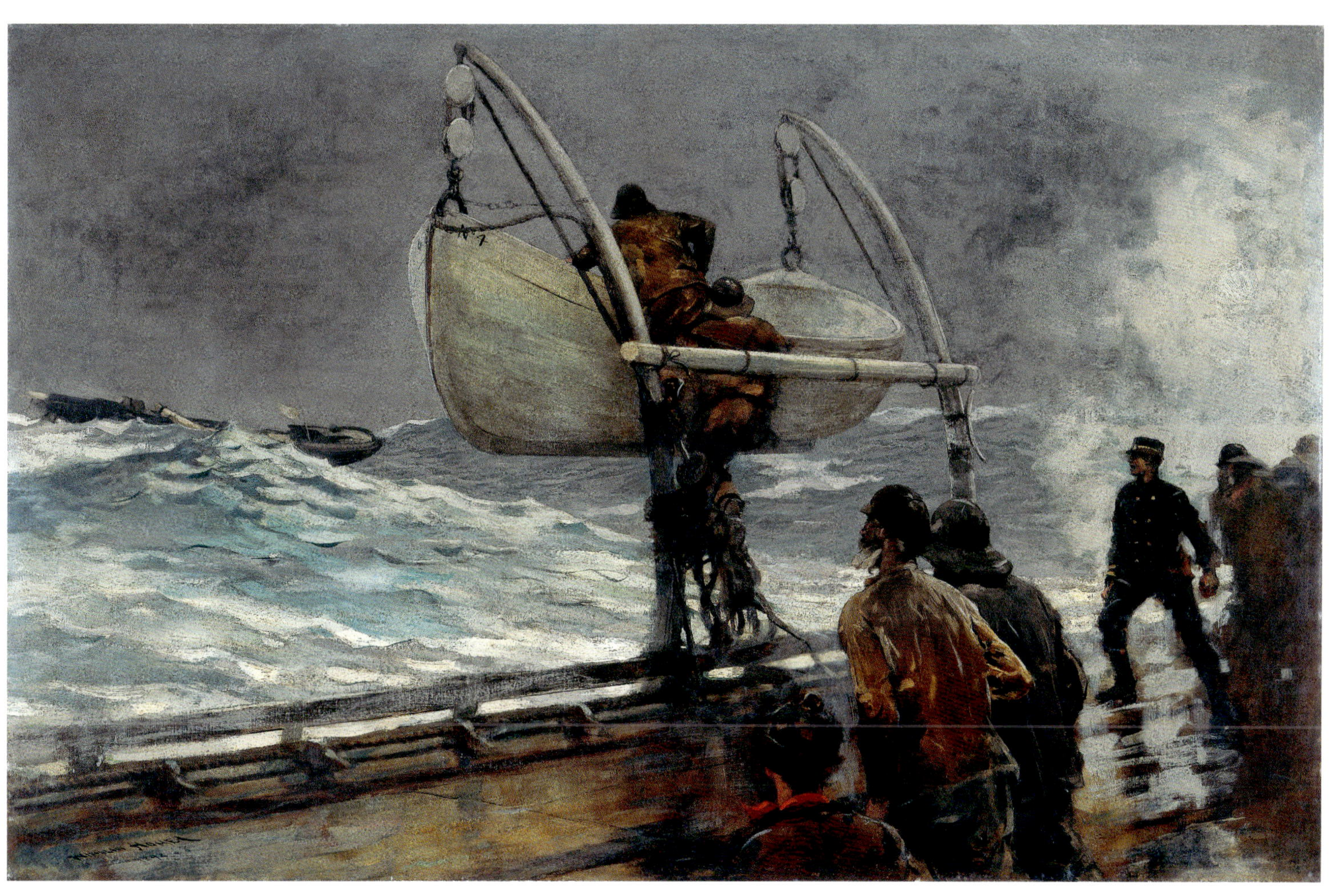

Fig. 56 *Signal of Distress*, 1890–6

Oil on canvas, 62 × 98 cm
Museo Nacional Thyssen-Bornemisza, Madrid (1980.71)

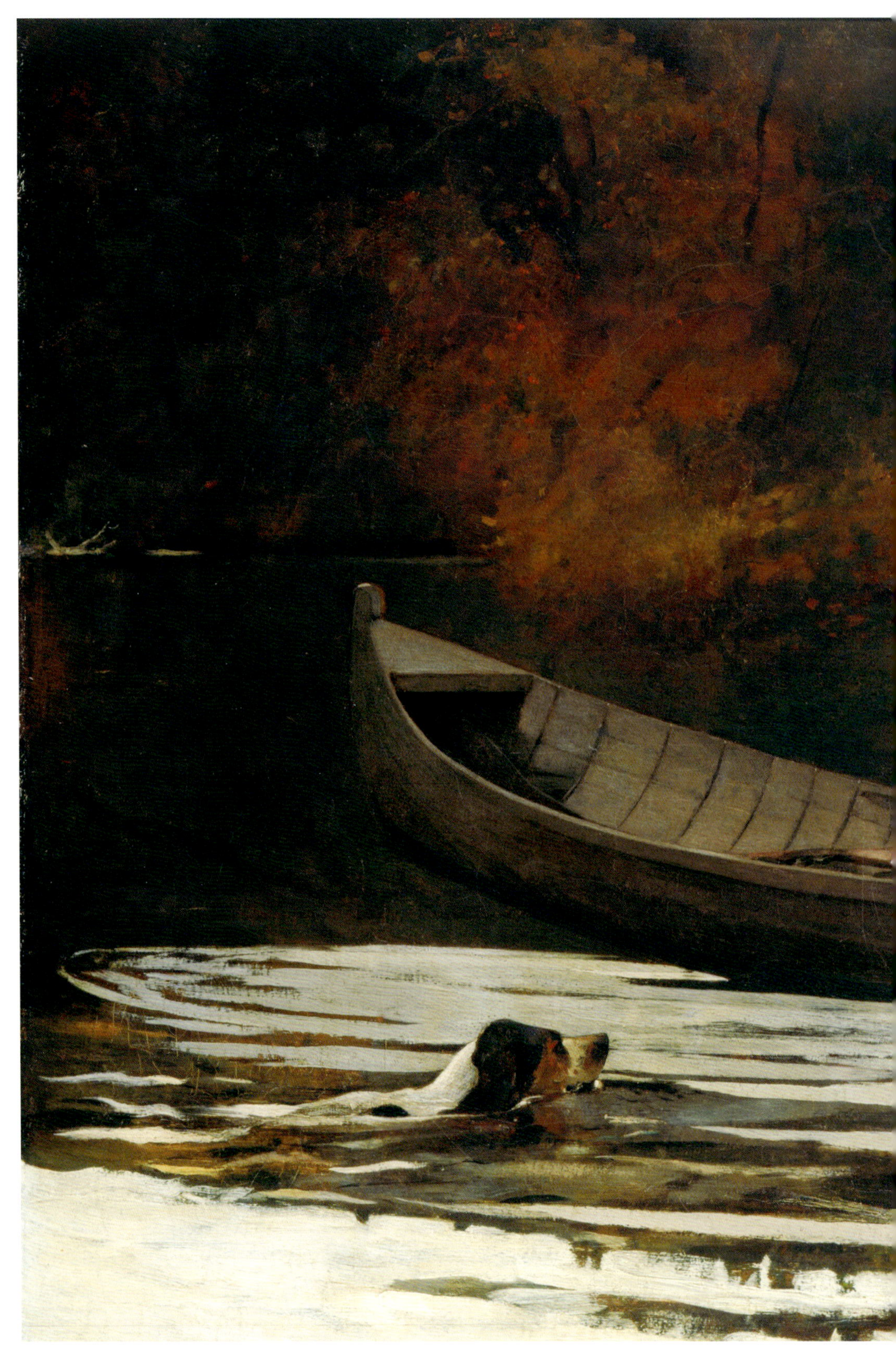

Fig. 57 *Hound and Hunter*, 1892

Oil on canvas, 71.8 × 122.3 cm
National Gallery of Art, Washington, DC.
Gift of Stephen C. Clark (1947.11.1)

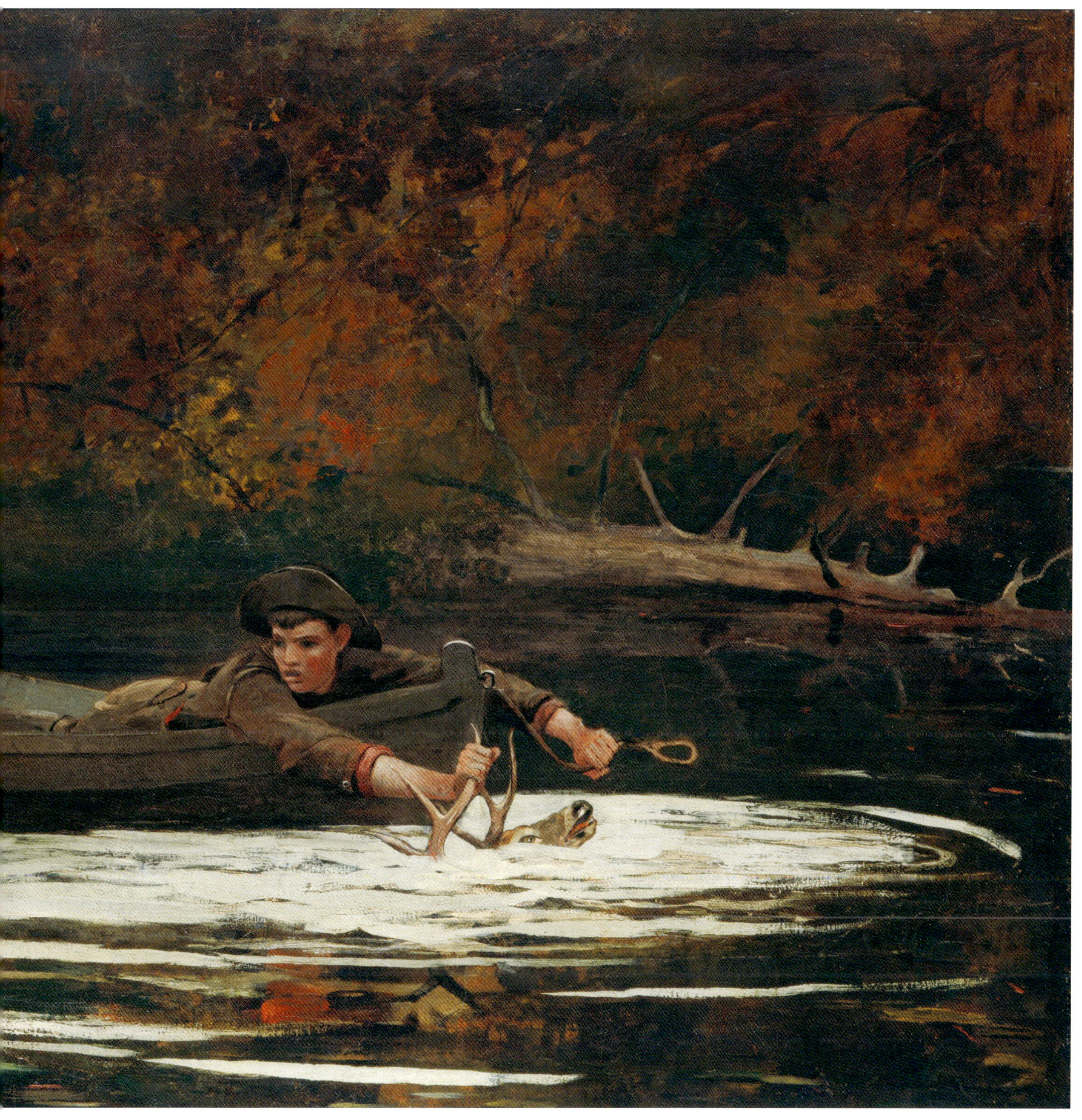

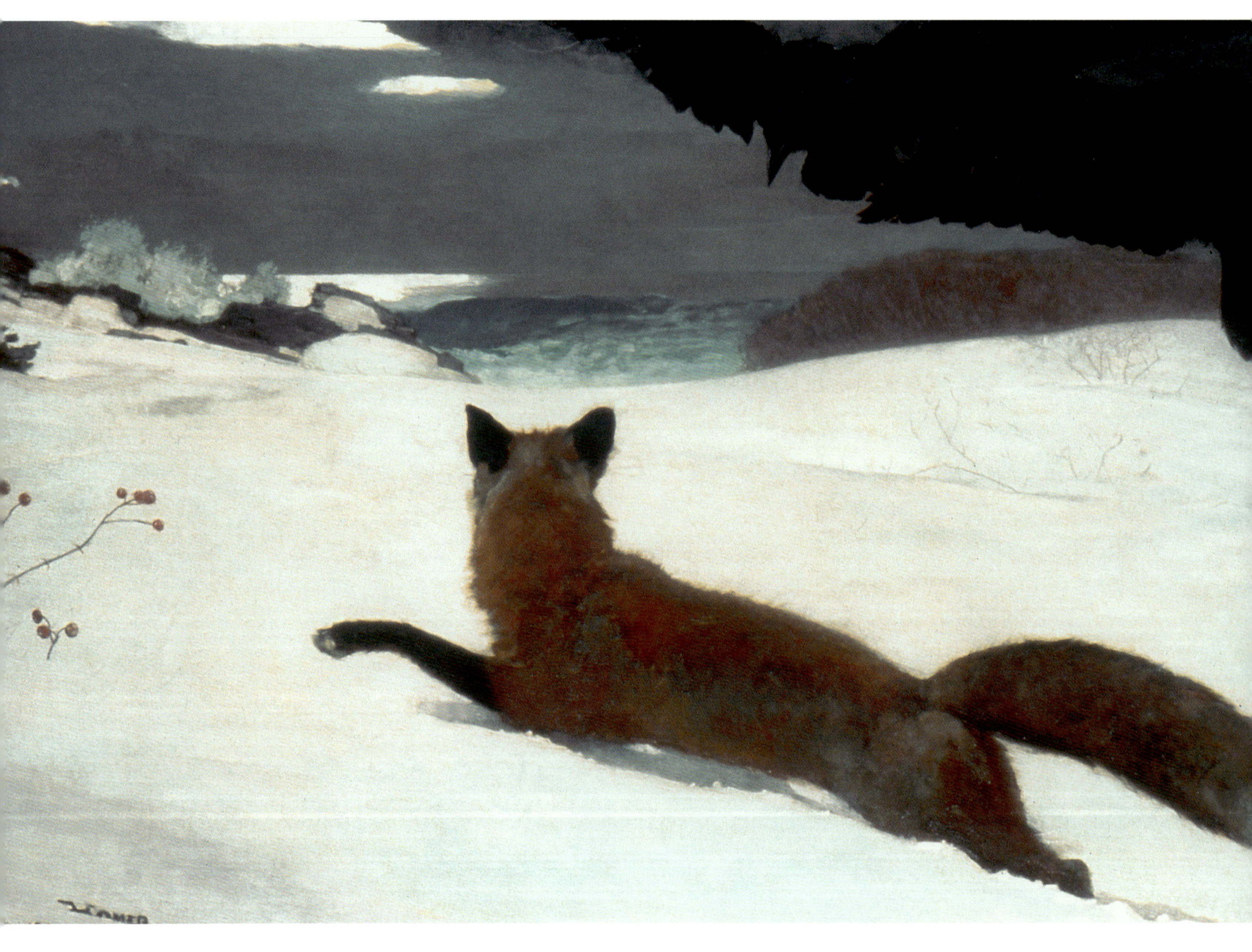

Fig. 58 *Fox Hunt*, 1893

Oil on canvas, 96.5 × 174 cm
Pennsylvania Academy of the Fine Arts, Philadelphia. Joseph E. Temple Fund (1894.4)

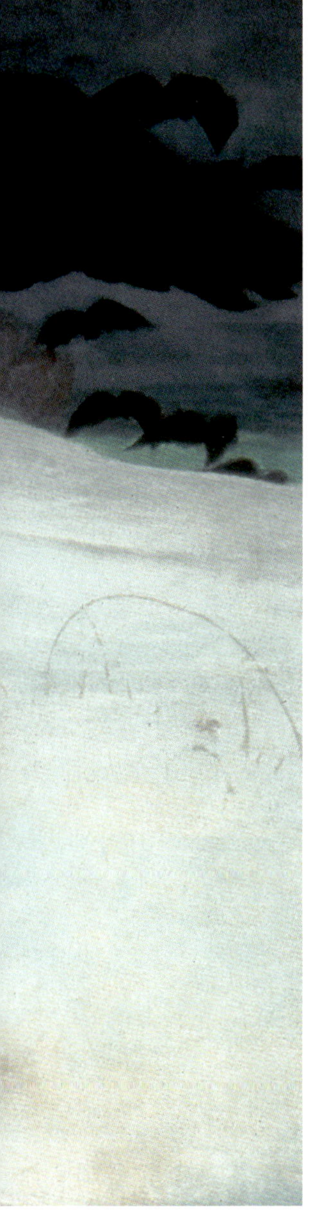

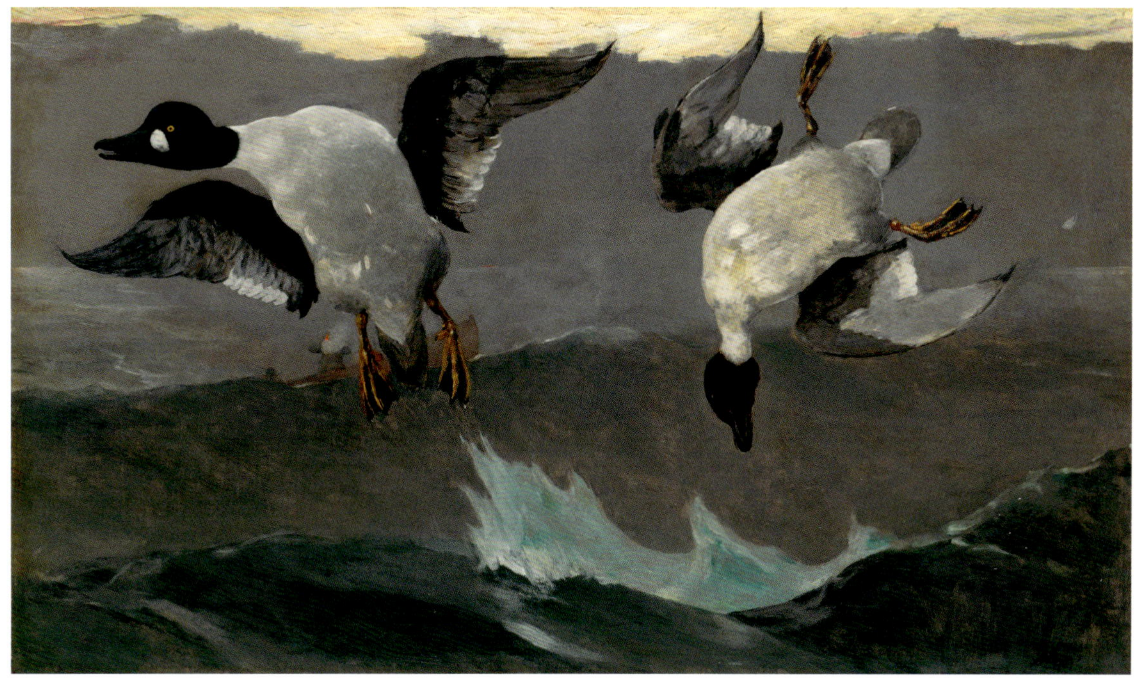

Fig. 59 *Right and Left*, 1909

Oil on canvas, 71.8 × 122.9 cm
National Gallery of Art, Washington, DC.
Gift of the Avalon Foundation (1951.8.1)

Going South: Florida and the Tropics

Chiara Di Stefano

Between 1884 and 1909, escaping the harsh winters on the Maine coast, Homer travelled frequently to Florida and the tropics, where he produced an astonishing array of watercolours. A first sojourn in The Bahamas, prompted by a commission from *The Century Magazine*,[1] was followed in February 1885 by a trip to Cuba. He visited Florida shortly after, returning there regularly until the end of his life.[2] A second voyage to The Bahamas – 'the best place I have ever found'[3] – was postponed for family reasons until December 1898. 'My father who has prevented any travel on my part of recent years died on August 22nd,'[4] he wrote in the autumn of 1898, resolving to 'go somewhere in the West Indies'.[5] In the end, he sailed to Nassau, where he spent three months. Less than a year later, at the turn of the century, he visited Bermuda: this would be his last journey to the tropics.

In striking contrast with his Cullercoats and Prouts Neck pictures, Homer's tropical watercolours show a renewed lightness and a brightened palette. Applied in flat masses and loose brushstrokes, the vibrant, saturated colours of his exotic views replace the greyish tones of his previous seascapes. Although the sea remained the central theme of the artist's repertoire, his pictorial interests varied widely. In Florida, Homer painted chiefly fishing and rainforest scenes (fig. 60);[6] and if Cuba intrigued him with its old Spanish architecture (fig. 61), Bermuda charmed him with its islands' geological formation and lush, colourful vegetation (figs 69 and 73).

The Bahamian watercolours, conversely, despite their chronological span over 15 years (1884–99), form a coherent group, mainly centred on the local population (figs 63, 64 and 72). Although based on careful observation, Homer's representation of the Black inhabitants

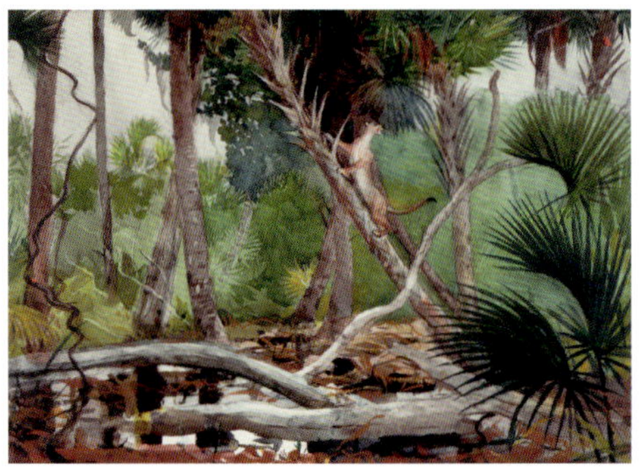

Fig. 60 *In the Jungle, Florida*, 1904, watercolour and graphite on paper, 35.2 × 50 cm. Brooklyn Museum, New York, Museum Collection Fund and Special Subscription (11.547)

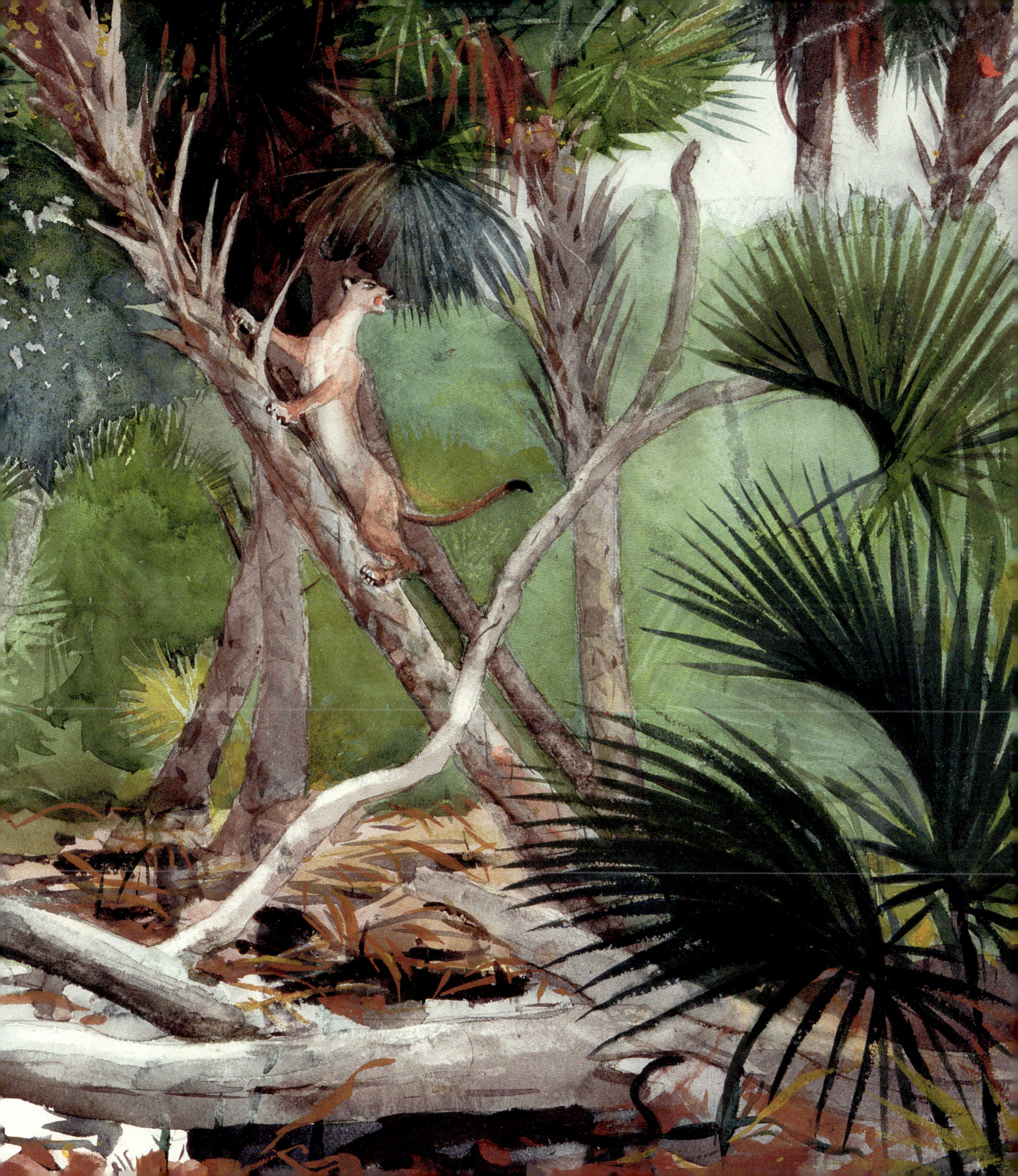

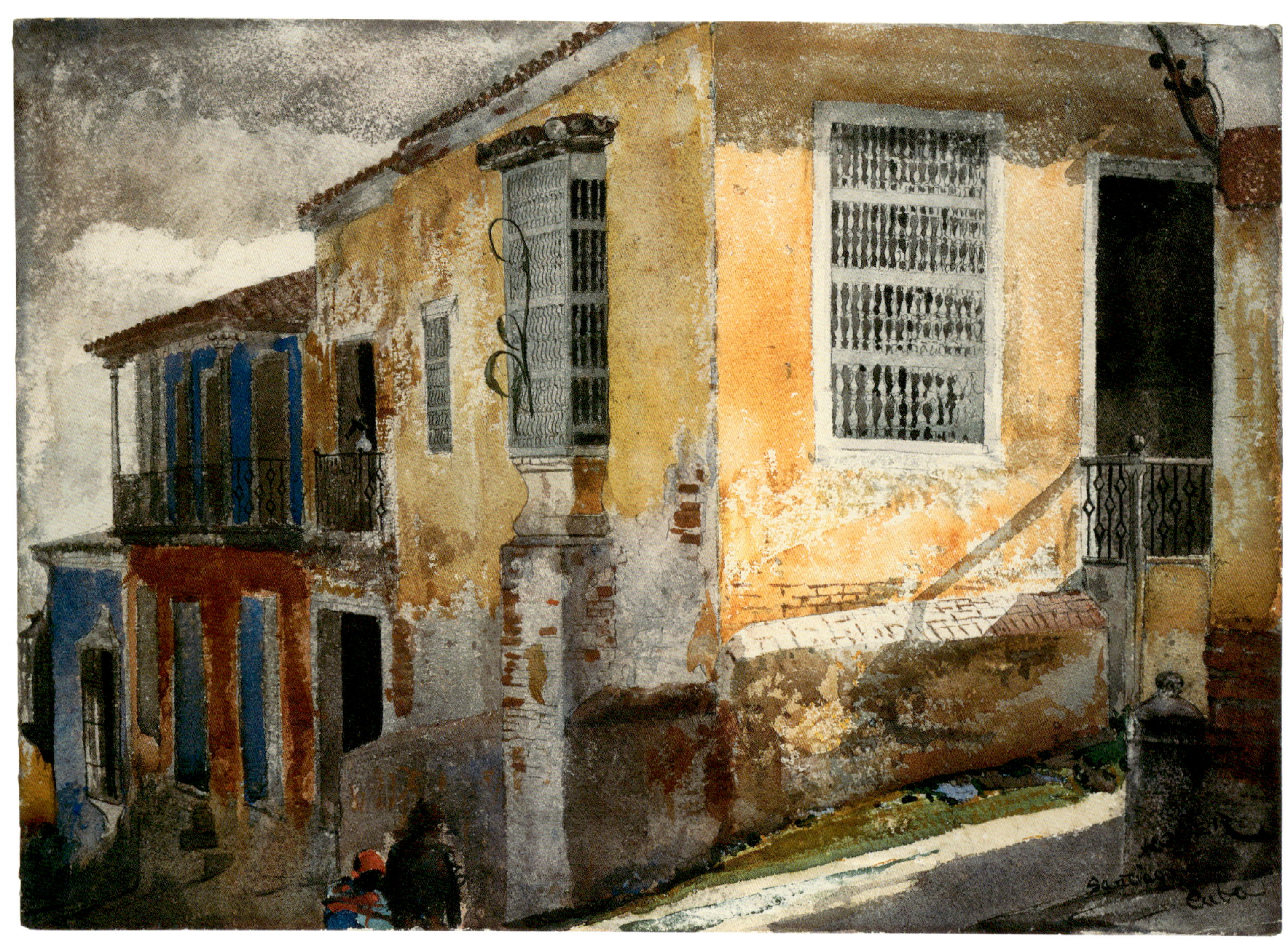

Fig. 61 *Street Corner, Santiago de Cuba*, 1885, watercolour over graphite pencil on paper, 35.6 × 50.9 cm. Museum of Fine Arts, Boston, Massachusetts. Anonymous gift in memory of Horace D. Chapin (1978.300)

is not exempt from stereotype. Produced to illustrate 'A Midwinter Resort', an article by William C. Church for *The Century Magazine*, Homer's first tropical works encouraged viewers 'to see Black Bahamian culture and its relationship to Africa as an unbroken, unchanged lineage'.[7] The picturesque huts, the fishermen at work, the boys bathing: all portray a paradise standing outside history. While several forms of segregation were still in place in The Bahamas, a rhetoric of racial harmony informs both Homer's works and Church's article, conveying an idealised image of the islands. 'Slavery was abolished in 1834 and with it seems to have disappeared the prejudice of color', the journalist wrote, perhaps to attract potential tourists, concluding that 'prosperity and the development of the faculty of accumulation will bring social success to the negro in our own country in time as it has here.'[8]

At the close of the nineteenth century, Homer painted another series of Bahamian watercolours. 'I have had a most successful winter in Nassau N. P. Bahamas', he told collector Thomas B. Clarke in February 1899. 'I found what I wanted & have many things to work up into *two paintings* that I have in mind.'[9] Based on his tropical works, these oils – *The Gulf Stream* (1899, reworked by 1906, fig. 84) and *Searchlight on Harbor Entrance, Santiago de Cuba* (1902, fig. 75) – count among Homer's masterpieces.

The latter depicts a crucial event in the Spanish–American War: the siege of Santiago de Cuba in the summer of 1898. Every night, the American fleet, arrayed around the mouth of the bay, shone a powerful searchlight on the entrance to the harbour, preventing the Spanish army from escaping. Widely reported by the press, the blockade and the subsequent Battle of Santiago de Cuba (3 July 1898) gained renewed interest in 1901, when a controversy arose as to which US commander had been responsible for the victory. A court of enquiry was convened in September. Three months later, his painting freshly finished, Homer wrote to his dealer M. Knoedler & Co. that it was 'just the time to show that picture as the subject is now before the people',[10] revealing his keen awareness of the painting's topicality. *Searchlight on Harbor Entrance, Santiago de Cuba* was exhibited in New York in early January 1902.[11]

Showing an astounding mastery of design, inspired chiefly by the Japanese prints then in vogue, Homer adopts an unusual view: the Castillo de San Pedro de la Roca, known as El Morro, a seventeenth-century fort overlooking the bay. This decadent colonial building, with its rusty cannons no longer in use and the silent traces of a lost grandeur, evokes a picturesque nightscape that vividly conveys the long, draining wait of the blockade. Drawing in part upon his memories of Cuba, where he sketched *Study for 'Searchlight, Harbor Entrance, Santiago de Cuba'* (fig. 62), Homer could also rely on first-

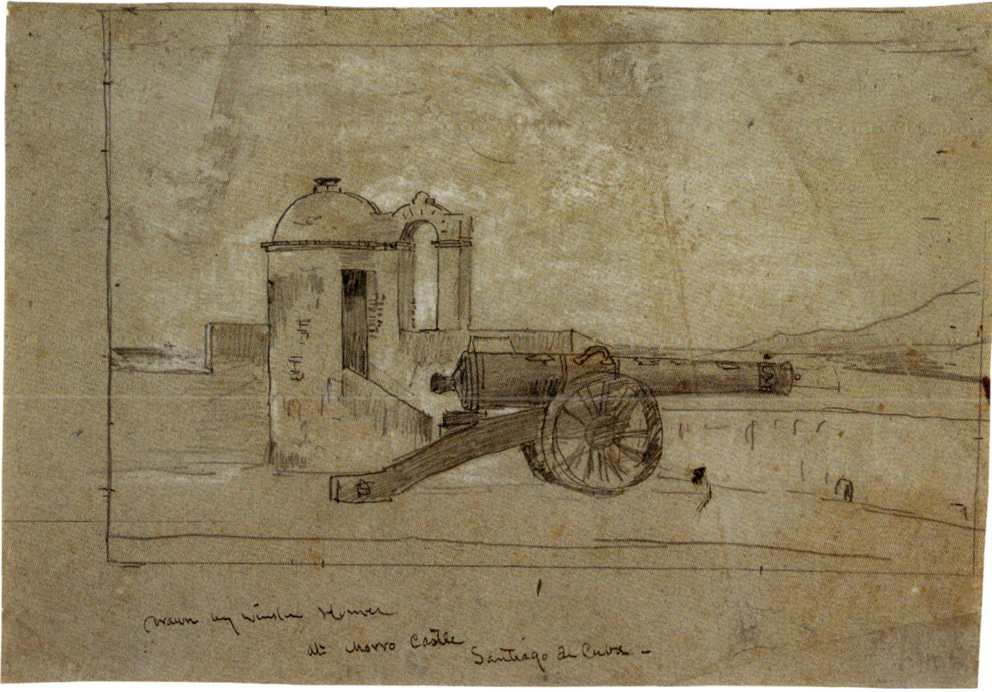

Fig. 62 *Study for 'Searchlight, Harbor Entrance, Santiago de Cuba'*, 1885, graphite and chalk on paper, 27.9 × 47.3 cm. Cooper Hewitt, Smithsonian Design Museum, Smithsonian Institution, New York. Gift of Charles Savage Homer, Jr (1912-12-1)

hand accounts: 'The scene on a moderately dark night was a very impressive one,' recalled US naval officer William T. Sampson in *The Century Magazine*, 'the path of the search-light having a certain massiveness, and the slopes and crown of the Morro cliff being lighted up with the brilliancy of silver.'[12]

Annoyed by one critic's pedantic review, Homer points out to Knoedler: 'That Santiago de Cuba picture *is not intended to be "beautiful"*. There are certain things (unfortunately for critics) that are stern facts but are worth recording as a matter of history as in this case.'[13] And yet in this painting, as in many of Homer's best works, even 'stern facts' can take on the proportions of a wider allegory. The moonlight, illuminating the Spanish cannons – beautiful and obsolete, poetic remnants of a fallen power – contrasts sharply with the beam of the American searchlight, which stands as the symbol of the US imperialist era. Nonetheless, as he often does, Homer plays here on the ambiguity of the scene, and the spectral atmosphere of the painting leaves a question unanswered: is this a celebration of the rising American Empire, or a sombre prophecy of its future decline?[14]

1 See Church 1887, pp. 499–506.
2 Homer visited The Bahamas between December 1884 and February 1885, from where he sailed to Cuba (February–March 1885). He went to Florida several times, although he did not always paint (December 1885–February 1886; February 1890; February–March 1899; December 1903–March 1904; December 1904–January 1905; January–February 1908; February–March 1909). He returned to The Bahamas between December 1898 and February 1899, and travelled to Bermuda between December 1899 and January 1900, and possibly again in December 1901.
3 W. Homer, letter to Louis Prang, 18 October 1905, quoted in Washington, DC, Fort Worth and New Haven 1986, p. 208.
4 W. Homer, letter to Thomas B. Clarke, 30 October 1898, quoted in Goodrich 1944, p. 153.
5 W. Homer, letter to J.W. Beatty, no date given, quoted in Goodrich 1944, p. 153.
6 For more on the photographs that Homer took in Florida, see Brunswick and Chadds Ford 2018–19.
7 D.E. Byrd, 'Trouble In Paradise? Homer in The Bahamas, Cuba, and Florida, 1884–1886', in Brunswick and Chadds Ford 2018–19, p. 112. See also M. Tedeschi, 'Memoranda of Travel. The Tropics', in Chicago 2008, pp. 170–98, and Hannaway 1974.
8 Church 1887, pp. 501–2. It should be noted that this quote shows a relatively 'progressive' position in 1887, despite the condescension and period terms that we would not use today.
9 W. Homer, letter to Thomas B. Clarke, 25 February 1899, quoted in Gerdts and Goodrich 2005–14, vol. 5, p. 34.
10 W. Homer, letter to M. Knoedler & Co., 30 December 1901, quoted in Spassky et al. 1985, p. 490.
11 See *A Group of Pictures by Living American Artists*, Union League Club, New York, January 1902.
12 Sampson 1899, p. 901. Quoted in Spassky et al. 1985, p. 491.
13 W. Homer, letter to M. Knoedler & Co., 14 January 1902.
14 Hélène Valance argues that the reading of *Searchlight on Harbor Entrance, Santiago de Cuba* must be revised. She proposes that the painting should be seen not as a celebration of US victory in the Spanish–American War, but as 'a prophecy in the form of jeremiad ... a meditation on the future of American imperial power'. See Valance 2018, pp. 91–110.

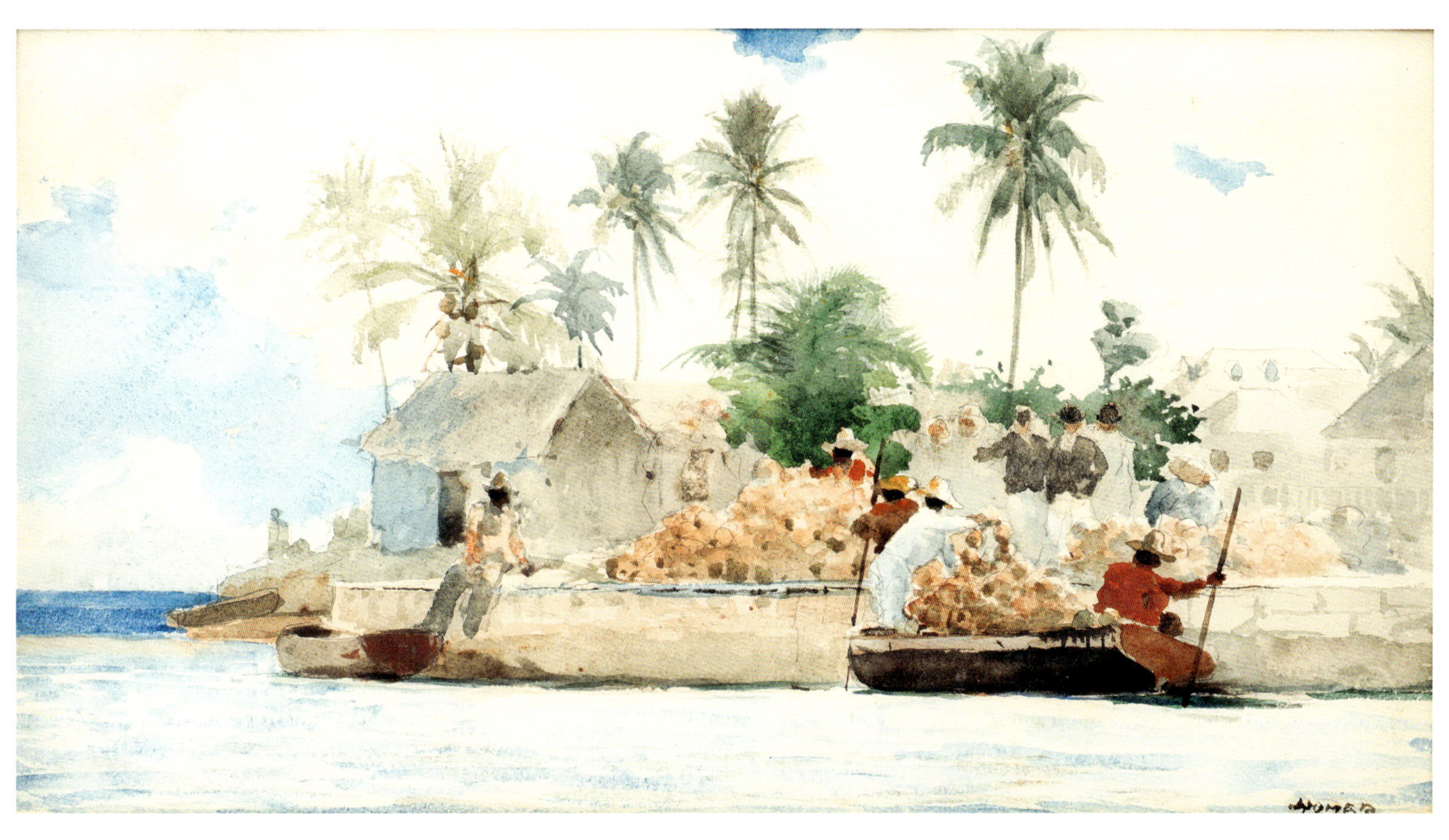

Fig. 63 *Sponge Fishermen, Bahamas*, 1885

Watercolour, gouache and graphite on paper, 27.9 × 51.1 cm
Private collection

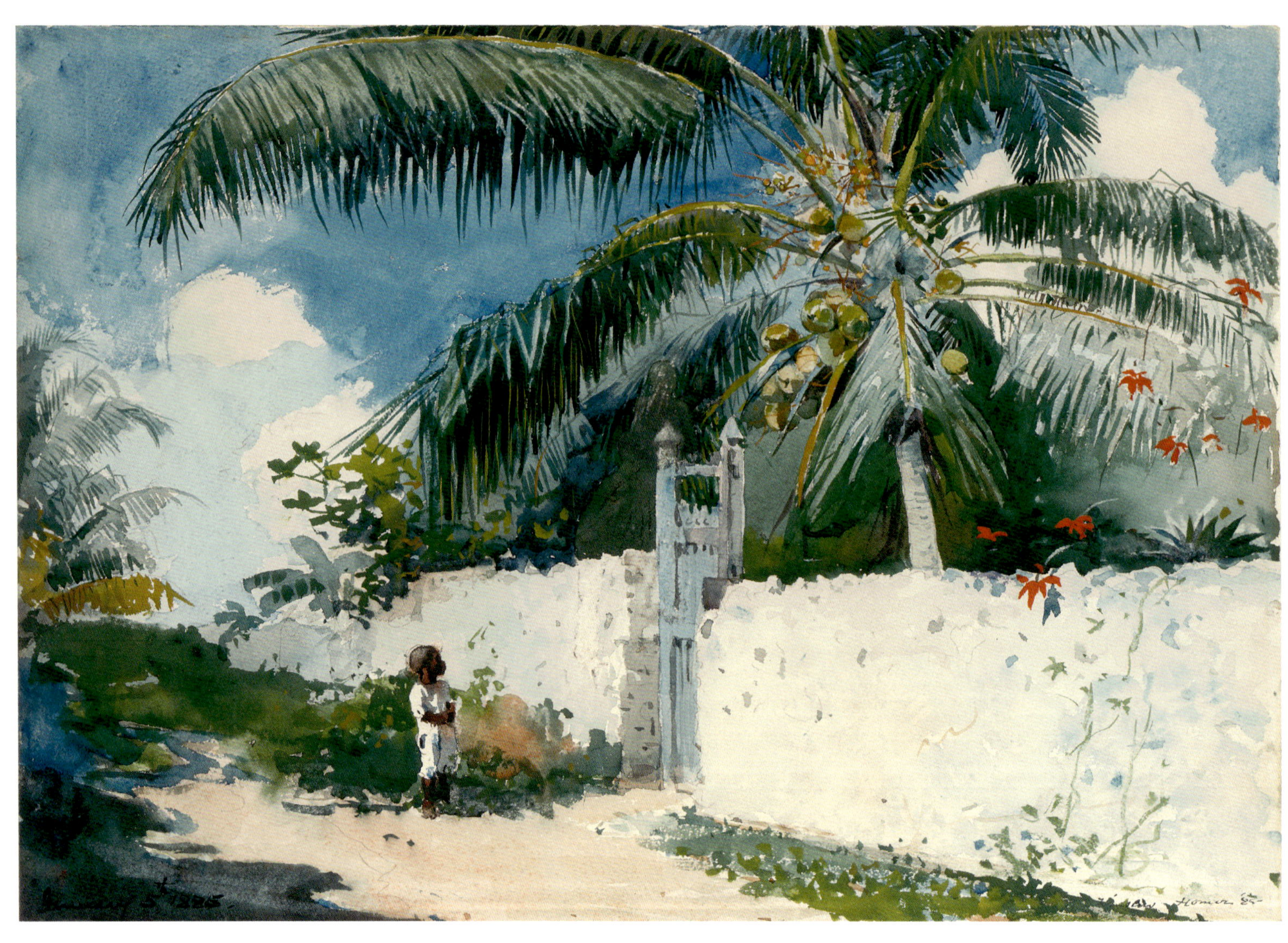

Fig. 64 *A Garden in Nassau*, 1885

Watercolour, gouache and graphite on wove paper, 36.8 × 53.3 cm
Terra Foundation for American Art, Chicago, Illinois. Daniel J. Terra Collection (1994.10)

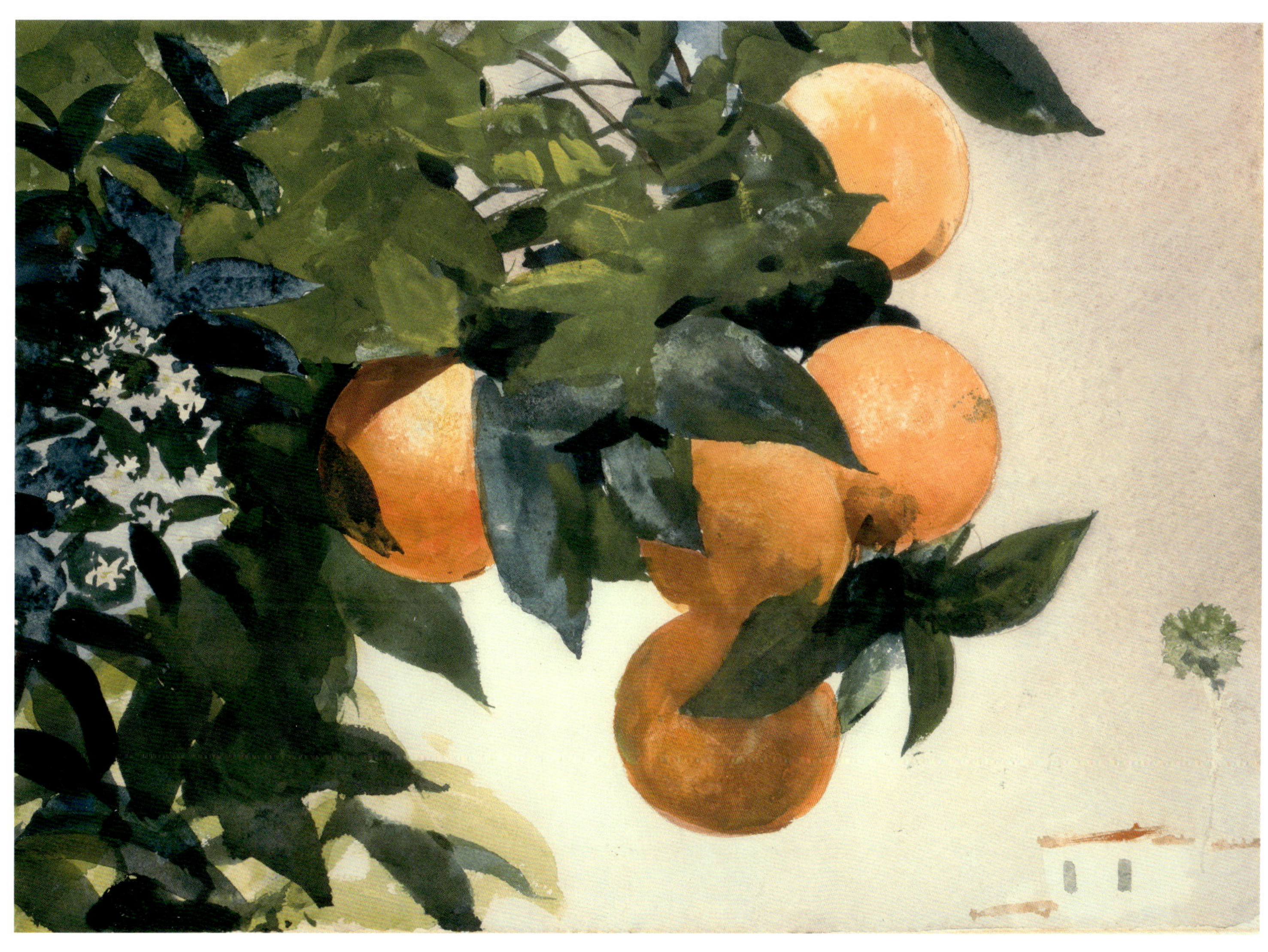

Fig. 65 *Oranges on a Branch*, 1885

Watercolour on paper, 35.6 × 49.8 cm
Erving and Joyce Wolf Collection

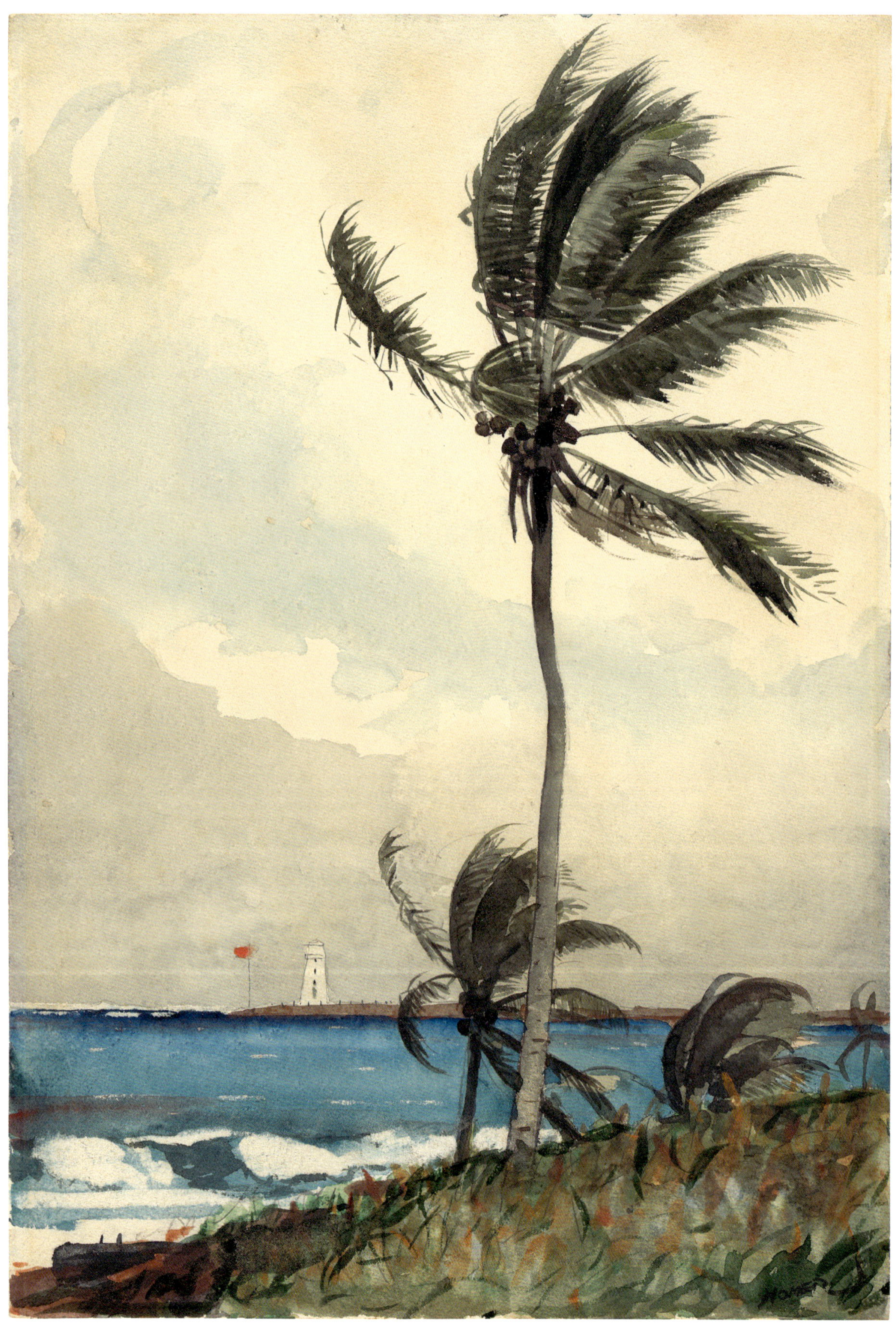

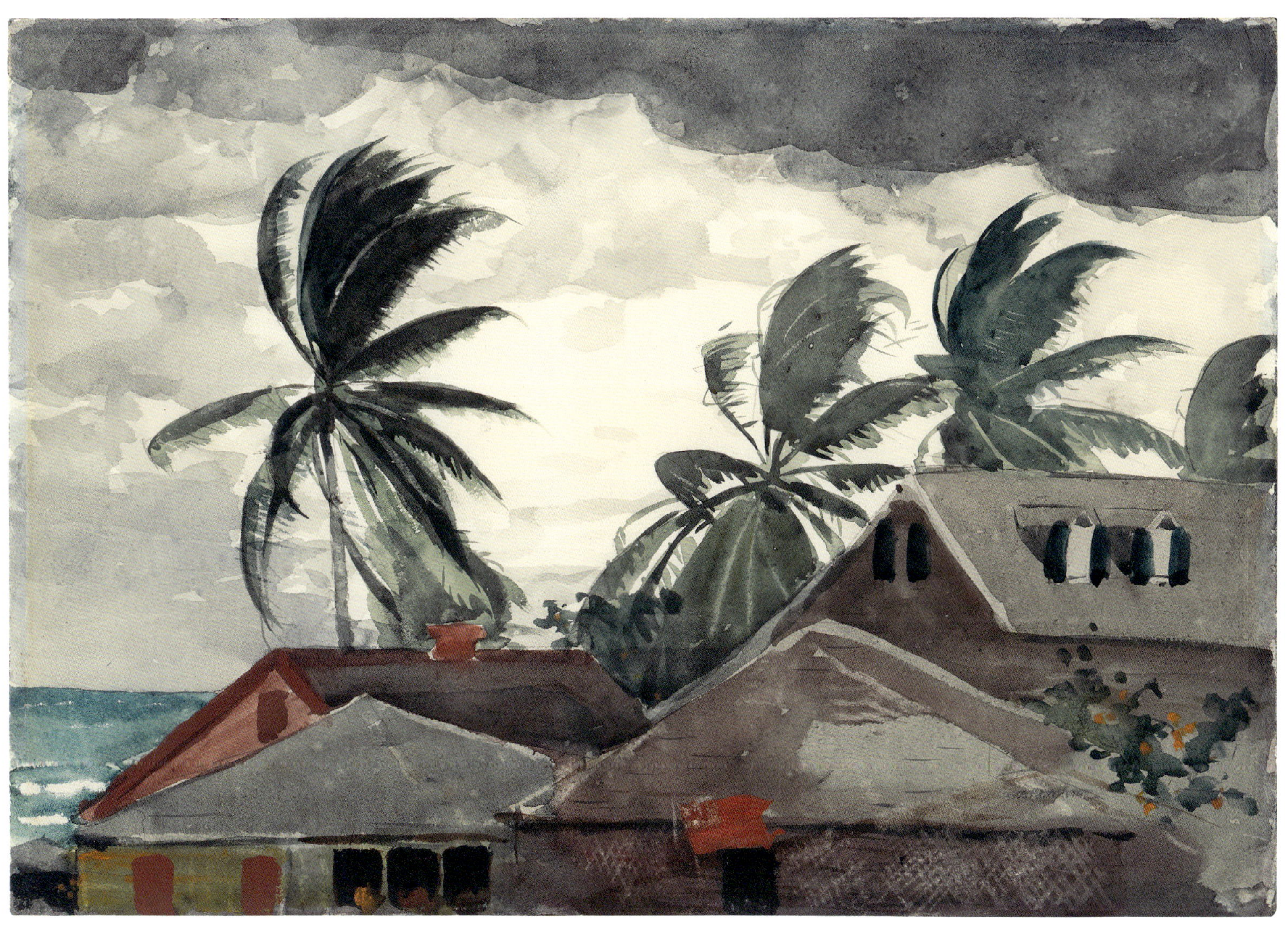

Opposite
Fig. 66 *Palm Tree, Nassau*, 1898

Watercolour and graphite on wove paper, 54.3 × 37.8 cm
The Metropolitan Museum of Art, New York. Amelia B. Lazarus Fund, 1910 (10.228.6)

Fig. 67 *Hurricane, Bahamas*, 1898

Watercolour and graphite on wove paper, 36.7 × 53.5 cm
The Metropolitan Museum of Art, New York. Amelia B. Lazarus Fund, 1910 (10.228.7)

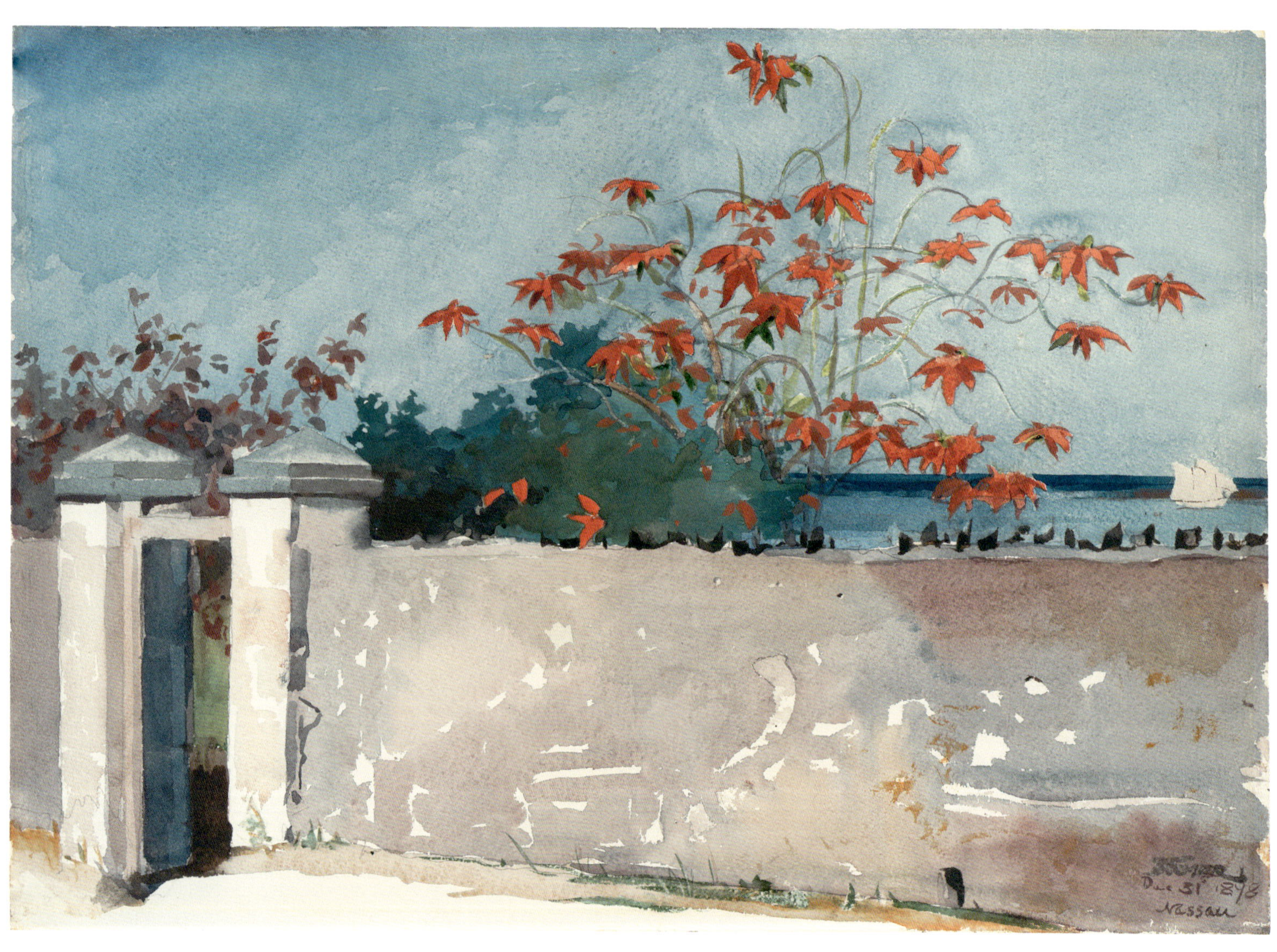

Fig. 68 *A Wall, Nassau*, 1898

Watercolour and graphite on wove paper, 37.8 × 54.3 cm
The Metropolitan Museum of Art, New York. Amelia B. Lazarus Fund, 1910 (10.228.9)

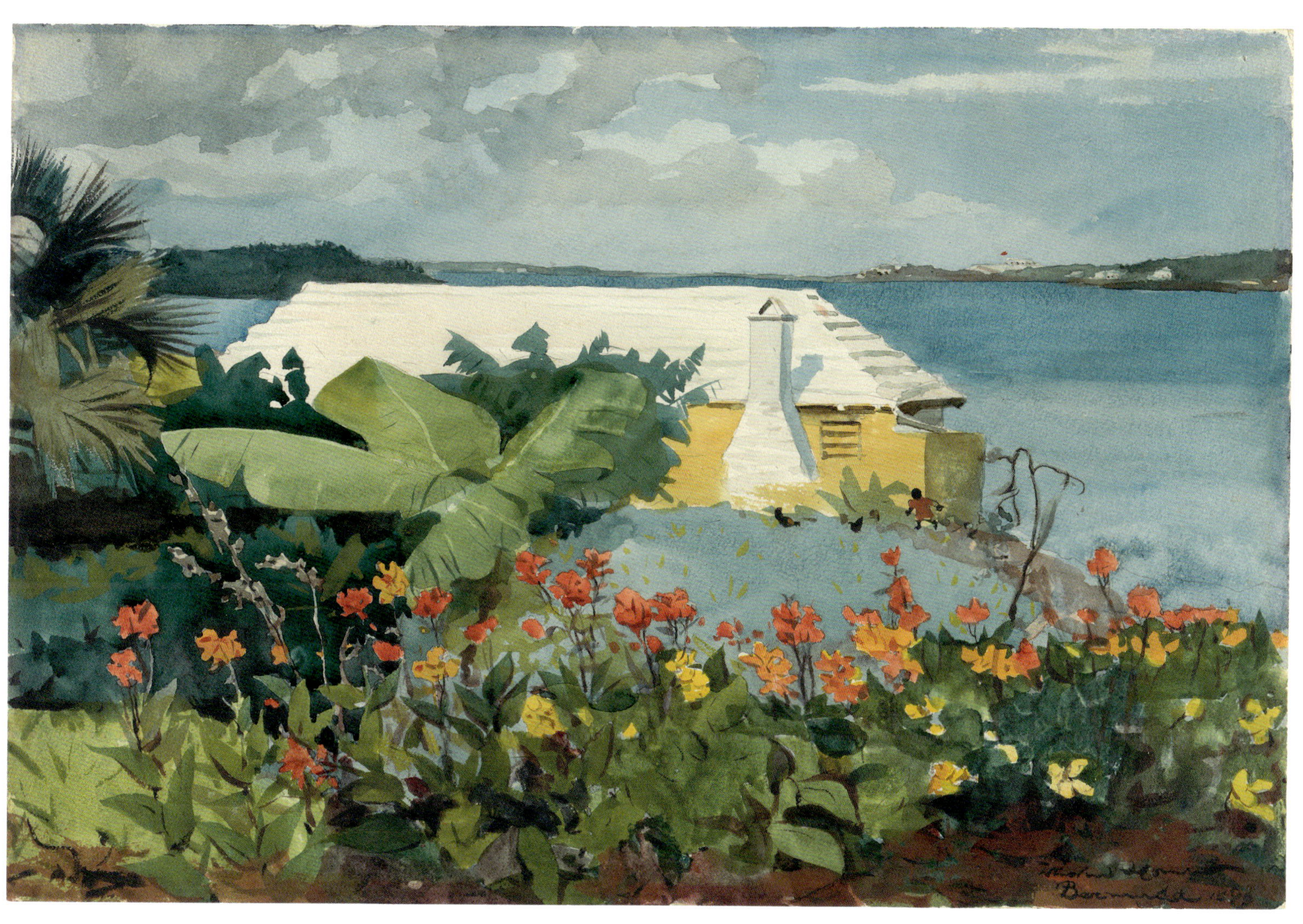

Fig. 69 *Flower Garden and Bungalow, Bermuda*, 1899

Watercolour and graphite on wove paper, 35.4 × 53.2 cm
The Metropolitan Museum of Art, New York. Amelia B. Lazarus Fund, 1910 (10.228.10)

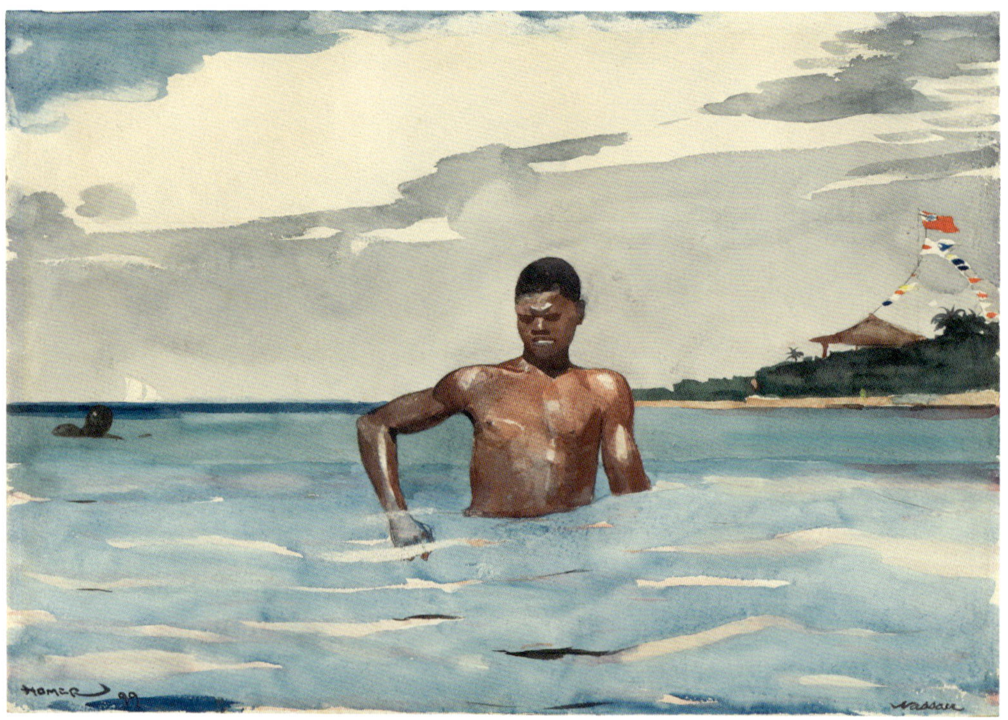

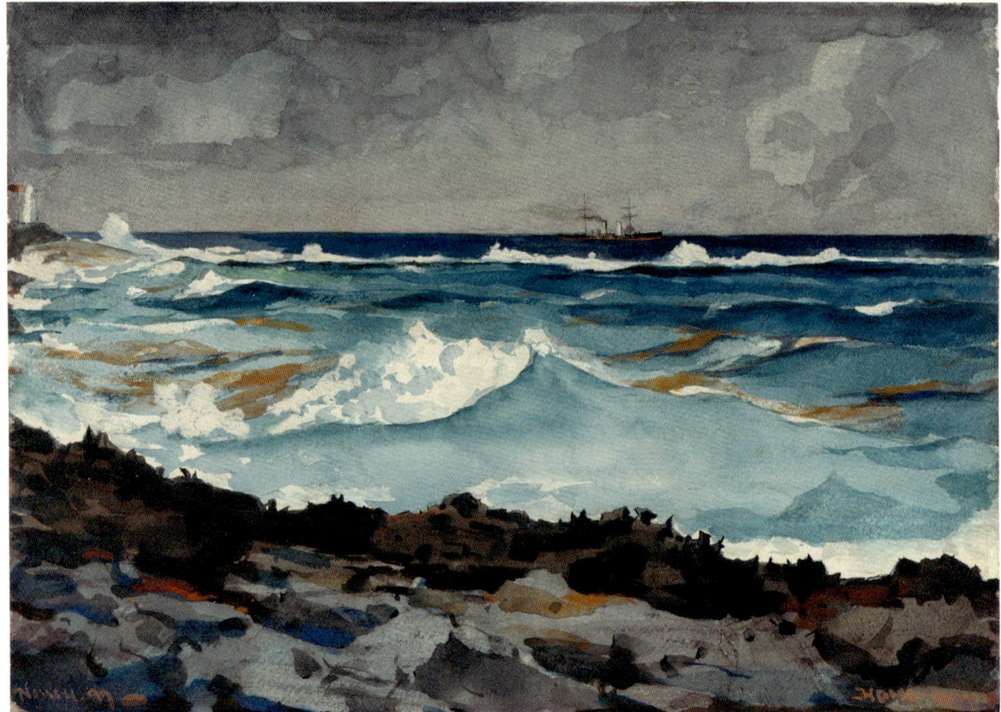

Top
Fig. 70 *The Bather*, 1899

Watercolour and graphite on wove paper, 36.7 × 53.5 cm
The Metropolitan Museum of Art, New York. Amelia B. Lazarus Fund, 1910 (10.228.8)

Bottom
Fig. 71 *Shore and Surf, Nassau*, 1899

Watercolour and graphite on wove paper, 37.9 × 54.3 cm
The Metropolitan Museum of Art, New York. Amelia B. Lazarus Fund, 1910 (10.228.5)

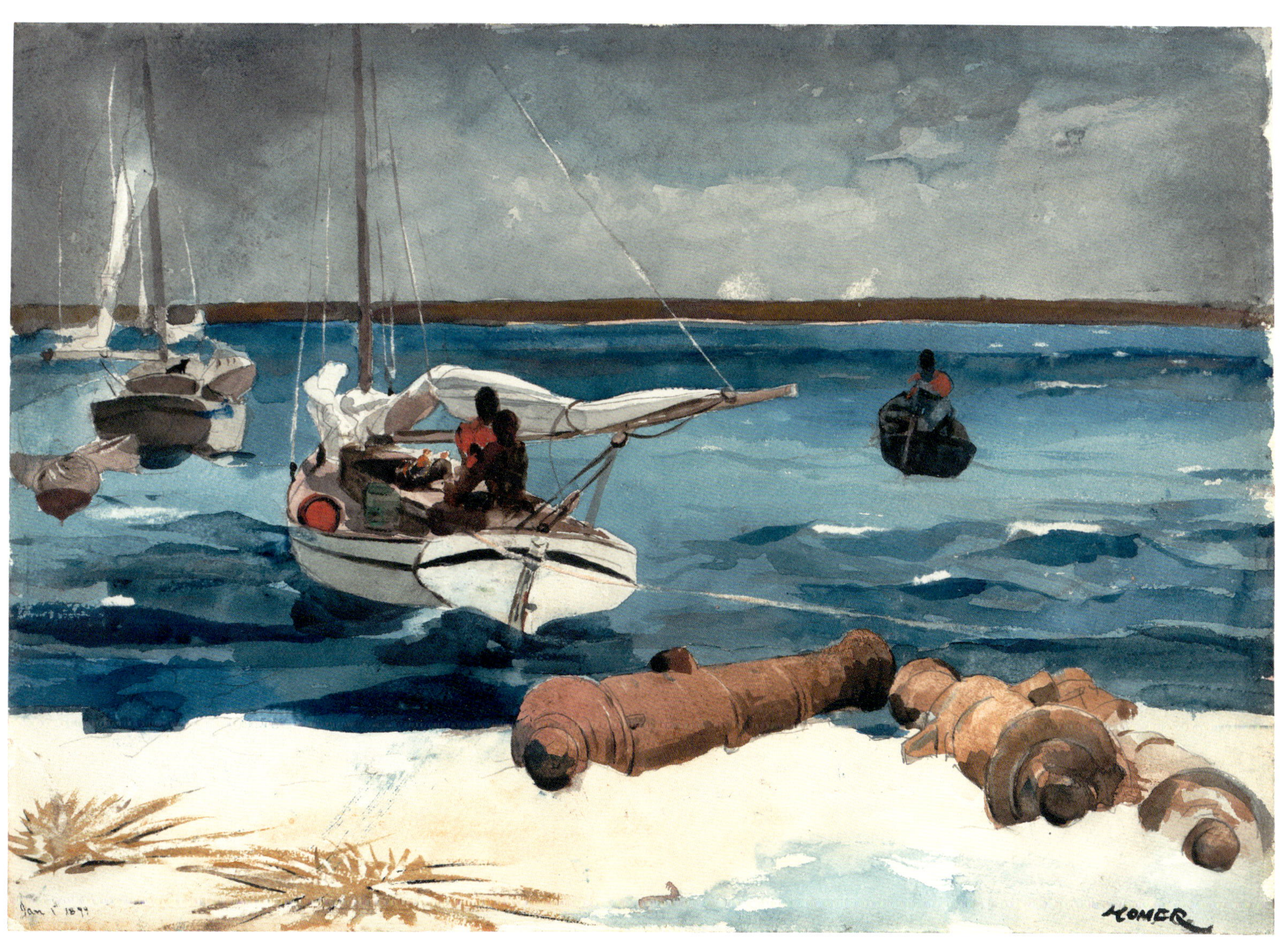

Fig. 72 *Nassau*, 1899

Watercolour and graphite on wove paper, 37.8 × 54.3 cm
The Metropolitan Museum of Art, New York. Amelia B. Lazarus Fund, 1910 (10.228.4)

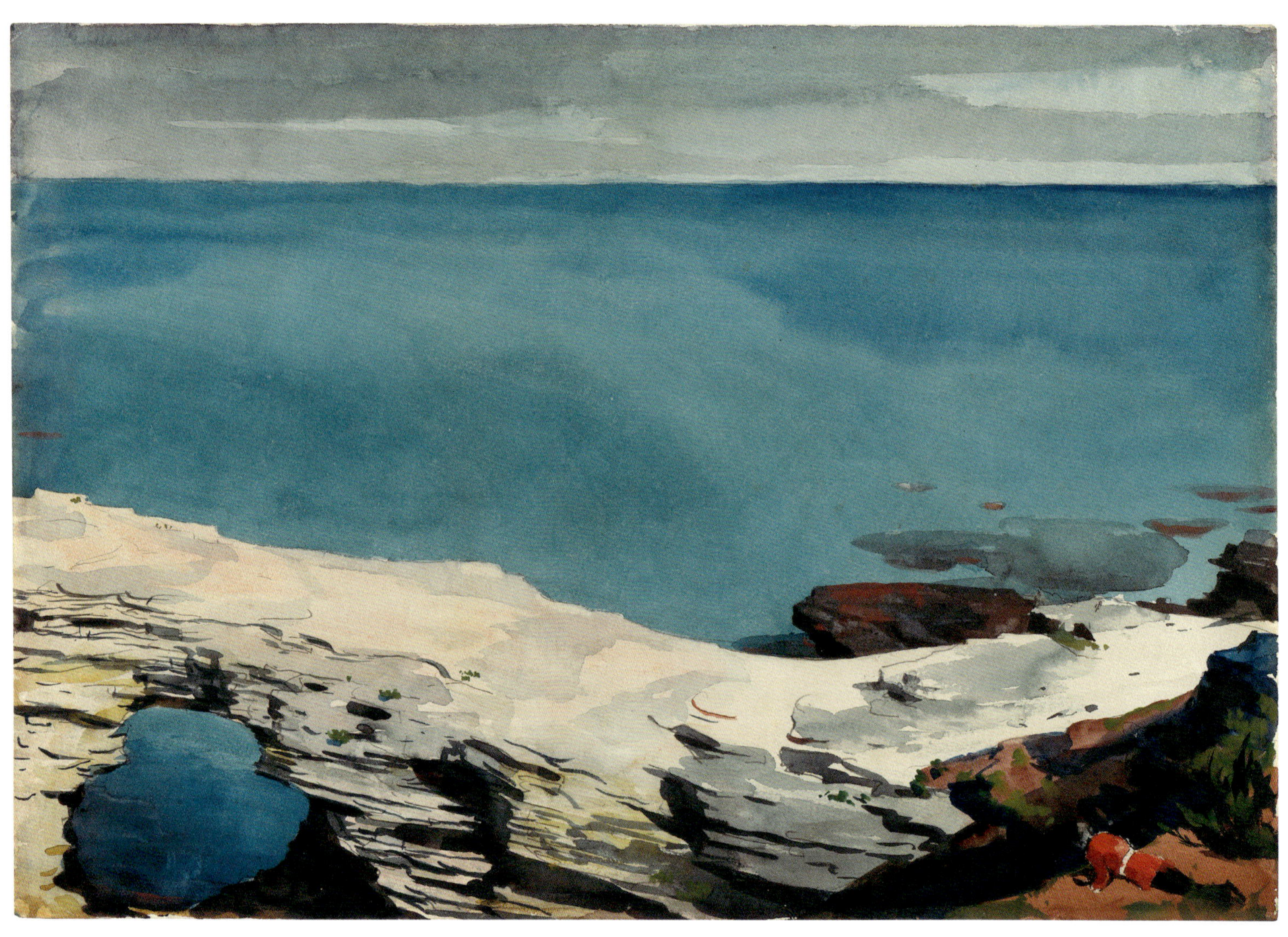

Fig. 73 *Natural Bridge, Bermuda*, about 1901

Watercolour and graphite on wove paper, 36.7 × 53.3 cm
The Metropolitan Museum of Art, New York. Amelia B. Lazarus Fund, 1910 (10.228.12)

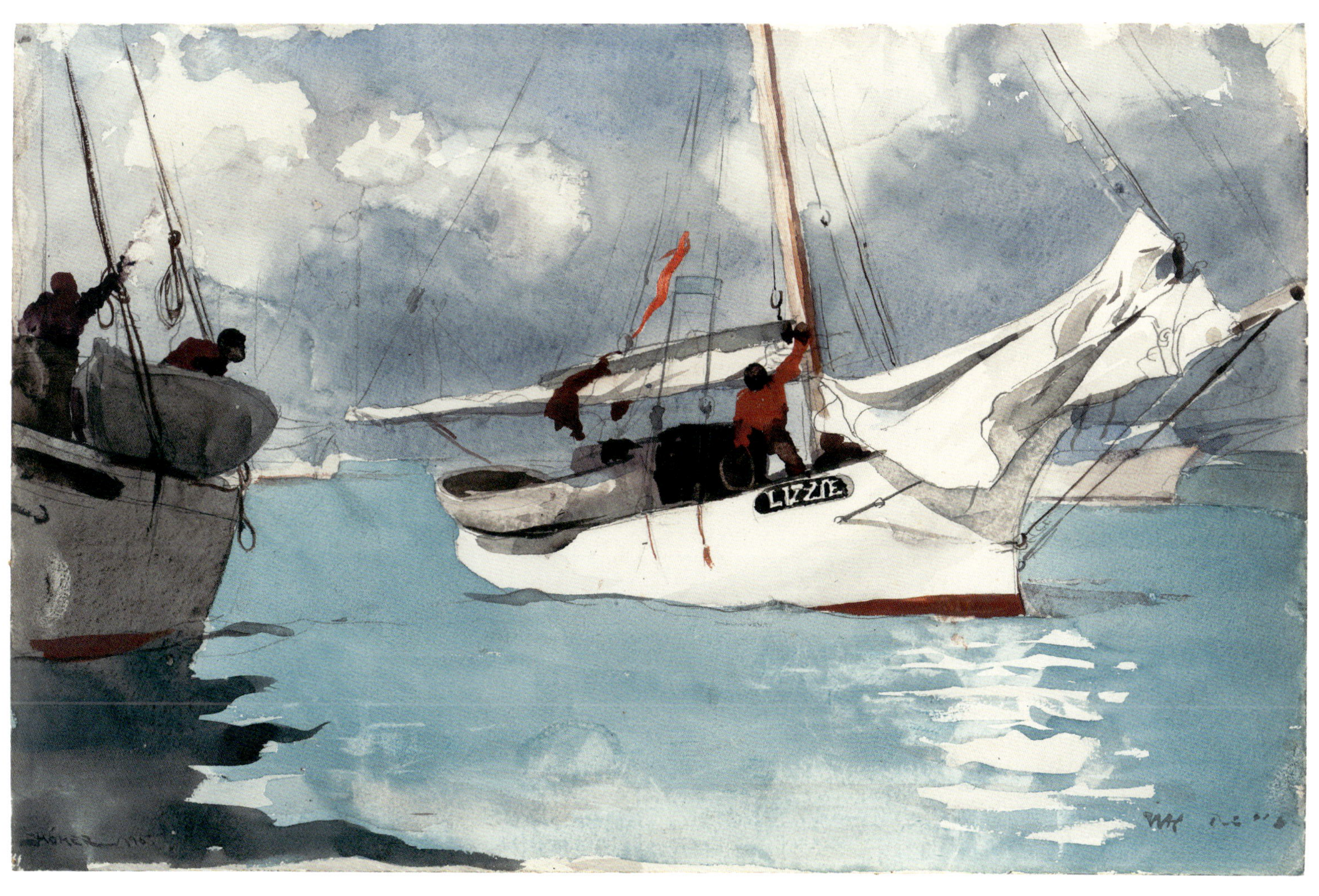

Fig. 74 *Fishing Boats, Key West*, 1903

Watercolour and graphite on wove paper, 35.4 × 55.2 cm
The Metropolitan Museum of Art, New York. Amelia B. Lazarus Fund, 1910 (10.228.1)

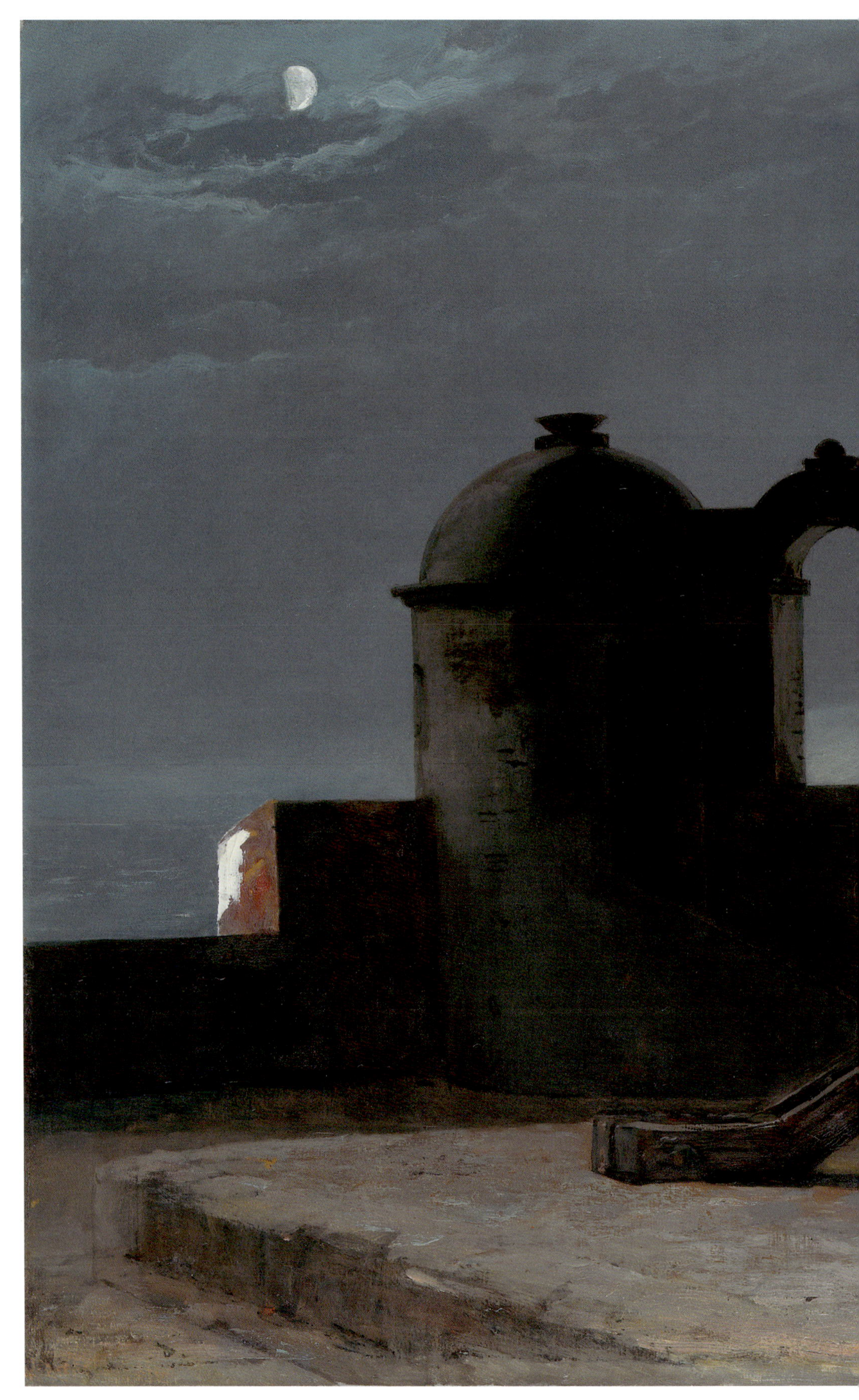

Fig. 75 *Searchlight on Harbor Entrance, Santiago de Cuba*, 1902

Oil on canvas, 77.5 × 128.3 cm
The Metropolitan Museum of Art, New York. Gift of George A. Hearn, 1906 (06.1282)

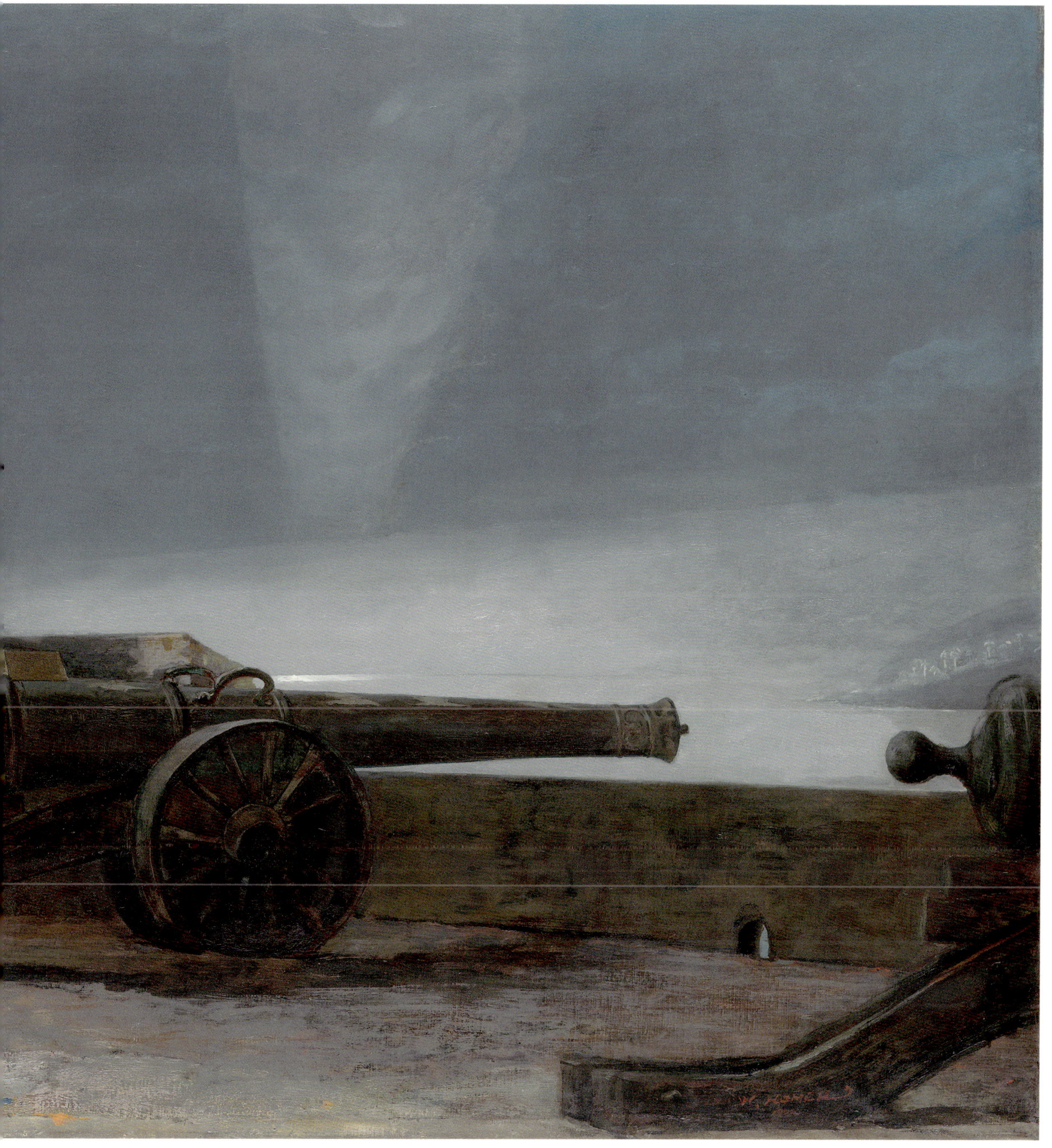

Painted in 1899 and soon after celebrated as 'a great dramatic picture',[1] *The Gulf Stream* is one of Homer's most acclaimed works (fig. 84). It shows a sailboat, its mast snapped, at the mercy of storm-tossed waters; on its deck, an exhausted Black sailor, resigned to his fate, seems oblivious to the menacing sharks, the waterspout on the horizon and the vessel in the far distance.

The genesis of the motif can be traced to Homer's first trip to The Bahamas in 1884 to 1885, where he sketched a sloop adrift in stormy waters (fig. 81) and a derelict boat encircled by sharks (fig. 82). Storms and shipwrecks were not uncommon in the Gulf Stream: most of the 'dangerous derelicts' in the North Atlantic Ocean, states *Frank Leslie's Illustrated Weekly* in 1893, 'drift to and from until some storm of exceptional fury sends them to the bottom' (fig. 78).[2] Produced during the same sojourn in the mid-1880s, *Shark fishing—Nassau Bar* (fig. 77) may also have served as a source for the picture. But it was not until 1899, after his second visit to The Bahamas and various watercolours (fig. 79), that Homer started working on the oil. 'I have painted in water colors three months last winter at Nassau,' he wrote to a friend

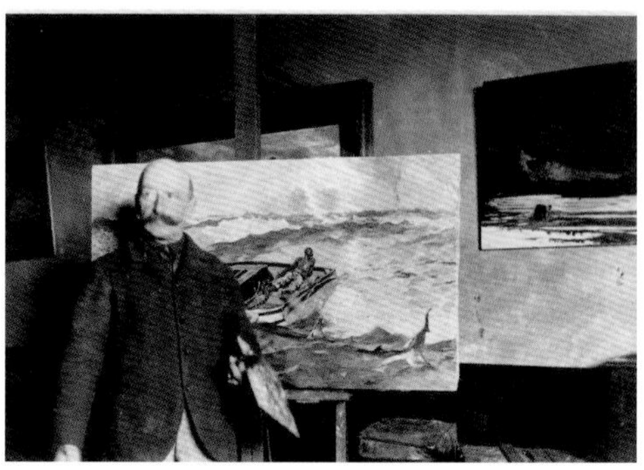

Fig. 76 Winslow Homer with *The Gulf Stream* in his studio in Prouts Neck, about 1899–1900. Bowdoin College Museum of Art, Brunswick, Maine. Gift of the Homer Family (1964.69.179.9)

in September of that year, '& have now just commenced arranging a picture from some of the studies' (fig. 76).[3] Two months later, *The Gulf Stream* was finished, packed and ready to ship: it would hang in Pennsylvania Academy of the Fine Arts in Philadelphia in January 1900. The following summer, though, the artist reported having 'painted on the picture since it was in Phil[a] & improved it very much – (more of the Deep Sea water than before)'.[4] Aside from the sea,

Around the Gulf Stream

Chiara Di Stefano

Fig. 77 *Shark Fishing—Nassau Bar* (detail), 1887, engraving, 9.8 × 13.5 cm. Brooklyn Museum of Art, New York. Gift of Harvey Isbitts (1998.105.211)

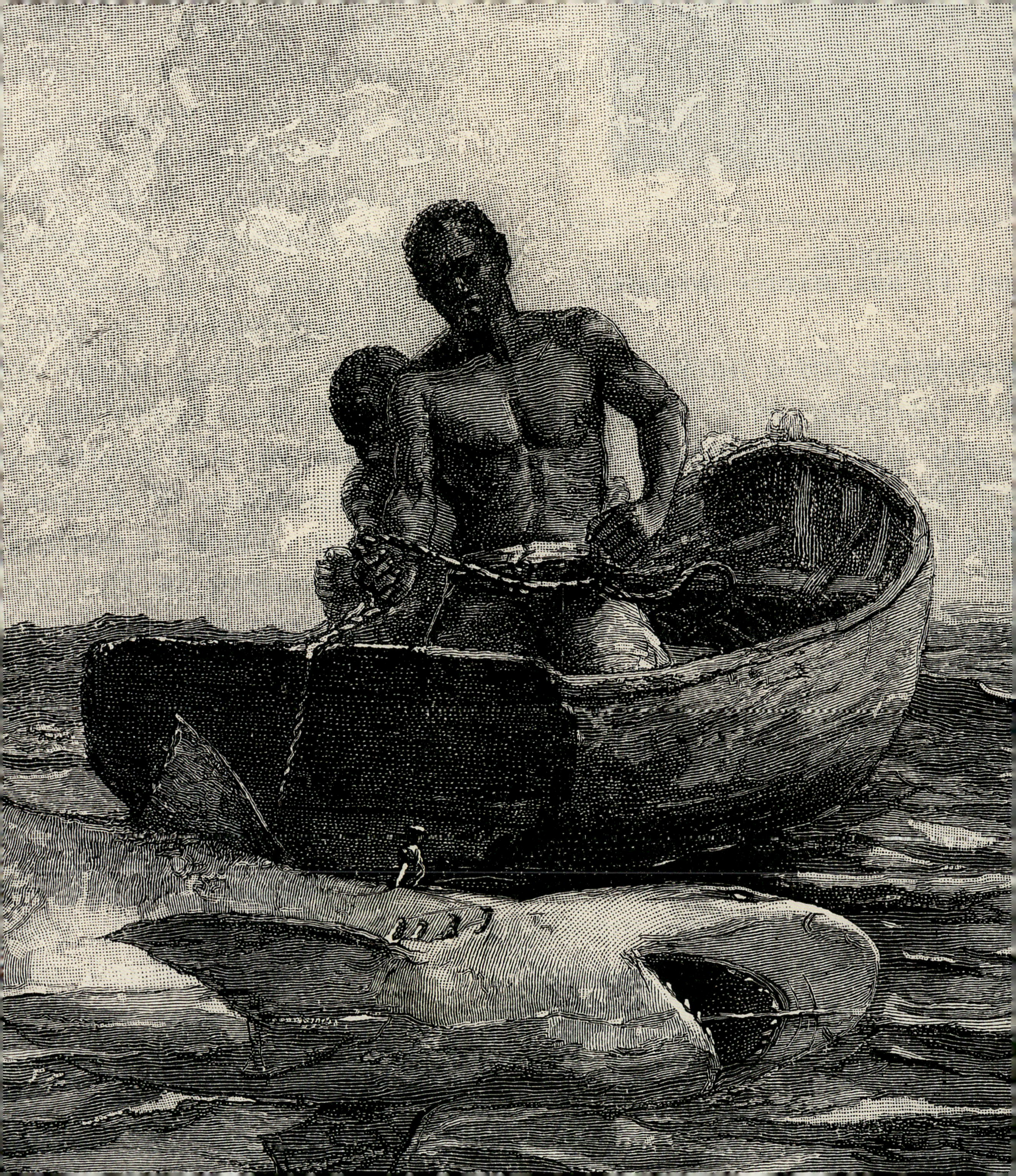

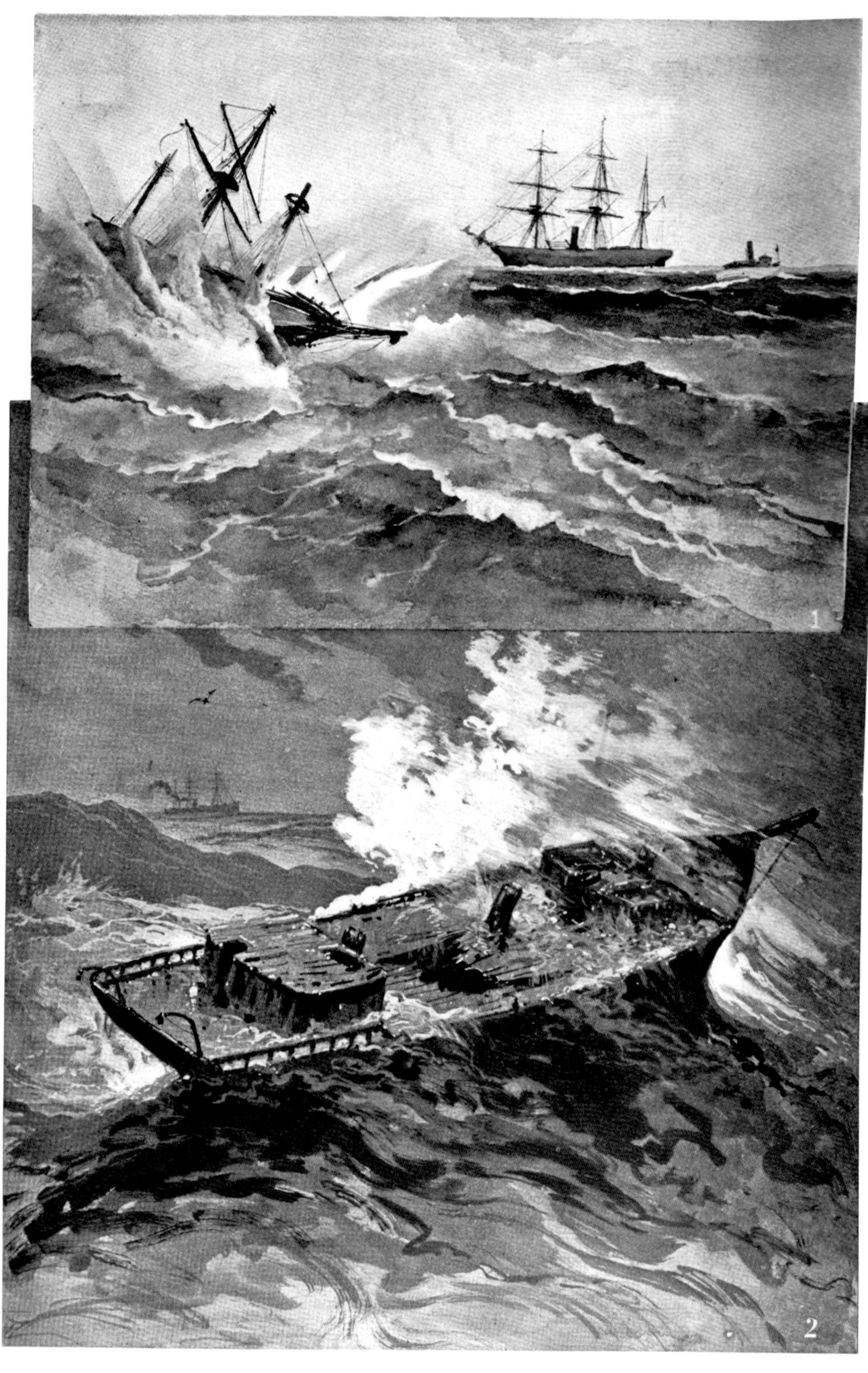

Fig. 78 Anonymous, *Frank Leslie's Illustrated Weekly*, 27 July 1893, p. 54

he modified several details of the boat: naming it *Anna – Key West*, adding a sail and breaking the starboard gunwale. Most importantly, he depicted a schooner in the far distance, opening the narrative to a less dreadful ending. The tragic nature of the subject was, in the artist's opinion, a major obstacle to the selling, as he suggested to his Chicago art dealer: 'Why do you not try & sell the Gulf Stream to ... [a] public Gallery? No one would expect to have it in a private house.'[5]

Rooted in the Romantic tradition, the painting was defined by one critic as 'Homer's *Raft of the Medusa*',[6] an allusion to Théodore Géricault's work in the musée du Louvre (fig. 80). More often, it was inscribed in the genealogy of Joseph Mallord William Turner's *Slave Ship* (1840, seen by Homer in April 1872 while in John Taylor Johnston's collection[7] and acquired in 1899 by the Museum of Fine Arts, Boston; fig. 17), as well as Thomas Cole's (1801–1848) *The Voyage of Life: Manhood* (1842) and John Singleton Copley's *Watson and the Shark* (1778, fig. 20), both now in Washington's National Gallery of Art,[8] which are considered masterpieces of American painting and were surely known to Homer. Perhaps to secure a public acquisition, Homer measured himself openly against these great masters. Turner's painting, for instance, is mentioned in a letter to a friend: 'You may remember "Turner's Slave Ship" with the chain cables floating on the water & the impossible arms & legs that have been admired by the public. These figures of mine [are of] the same value to the picture.'[9] Despite this neutral reading of Turner's picture, Homer was certainly aware of what *Slave Ship* meant and implied. A provocative denunciation of the horrors of slavery through the chronicle of a real event, its subject was deemed so unpleasant that its first owner, critic John Ruskin, despite considering it 'Turner's noblest work',[10] attempted (unsuccessfully) to sell it at Christie's in 1869.[11] More suitable for a public space than a private dwelling, *Slave Ship* engaged with a burning issue in the age of abolition.

An enigmatic painting, *The Gulf Stream* has been open to various interpretations. While it would be unfruitful to relay all the readings of this

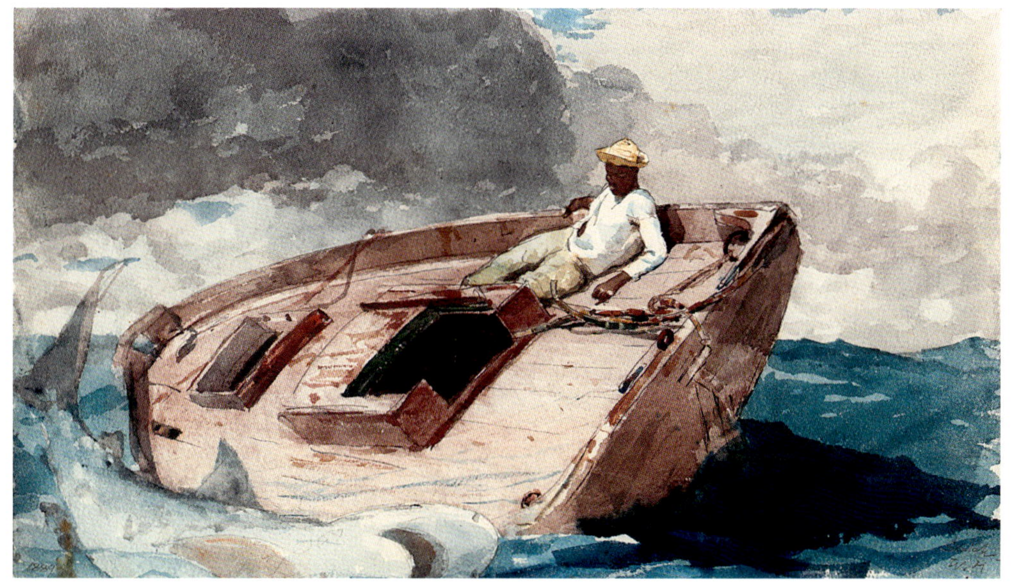

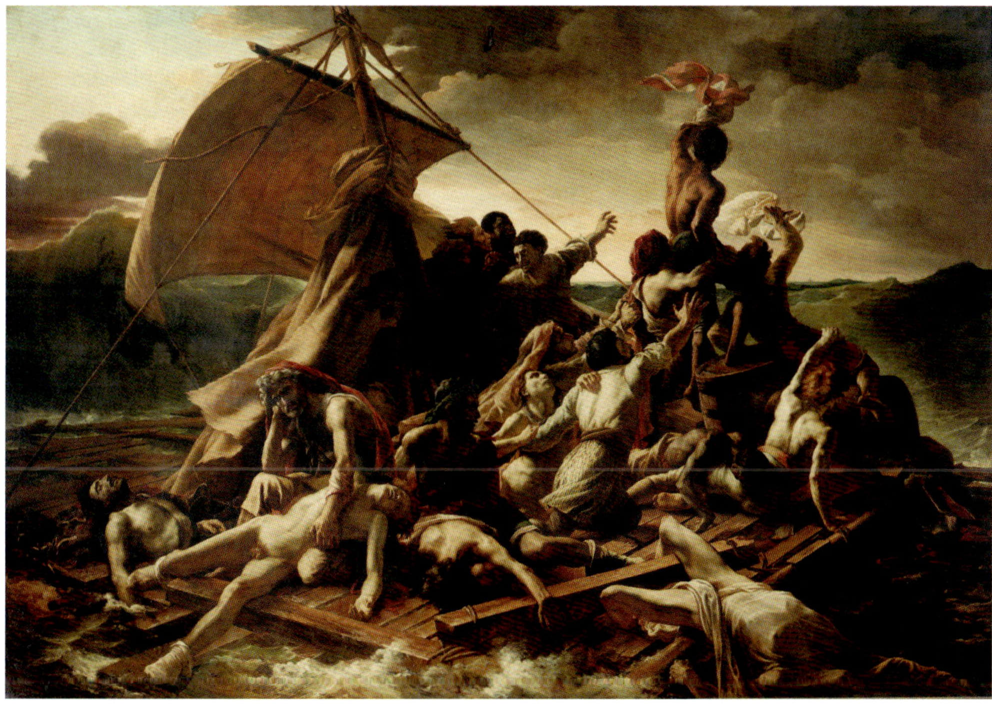

Top
Fig. 79 *The Gulf Stream*, probably 1899, watercolour and graphite on wove paper, 28.8 × 50.9 cm. The Art Institute of Chicago, Illinois. Mr and Mrs Martin A. Ryerson Collection (1933.1241)

Bottom
Fig. 80 Théodore Géricault (1791–1824), *The Raft of the Medusa*, 1818–19, oil on canvas, 490 × 716 cm. Musée du Louvre, Paris (INV 4884)

picture, it is useful to outline some aspects of its multifaceted – and often conflicting – reception. Broadly speaking, the first reviews of the work tended to highlight its narrative aspect. Though often praised for its 'honest, virile and rugged, yet not brutal'[12] style, the 'unusually strong canvas'[13] was initially perceived as a narrative image: 'elaborately literary ... frankly a story-telling piece of work'[14] said one critic; it showed for another 'a return to [Homer's] old fondness for anecdotal subject'.[15]

However, these readings seem at odds with Homer's own intent, focusing on the ocean's fury more than the sailor's fate. As he pointed out in a letter to Harrison Morris, Director of Pennsylvania Academy of the Fine Arts: 'This picture is called "The Gulf Stream". Please [do] *not change this title*. I have some landscape figures in it – enough to give interest to it but of little account in this great subject of "Gulf Stream".'[16] And, in 1902, he famously wrote to his art dealer Roland Knoedler, 'I regret very much that I have painted a picture that requires any description,' adding wryly:

> The subject of this picture is comprised in *its title* & I will refer these inquisitive Schoolma'ms to Lieut Maury. I have crossed the Gulf Stream ten times & I should know something about it. The boat & sharks are outside matters of very little consequence. *They have been blown out to sea by a hurricane*. You can tell these ladies that the unfortunate negro who now is so dazed & parboiled will be rescued & returned to his friends and home & ever after live happily.[17]

Matthew Fontaine Maury ('Lieut Maury', 1806–1873), oceanographer and meteorologist, was the author of *The Physical Geography of the Sea* (1855). In the chapter on the Gulf Stream, he defined it as 'the great "weather breeder" of the North Atlantic Ocean', whose path is 'marked by wreck and disaster'.[18] After describing a major deluge in the Florida Keys, he concluded that the flood 'in the Gulf Stream was never surpassed in awful sublimity on the ocean'.[19] Homer may allude to this specific episode in his painting with his later addition of the boat's home port (Key West).

Across the twentieth century, the interpretations varied widely, ranging from formalism to psychoanalysis. From Nicolai Cikovsky Jr's biographical perspective, Homer, feeling 'alone, abandoned and mortally vulnerable'[20] after his father's death, depicts a metaphor of human mortality. Similarly, art historian Hugh Honour believes the artist 'identified himself with the figure in the boat, alone on the cruel sea that had been the means of his livelihood'.[21] Another line of interpretation focuses on the racial tensions and the representation of Black people. For Alain Locke, a key figure of the 1920s Harlem Renaissance and editor of *The New Negro*, Homer's *Gulf Stream* marks 'the artistic emancipation of the Negro in American art',[22] while for art historian Albert Boime it portrays 'an allegory of black man's victimization at the end of the nineteenth century'.[23]

More recently, scholars have contextualised the work in the wider frame of Black Atlantic studies, with a particular focus on the transatlantic slave trade.[24] The same is true for contemporary artists: although *The Gulf Stream* was more likely conceived as a 'mute witness of the force of nature'[25] than as a metaphor of 'the paradoxical destiny of a freed black people in modern society',[26] its resonance in the collective imagination defies Homer's resistance to allegorical readings, making it a modern icon of Black imagery.

Studied, interpreted and ubiquitously reproduced since its creation, the painting has been quoted in the work of major African American artists such as Kehinde Wiley (b. 1977) and Kara Walker (b. 1969), acquiring new, transformative meanings, often in the light of Black Atlantic theory. Both Wiley and Walker engaged with *The Gulf Stream* in critical ways, reflecting on the visual representation of Black people and opening the debate on alternative views of the Black body.[27] Other voices are joining this polyphonic choir. Proposing a fresh consideration of the sailor's attitude, scholar Genevieve Hyacinthe interprets his behaviour not as passive resignation but as a bold example of 'black endurance', concluding: 'work must be done to transform the performance of the black man in *The Gulf Stream* from passive matter taken up by the thermodynamics of water into one of an active agent intent on survival.'[28] Opening up new critical space around *The Gulf Stream*, these perspectives are extending its fame as 'one of the greatest pictures ever painted in America'[29] to new generations of enthralled and challenged viewers.

1 *New York Evening Post*, 29 December 1906, p. 5.
2 Anonymous, 'Derelicts at sea', *Frank Leslie's Illustrated Weekly*, 1893, p. 64 (first mentioned in Cikovsky 1990, p. 153).
3 W. Homer, letter to J.W. Beatty, September 1899, quoted in Spassky et al. 1985, p. 487.
4 W. Homer, letter to J.W. Beatty, 18 September 1900, quoted in Gerdts and Goodrich 2005–14, vol. 5, p. 187.
5 W. Homer, quoted in Downes 1911, p. 149.
6 Cortissoz 1923, p. 122.
7 See this volume, p. 26.
8 Two other versions of *Watson and the Shark* are held in the Museum of Fine Arts, Boston, and the Detroit Institute of Art.
9 W. Homer, letter to H. Morris, 26 November 1899, quoted in Gerdts and Goodrich 2005–14, vol. 5, p. 286.
10 J. Ruskin, *Modern Painters*, London 1848, vol. 1, pp. 376–7.
11 See R. Hewison (ed.), *Ruskin, Turner and the Pre-Raphaelites*, exh. cat., Tate Britain, London 2000, p. 71; and J. McCoubrey, 'Turner's *Slave Ship*: Abolition, Ruskin, and Reception', *Word & Image*, vol. 14, no. 4 (October–December 1998), pp. 319–53.
12 Cleveland, Columbus and Washington, DC 1990–1, p. 69.
13 Anonymous, *New York Herald*, 21 December 1906, p. 12.
14 Downes 1911, p. 133.
15 H. Caffin in *The Artist*, vol. 27, 1900, p. vi.
16 W. Homer, letter to H. Morris, 26 November 1899, quoted in Gerdts and Goodrich 2005–14, vol. 5, p. 286.
17 W. Homer, letter to R. Knoedler, 19 February 1902, quoted in Gerdts and Goodrich 2005–14, vol. 5, p. 288.
18 Maury 1855, pp. 54–55.
19 Ibid, p. 55.
20 Washington, DC, Boston and New York 1995, p. 369.
21 Honour 1989, p. 202.
22 A. Locke quoted in Kaplan 1966, p. 112.
23 Boime 1989, p. 36.
24 See New York 2022.
25 F.W. Morton, 'The Art of Winslow Homer', *Brush and Pencil*, vol. 10, no. 1, April 1902, p. 54.
26 Boime 1989, p. 44.
27 Both artists recently exhibited in London galleries: Kara Walker, *Fons Americanus*, Tate Modern (Hyundai Commission; 2 October 2019–7 February 2021); and Kehinde Wiley, *The Prelude*, National Gallery (10 December 2021–18 April 2022).
28 G. Hyacinthe, 'The Shape of Humidity: Performing Black Atlantic Theory Making', *Performance Philosophy* 4.2, 2019: www.performancephilosophy.org/journal/article/view/237/342 (accessed 7 April 2022). I am extremely grateful to Dr John Fagg for his attentive and insightful reading, and for bringing Hyacinthe's article to my attention.
29 S. Hartmann, *A History of American Art*, vol. 1, 1901, p. 200, quoted in Spassky et al. 1985, p. 493.

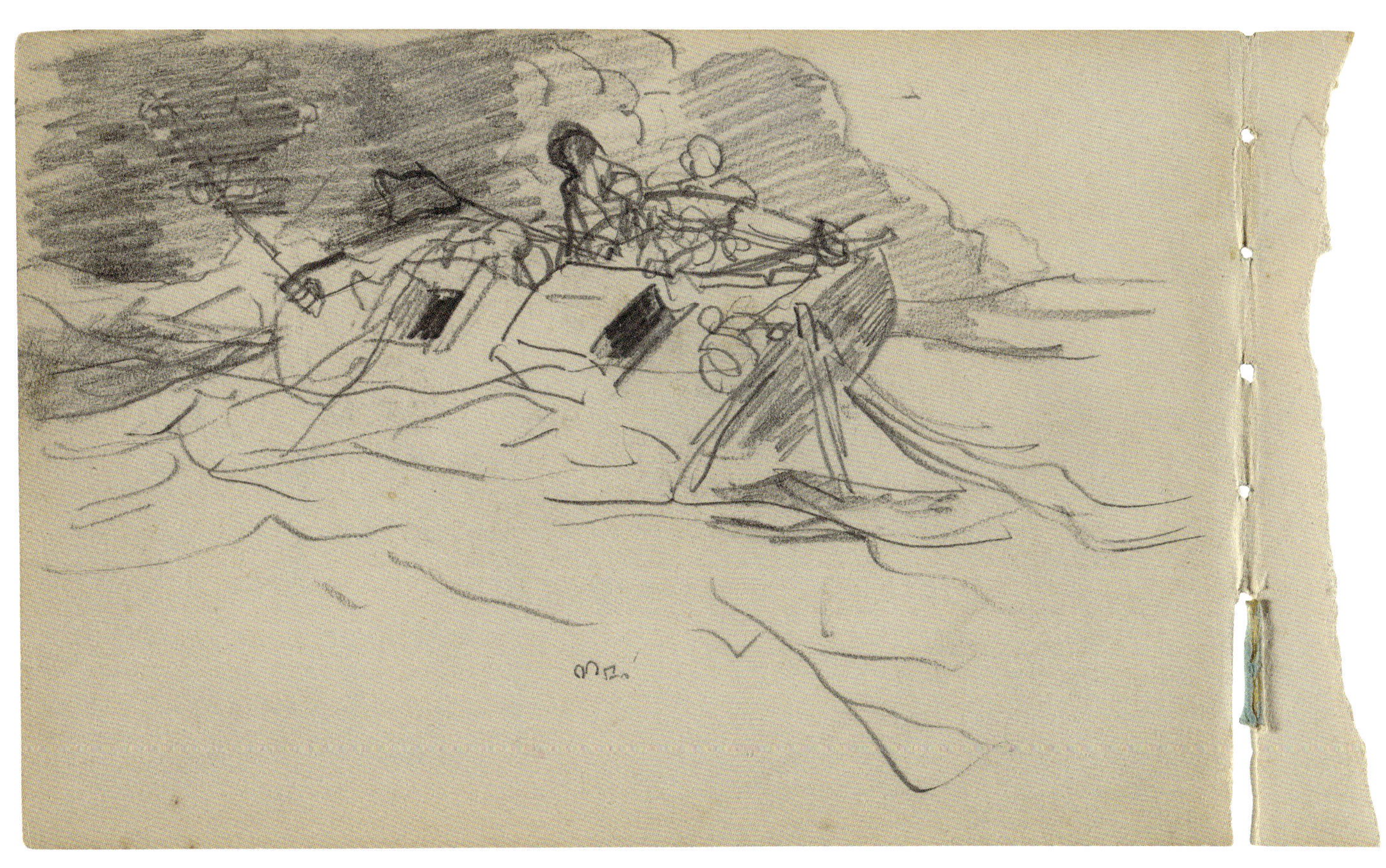

Fig. 81 *Distressed Boat (Sketch for 'The Gulf Stream')*, 1885

Graphite on paper, 10.2 × 16 cm
The Metropolitan Museum of Art, New York. Morris K. Jesup Fund, 2016 (2016.1 recto)

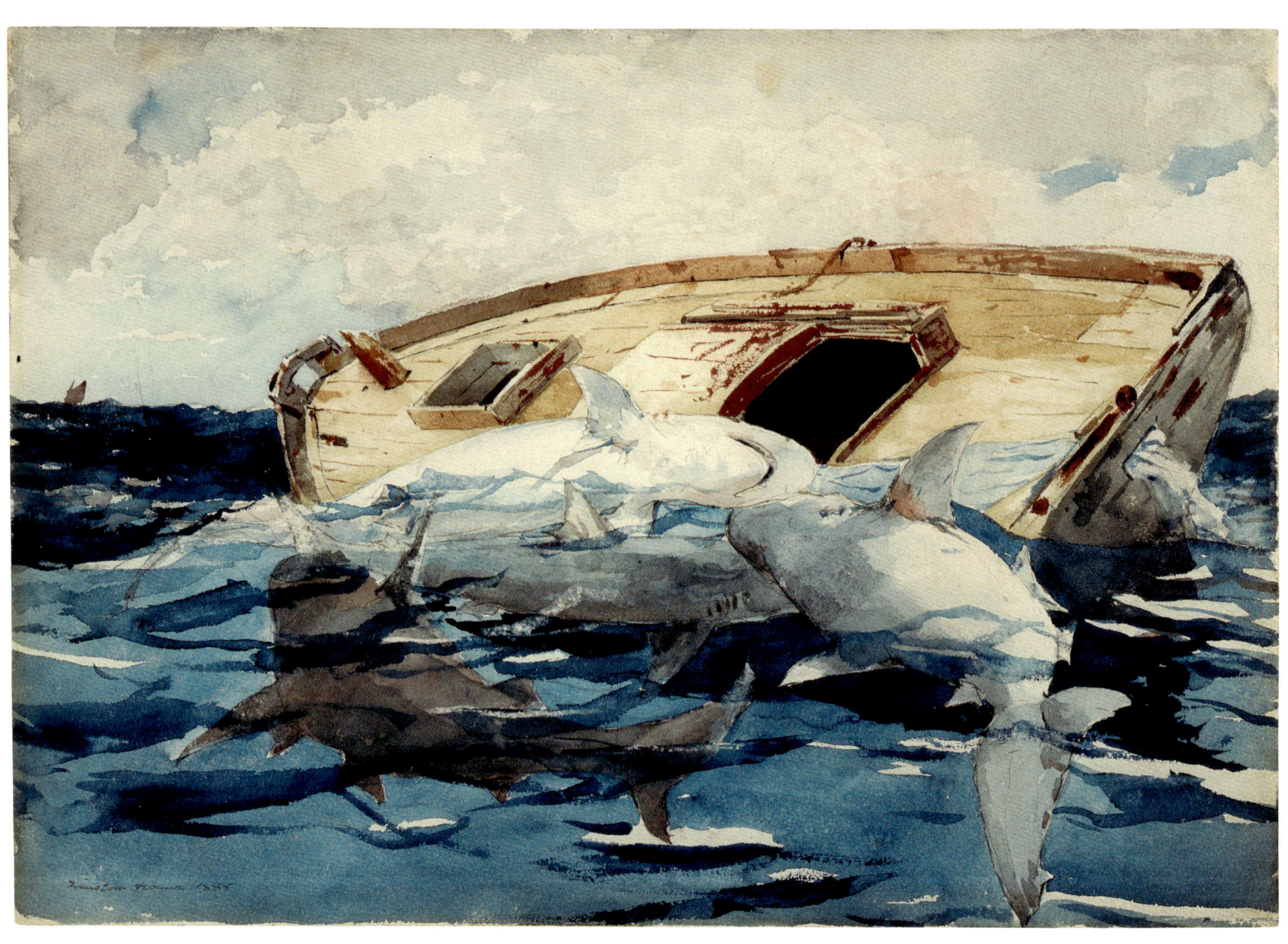

Fig. 82 *Sharks (The Derelict)*, 1885

Watercolour over graphite on wove paper, 36.8 × 53.2 cm
Brooklyn Museum, New York. Gift of the Estate of Helen Babbott Sanders (78.151.4)

Opposite
Fig. 83 *Study for 'The Gulf Stream'*, 1898–9

Watercolour and chalk on wove paper, 36.8 × 25.6 cm
Cooper Hewitt, Smithsonian Design Museum, Smithsonian Institution, New York. Gift of Charles Savage Homer, Jr (1912-12-36)

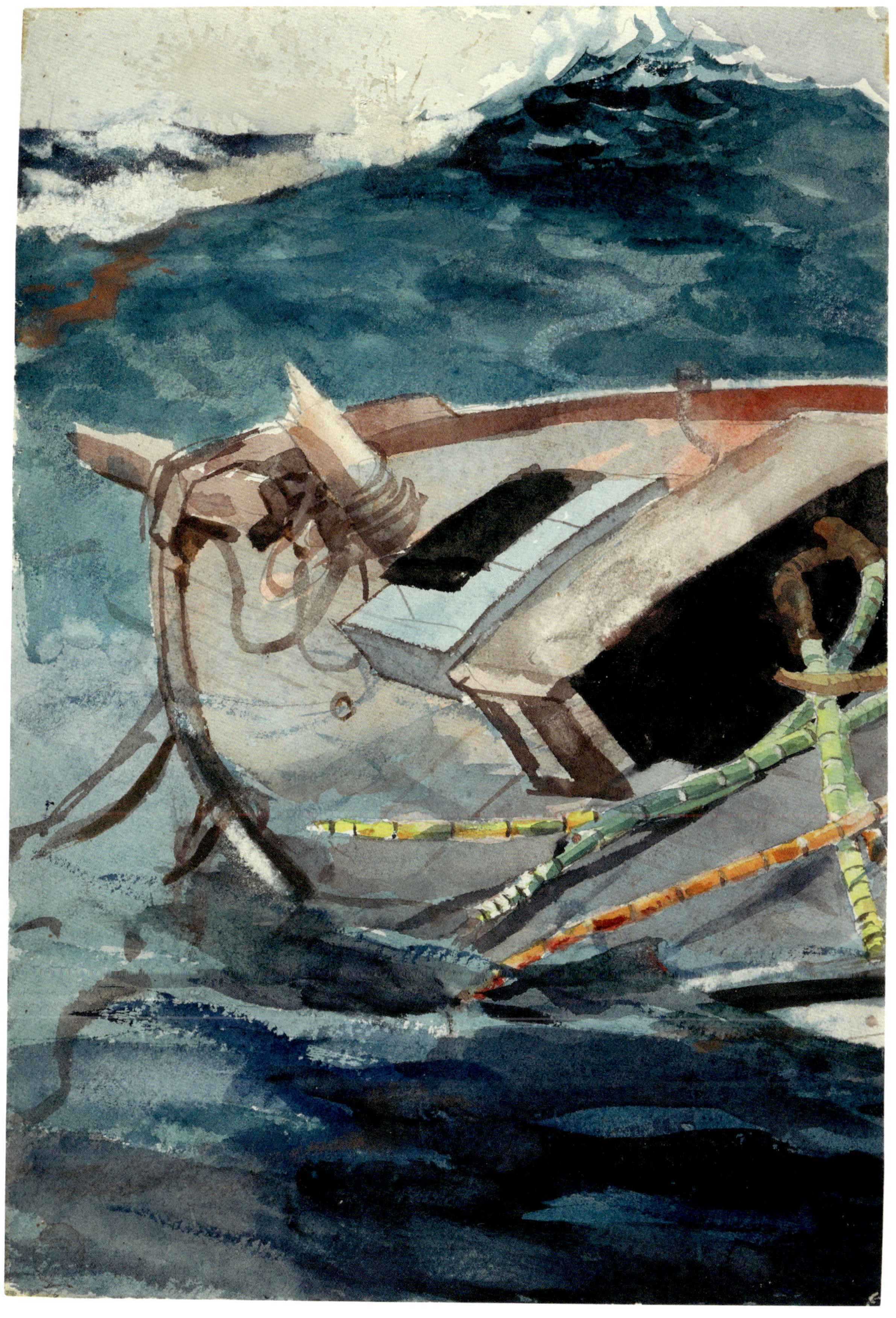

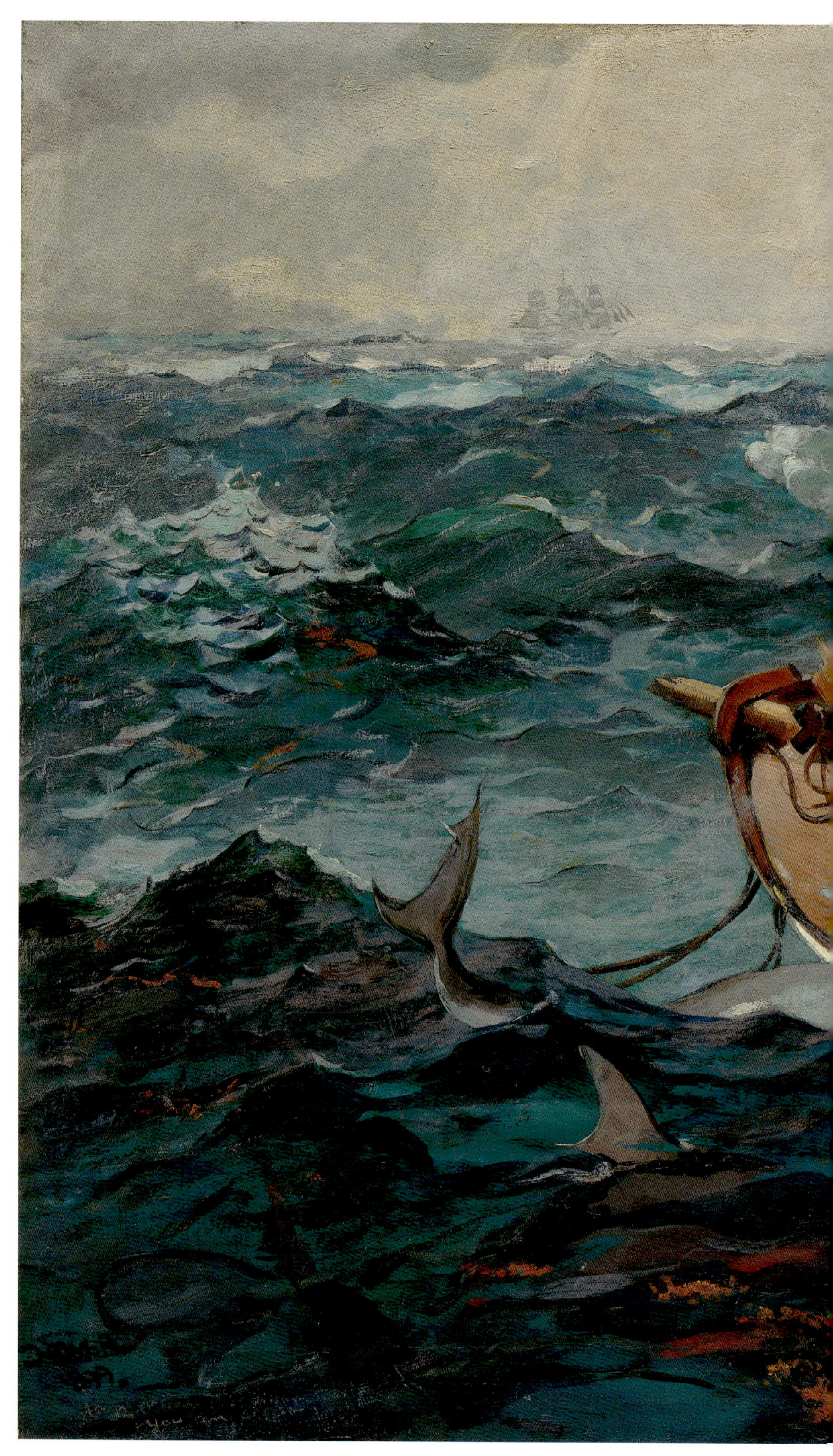

Fig. 84 *The Gulf Stream*, 1899, reworked by 1906

Oil on canvas, 71.4 × 124.8 cm
The Metropolitan Museum of Art, New York. Catharine Lorillard Wolfe Collection, Wolfe Fund, 1906 (06.1234)

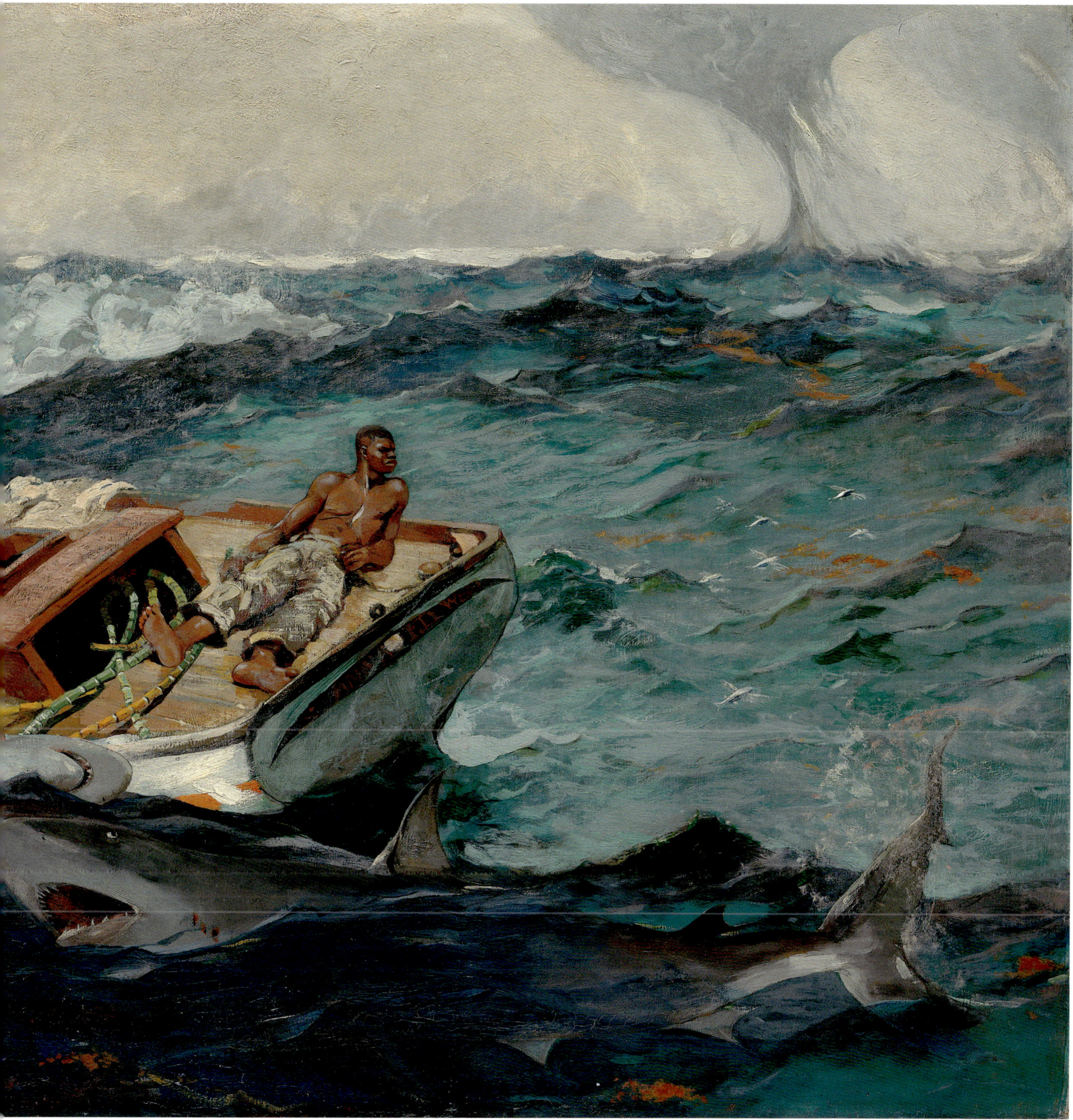

‘The Great Ocean Symphony’: Homer’s Late Seascapes

Chiara Di Stefano

In 1883 Homer moved to Prouts Neck, Maine, where he would live until the end of his life. From his house and studio overlooking the coast, he tirelessly observed the moods of the ocean (fig. 85). A profound change occurred at this time in his art: human beings became less and less important, often reduced to tiny, insignificant presences facing the power of nature. Conversely, the ocean acquired a pivotal role.

While the sea had always been central to Homer’s work, it featured until the late 1880s as either a background or an actor in human chronicles: sometimes an idyllic setting for leisure activities, more often a merciless antagonist to survival. From the 1890s, however, the raw beauty of the waves became a subject in its own right. Hugely admired by his contemporaries, Homer’s peopleless seascapes eclipsed the celebrity of his earlier pictures, securing his fame as the greatest American painter of his time. Yet they also nurtured the myth of the artist as a recluse, living in isolation on the rocky shores of Prouts Neck – an image Homer himself liked to promote. And although recent studies have countered this reading, which romantically entwines the painter with his subjects, his reputation as a ‘hermit of the brush’[1] proves difficult to shake.

‘There is something rugged, austere, even Titanic in almost everything Homer has done,’ wrote one critic in 1902, adding, ‘His sea is the watery waste as the expression of tremendous force, mystery, peril.’[2] The motif of the untamed sea was not new in Western art. And the sublime – the aesthetic response of grandeur and horror

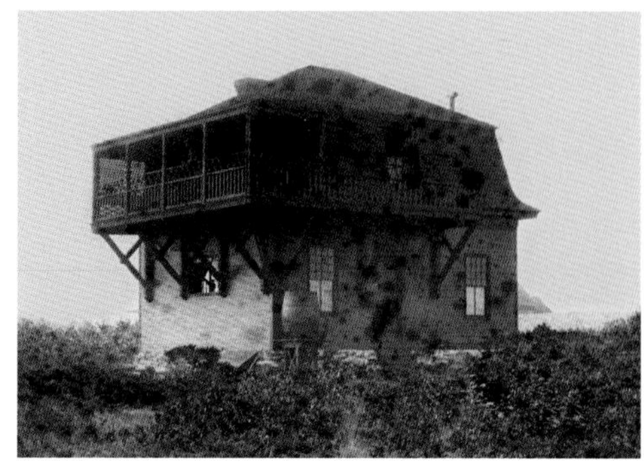

Fig. 85 Winslow Homer on the gallery of his Prouts Neck studio, about 1884, albumen silver print, Bowdoin College Museum of Art, Brunswick, Maine. Gift of the Homer Family (1964.69.153.11)

Detail of fig. 96

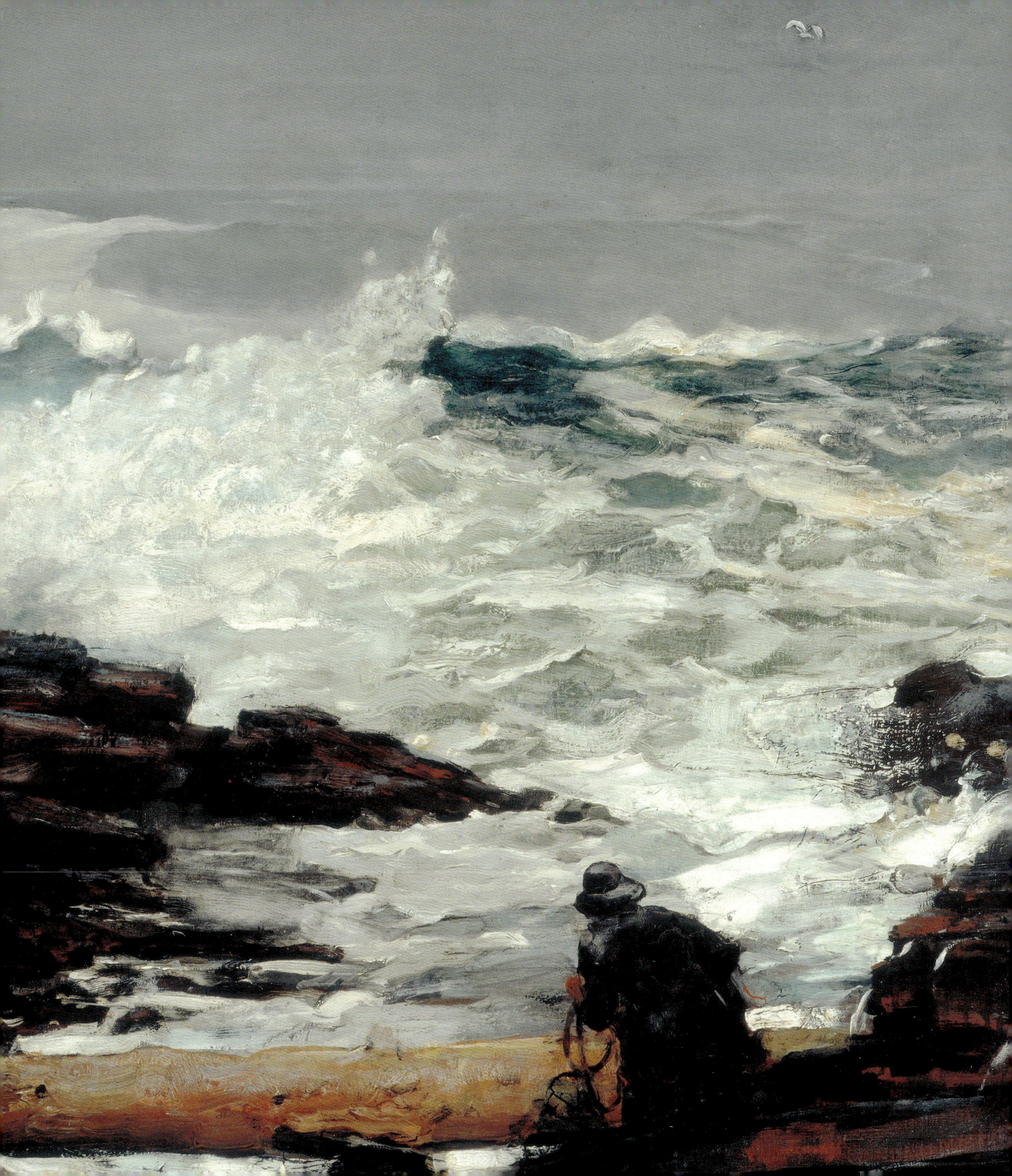

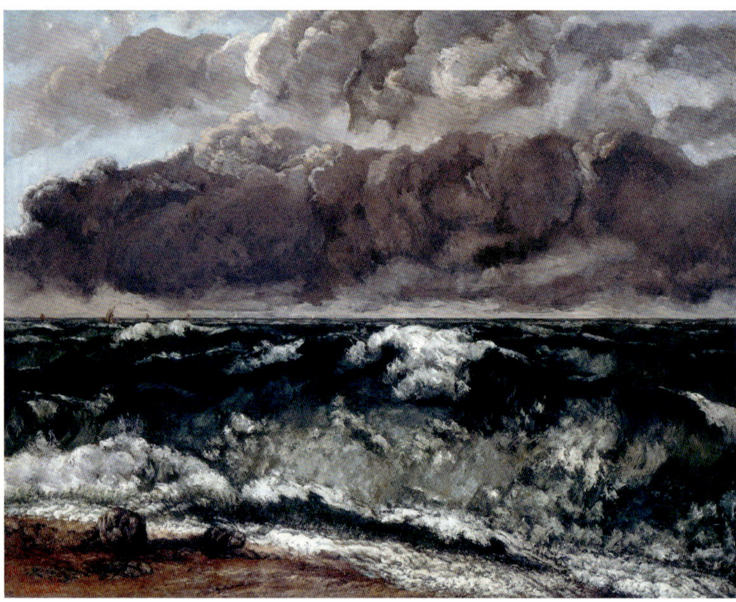

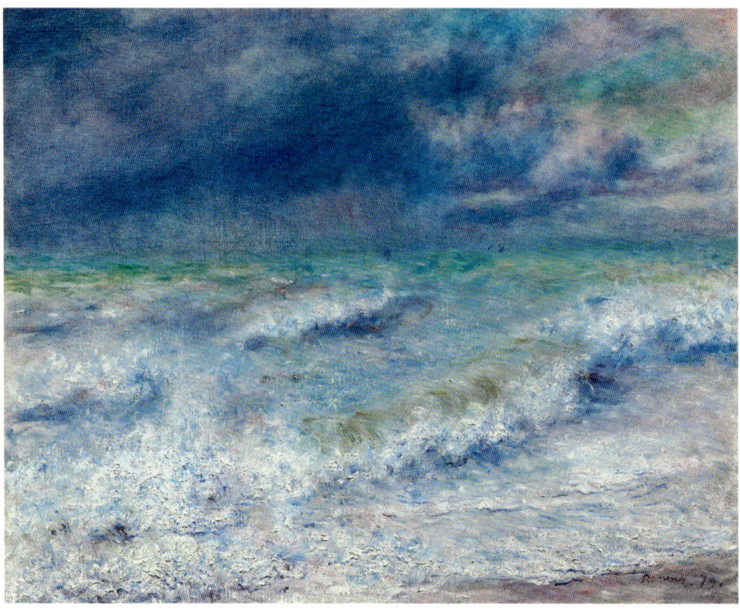

Top
Fig. 86 Gustave Courbet (1819–1877), *Wave*, 1870, oil on canvas, 112 × 144 cm. Alte Nationalgalerie, Berlin

Bottom
Fig. 87 Pierre-Auguste Renoir (1841–1919), *Seascape*, 1879, oil on canvas, 72.6 × 91.6 cm. The Art Institute of Chicago, Illinois. Potter Palmer Collection (1922.438)

before nature's fury – as theorised by Edmund Burke in the mid-eighteenth century and a source of inspiration since the Romantic era, revived this iconographic tradition.[3] 'The ocean is an object of no small terror,' Burke wrote, 'Indeed terror is in all cases whatsoever, either openly or latently the ruling principle of the sublime.'[4] These emotions were not limited to the canvas. John W. Beatty recalled Homer's astonishing reaction in the face of the stormy sea: 'This placid, self-contained little man was in a fever of excitement, and his delight in the thrilling and almost overpowering expression of the ocean, as it foamed and rioted, was truly inspiring.'[5]

Meanwhile, on the other side of the Atlantic, following the success of Gustave Courbet's stormy seascapes of 1869 to 1870 (fig. 86), Claude Monet, Pierre-Auguste Renoir (1841–1919) and other impressionists had started to depict the rough sea (fig. 87) – a motif that Guy de Maupassant would soon ascribe to the modernist repertoire.[6] Homer might have known these paintings; despite his fiercely proclaimed artistic independence, he was very appreciative of the European art scene. In a letter to his brother Charles in October 1891, after mentioning two 'great works' he had just completed, he added: 'Your eye being fresh from European pictures, great care is required to make you proud of your brother.'[7]

Sunlight on the Coast, painted in 1890 (fig. 88), is Homer's first pure marine in oil. Other canvases followed, such as *Northeaster* and *Maine Coast* (figs 90 and 91). Showing no historical elements nor human traces, capturing only the waves crashing on the rocky shores, these paintings evoke the eternal presence of the sea.

Northeaster is an ode to the savage beauty of the ocean.[8] Homer exhibited a first version of it in 1895 at M. Knoedler & Co. But despite its prompt success, in 1900 he painted out the two men crouching in the foreground, along with some narrative details, to give more prominence to the magnificent burst of spray. Acquired by collector George A. Hearn in 1901, the painting was later lent to the Metropolitan Museum of Art in New York, where curator Bryson Burroughs

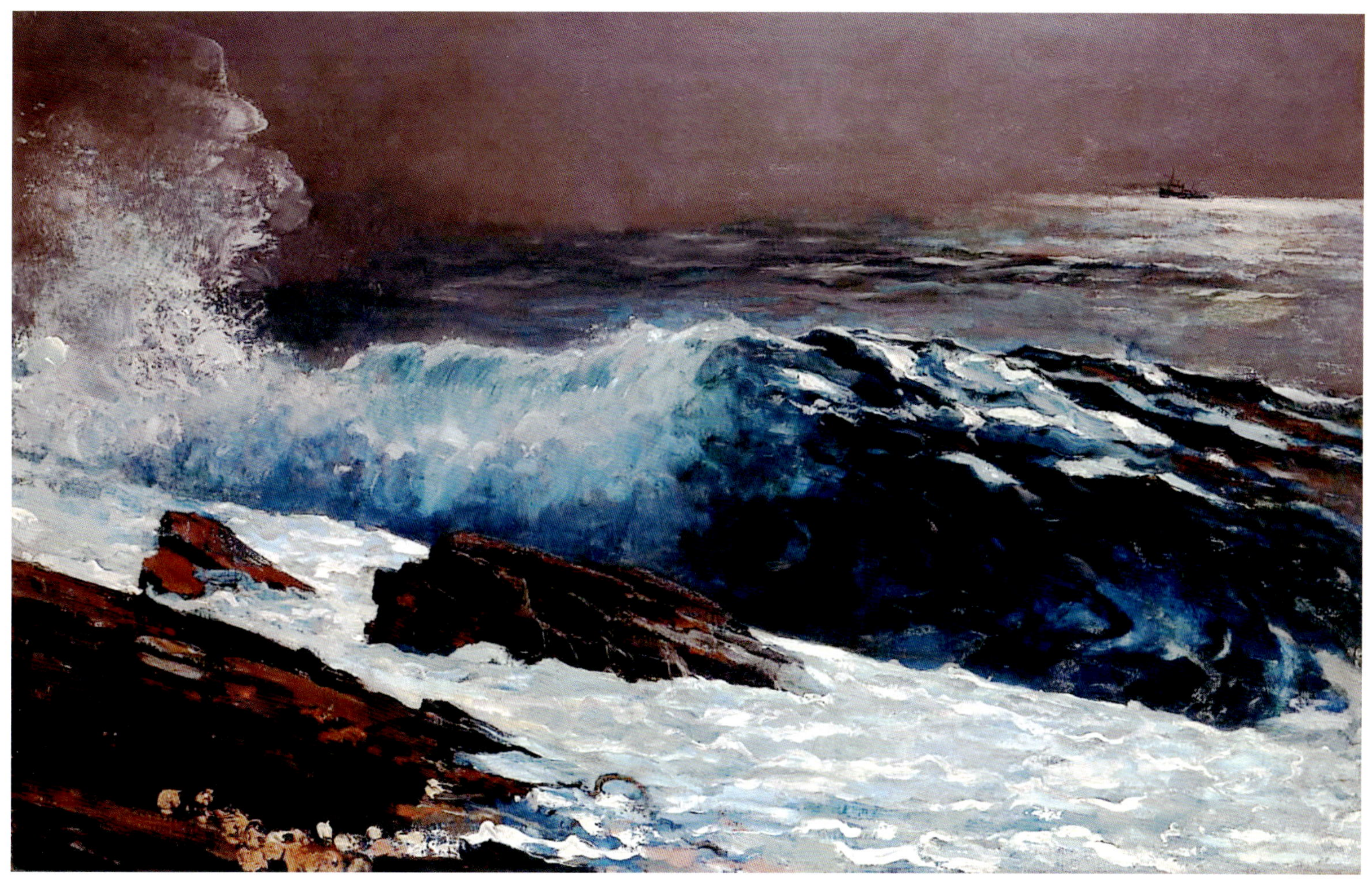

Fig. 88 *Sunlight on the Coast*, 1890, oil on canvas, 76.8 × 123.2 cm. Toledo Museum of Art, Toledo, Ohio. Gift of Edward Drummond Libbey (1912.507)

praised its austere beauty, concluding: 'In the opinion of many people, *Northeaster* is Homer's masterpiece. Certainly one can rarely find so vigorously expressed the dynamic energy and weight of moving water.'[9] The fury of the gale is also captured in *Maine Coast*, where the billowing surf and receding waves convey a feeling of overwhelming grandeur. In the same vein, *Winter Coast* (1890, fig. 89) depicts the brutal cold of Maine's winters. The asymmetrical composition, whose design owes much to Japanese prints, shows the frozen cliff imposing its mass on the puny figure of the hunter. Hardly distinguishable from the background and carrying a duck over his shoulder, the tiny huntsman looks dumbfounded at the towering surf.

In portraying the ocean's power and vastness – elusive in both space and time – Homer's late pictures seem to bear a transcendental meaning. One perhaps connected to the divine, a 'strange power that has some overlook on me and (is) directing my life', as he mentioned in 1899 in a letter to his brother Charles.[10] A spiritual undertone can also be perceived in his moonlit scenes, such as *Kissing the Moon* and *Cape Trinity, Saguenay River, Moonlight* (1904, figs 92 and 93).

Despite suffering a mild stroke and a prolonged illness, this 'ordinary old man', as Homer described himself in 1906, travelled and painted relentlessly. In November 1909, aged 73, he was still working feverishly: 'I cannot accept your invitation to Thanksgiving,' he wrote to his brother Arthur, 'I have little time for anything—many letters unanswered and work unfinished. I am painting.'[11] *Driftwood*, 1909, would be his last canvas (fig. 96).

'Strong, simple, honest, true',[12] according to one critic, while another describes them as unambiguously 'virile' and 'thoroughly national in style and character',[13] Homer's late works fit the hagiographic narrative of a 'purely American and purely realist' painter.[14] His subjects, encompassing the wild North and the tropical South, paved the way for an American declination of modern art that was not exempt from nationalistic rhetoric. This reading, long in vogue and now increasingly challenged, nonchalantly resolves the contradiction between Homer's truth to nature and his late tendency towards abstraction and formalism – making him at the same time a disciple of nineteenth-century realism and a quintessentially modernist painter. New critical approaches are complicating this narrative.[15]

On one aspect, however, the literature seems to agree: whether depicting the Civil War, the seafolks' heroic actions or the 'movements of the great Ocean Symphony',[16] Homer carefully constructed his paintings in the manner of a great storyteller. As one of his first biographers, Lloyd Goodrich, noted in 1944: 'The straight storytelling of earlier works like *The Life Line* was now replaced by a less obvious kind – the drama of the sea and its never-ending battle with the land. Human actors gave way to the impersonal forces of nature.'[17]

1 W.H. Downes and F.T. Robinson, 'Later American Masters', *The New England Magazine*, no. 14, April 1896, p. 140.
2 F.W. Morton, 'The Art of Winslow Homer', *Brush and Pencil*, vol. 10, no. 1, April 1902, pp. 40–54.
3 See C. Riding, 'Shipwreck, Self-preservation and the Sublime', in N. Llewellyn and C. Riding (eds), *The Art of the Sublime*, Tate Research Publication, January 2013: https://www.tate.org.uk/art/research-publications/the-sublime/christine-riding-shipwreck-self-preservation-and-the-sublime-r1133015 (accessed 21 March 2022).
4 Burke 1998, p. 102, quoted in ibid.
5 J.W. Beatty, 'Introductory note', in Downes 1911, p. xxvii.
6 See Guy de Maupassant, 'La vie d'un paysagiste', *Gil Blas*, 28 September 1886, p. 1.
7 W. Homer, letter to Charles Homer, Jr, 15 October 1891, quoted in Washington, DC, Boston and New York 1995, p. 398.
8 A northeaster is a storm along the East Coast of North America, so called because the winds are typically from the northeast.
9 B. Burroughs, in *The Metropolitan Museum of Art Bulletin*, no. 3, May 1908, p. 100.
10 W. Homer, letter to Charles Homer, Jr, 25 November 1899, Bowdoin College.
11 W. Homer, letter to Arthur Homer, 19 November 1909, quoted in Gerdts and Goodrich 2005–14, vol. 5, p. 59.
12 R. Kent, *World Famous Paintings*, New York, 1947, entry 93.
13 Downes 1911, p. 3.
14 Burns 1997.
15 For an overview of the latest literature on Homer, see S. Yount, 'Reconsidering Winslow Homer: Methods and Meanings', in New York 2022, pp. 15–19.
16 W. Stanton Howard, *The Metropolitan Museum of Art Bulletin*, March 1906. Quoted in Downes 1911, p. 178.
17 Goodrich 1944, p. 135.

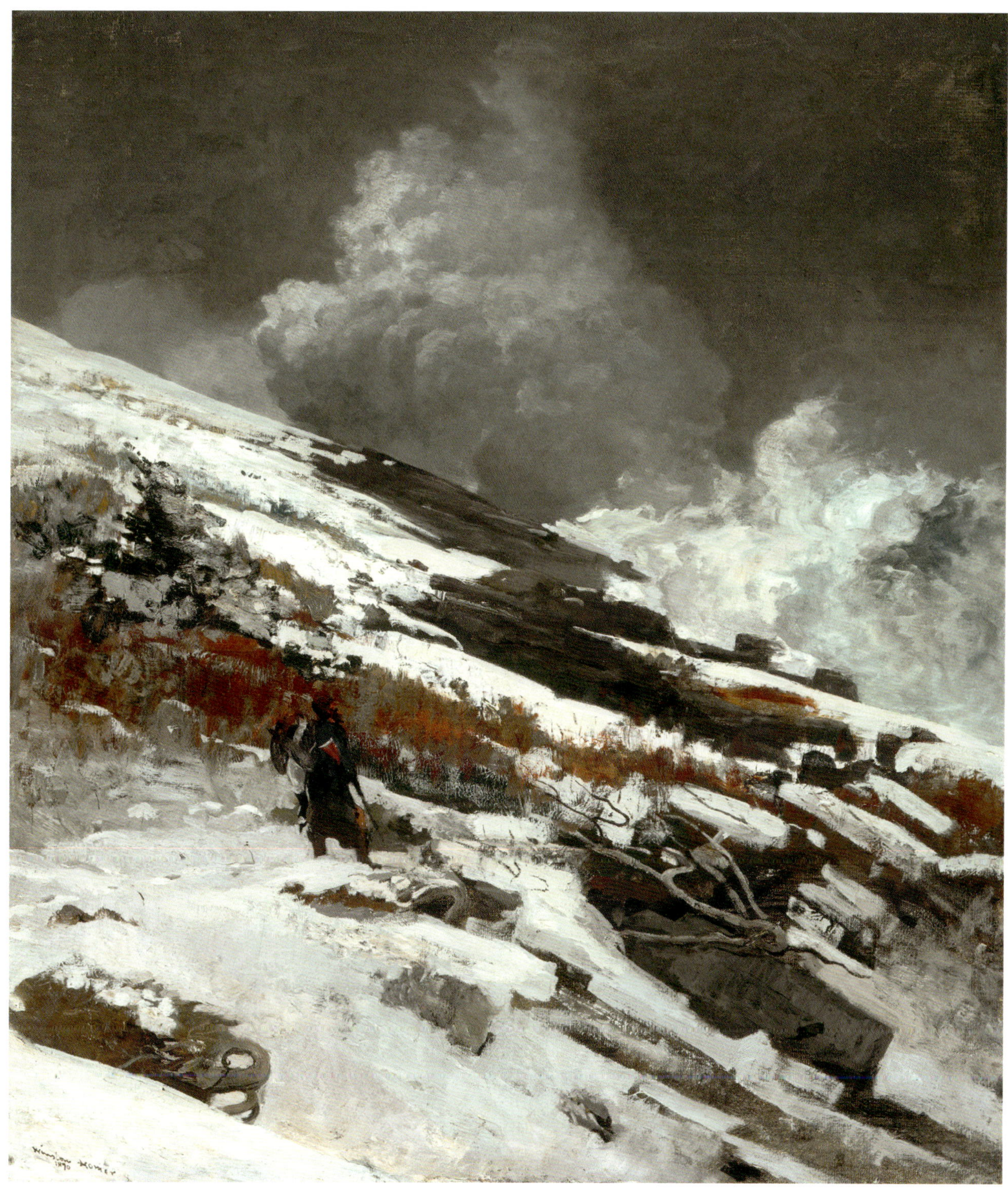

Fig. 89 *Winter Coast*, 1890

Oil on canvas, 91.8 × 80.5 cm
Philadelphia Museum of Art, Philadelphia, Pennsylvania. John G. Johnson Collection, 1917 (cat. 1004)

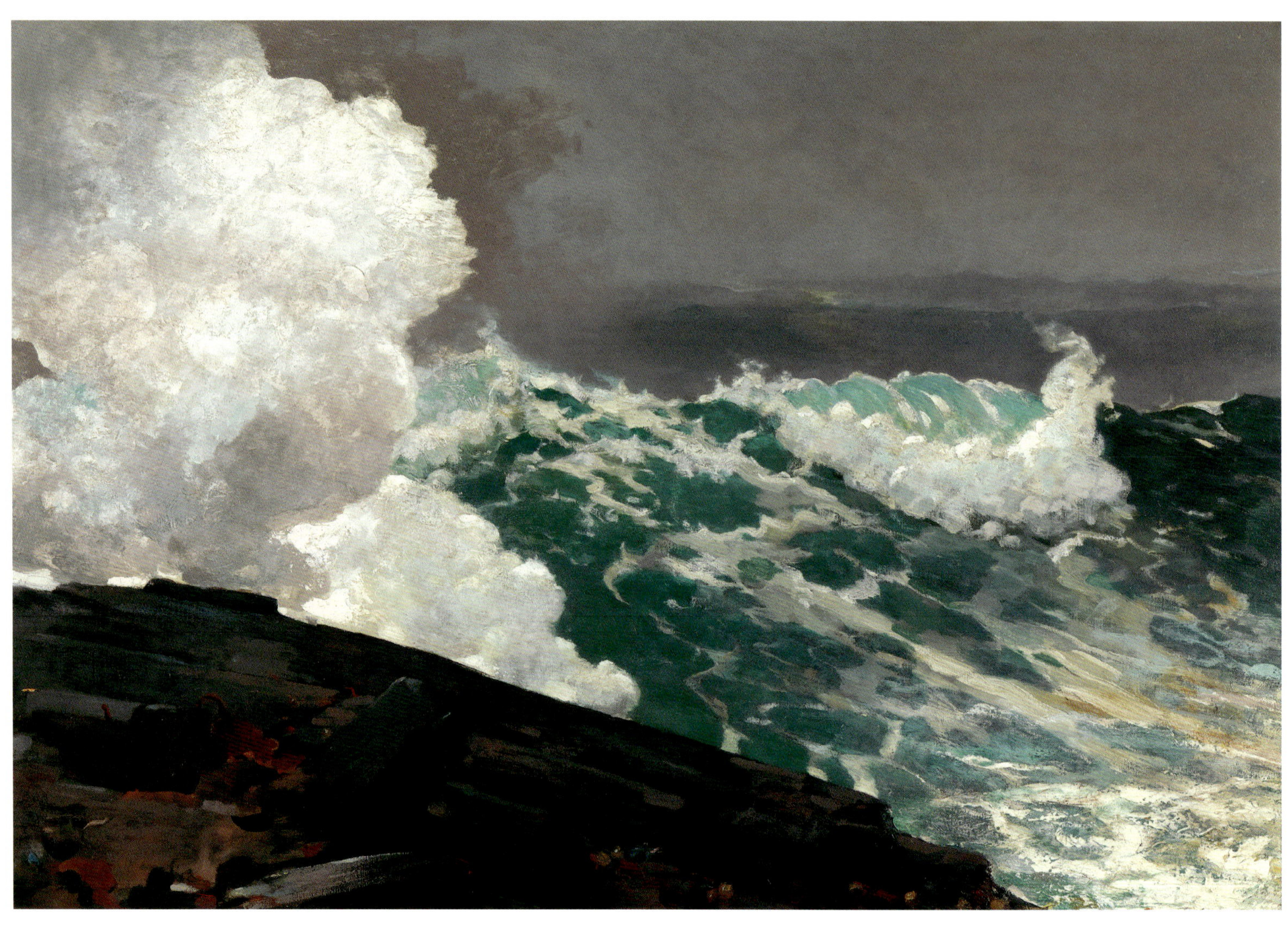

Fig. 90 *Northeaster*, 1895, reworked by 1901

Oil on canvas, 87.6 × 127 cm
The Metropolitan Museum of Art, New York. Gift of George A. Hearn, 1910 (10.64.5)

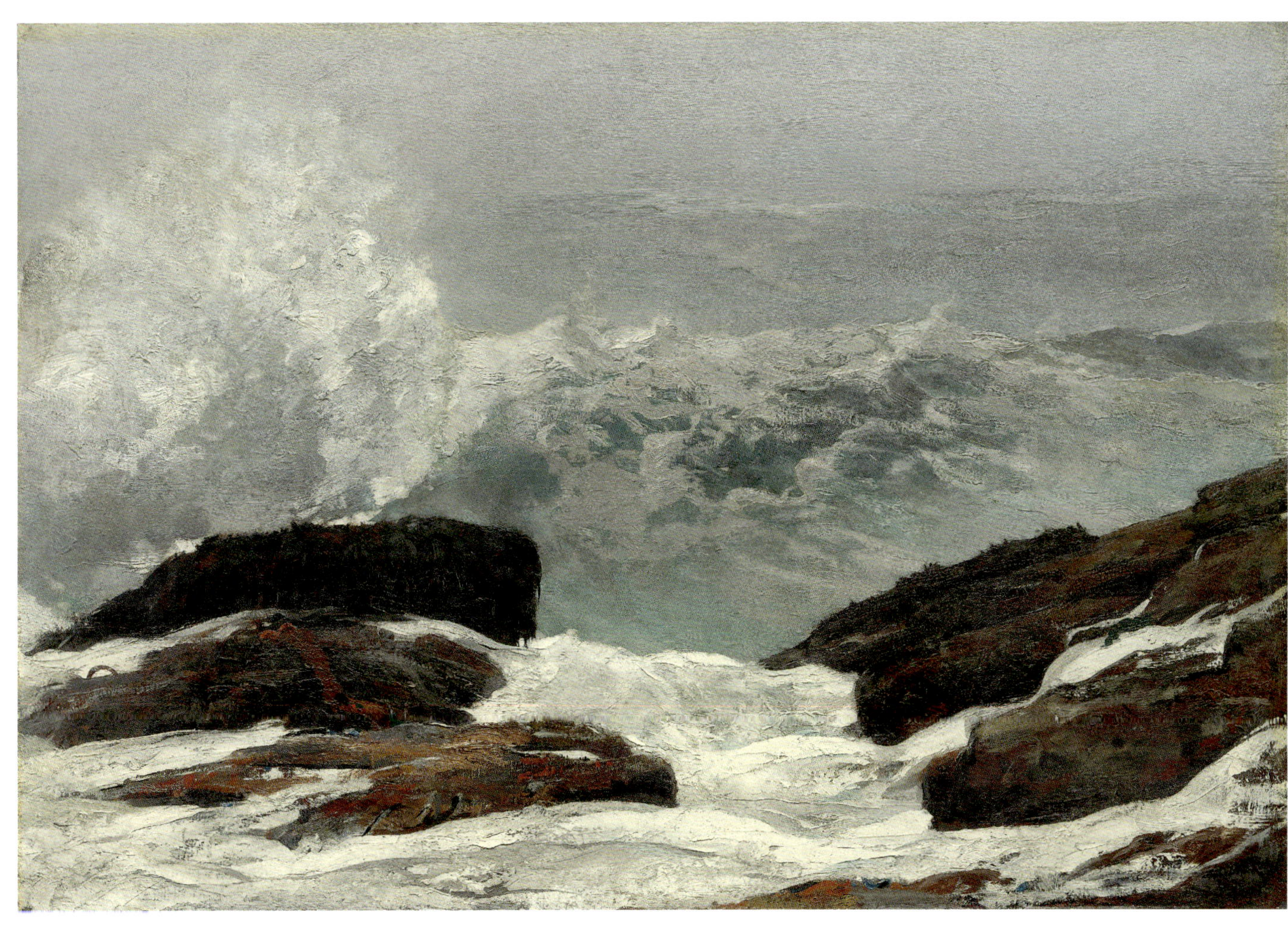

Fig. 91 *Maine Coast*, 1896

Oil on canvas, 76.2 × 101.6 cm
The Metropolitan Museum of Art, New York. Gift of George A. Hearn, in memory of Arthur Hoppock Hearn, 1911 (11.116.1)

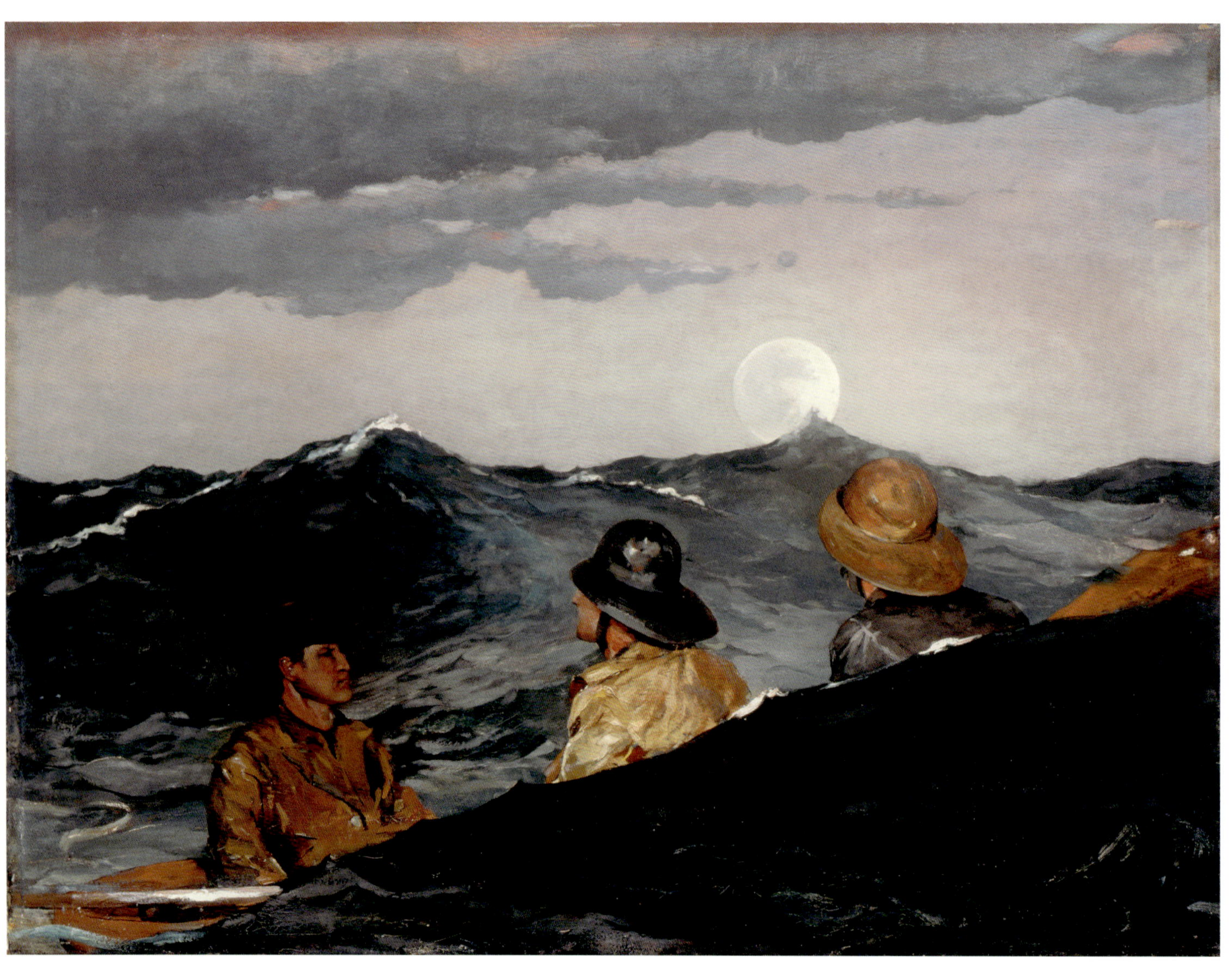

Fig. 92 *Kissing the Moon*, 1904

Oil on canvas, 76.8 × 101.6 cm
Addison Gallery of American Art, Phillips Academy, Andover, Massachusetts. Bequest of Candace C. Stimson (1946.19)

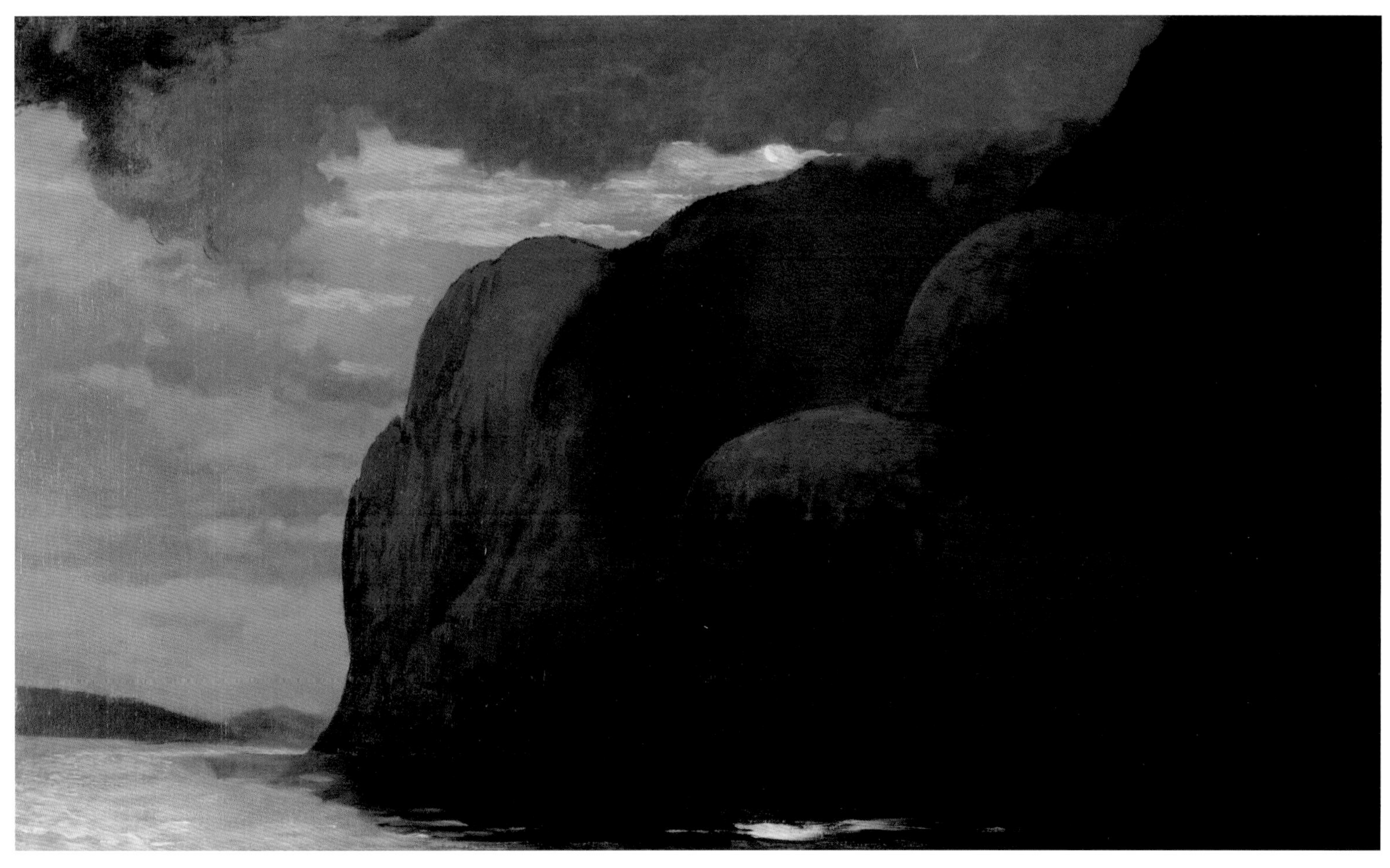

Fig. 93 *Cape Trinity, Saguenay River, Moonlight*, 1904

Oil on canvas, 73 × 123.8 cm
Myron Kunin Collection of American Art, Minneapolis, Minnesota
(1986.05.19.1)

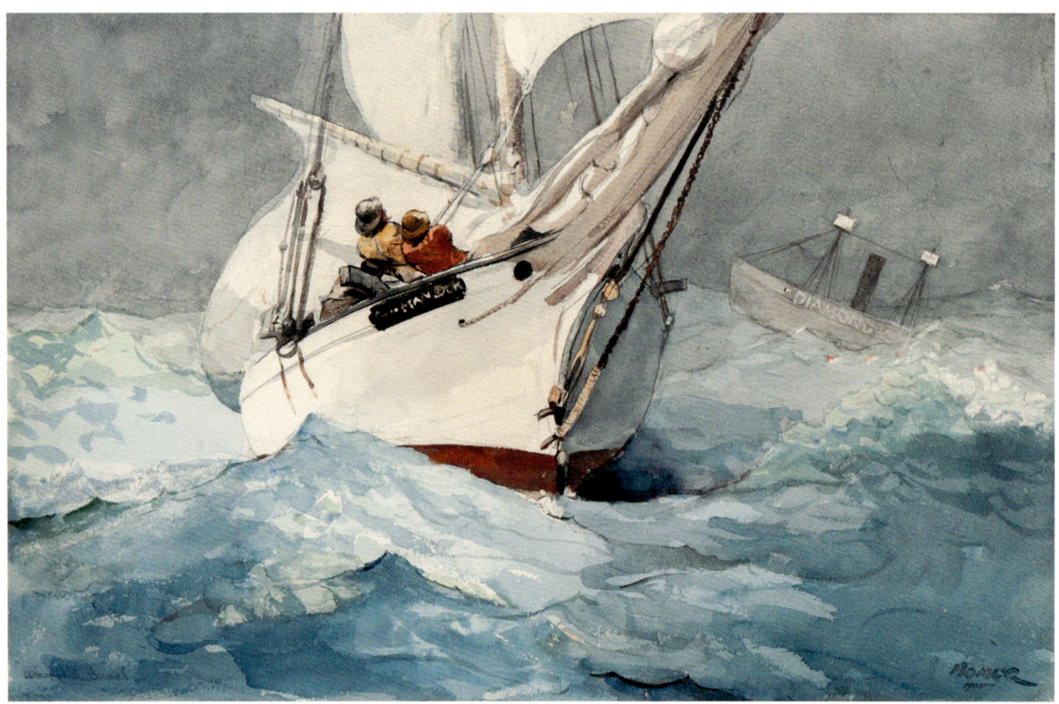

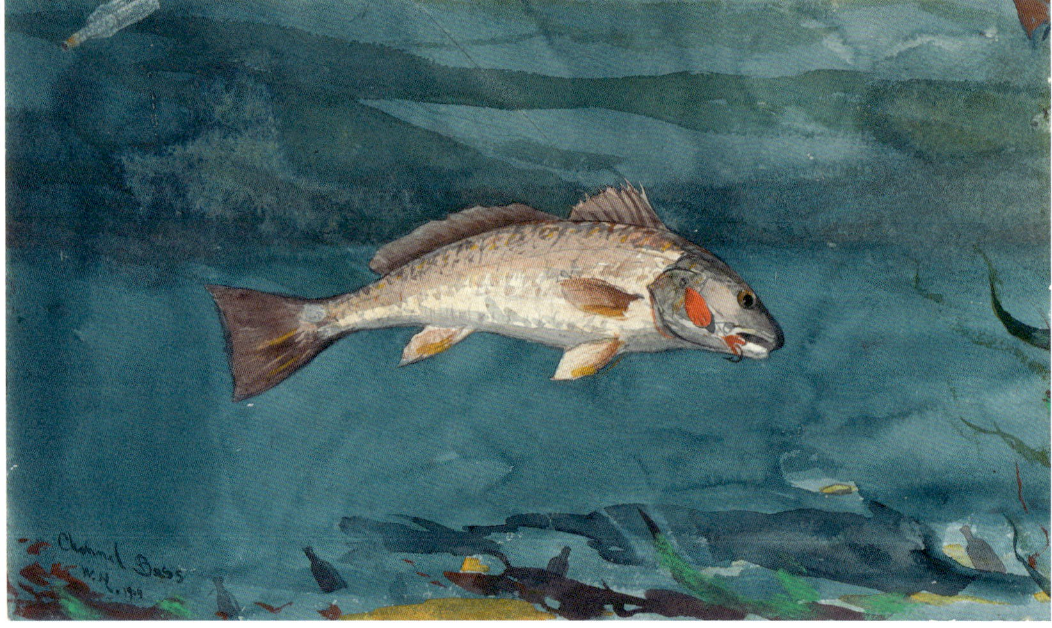

Top
Fig. 94 *Diamond Shoal*, 1905

Watercolour and graphite on paper, 35.5 × 55.2 cm
Private collection

Bottom
Fig. 95 *Channel Bass*, 1904

Watercolour and graphite on wove paper, 28.6 × 49.2 cm
The Metropolitan Museum of Art, New York. George A. Hearn Fund, 1952 (52.155)

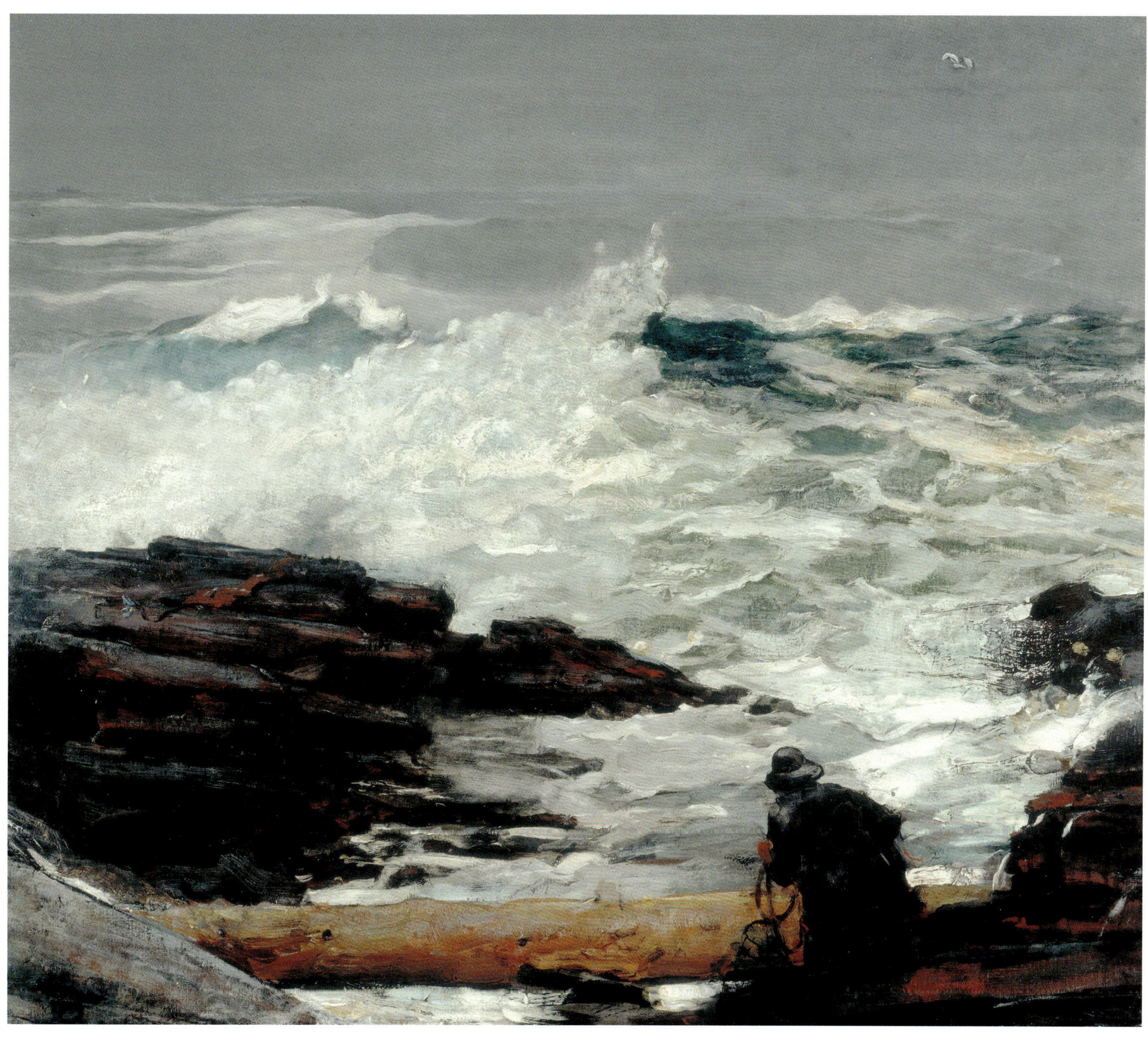

Fig. 96 *Driftwood*, 1909

Oil on canvas, 62.2 × 72.4 cm
Museum of Fine Arts, Boston,
Massachusetts. Henry H. and Zoe
Oliver Sherman Fund and other funds
(1993.564)

Selected Bibliography

For an extensive bibliography on Winslow Homer, see Gerdts and Goodrich 2005–14, vol. 1 (2005), pp. 41–55, and vol. 5 (2014), pp. 472–3.

Exhibition Catalogues

Brunswick and Chadds Ford 2018–19
D.E. Byrd and F.H. Goodyear III, *Winslow Homer and the Camera: Photography and the Art of Painting*, exh. cat., Bowdoin College Museum of Art, Brunswick, and Brandywine River Museum of Art, Chadds Ford; New Haven 2018

Buffalo and Albany 1972
N. Spassky, *Winslow Homer: A Selection of Watercolors, Drawings and Prints from The Metropolitan Museum of Art*, exh. cat., Albright-Knox Art Gallery, Buffalo, and Albany Institute of History and Art; New York 1972

Chicago 2008
M. Tedeschi with K. Dahm et al., *Watercolors by Winslow Homer: The Color of Light*, exh. cat., Art Institute of Chicago; New Haven 2008

Cleveland, Columbus and Washington, DC 1990–1
B. Robertson (ed.), *Reckoning with Winslow Homer: His Late Paintings and Their Influence*, exh. cat., Cleveland Museum of Art, Columbus Museum of Art and Corcoran Gallery of Art, Washington, DC; Bloomington, Indiana 1990

Kansas City, Los Angeles and Atlanta 2001–2
M.C. Conrads, *Winslow Homer and the Critics: Forging a National Art in the 1870s*, exh. cat., Nelson-Atkins Museum of Art, Kansas City, Los Angeles County Museum of Art and High Museum of Art, Atlanta; Princeton, New Jersey 2001

London and Giverny 2006
S. Levy (ed.), *Winslow Homer: Poet of the Sea*, exh. cat., Dulwich Picture Gallery, London, and Musée d'Art Américain Giverny; Chicago 2006

New York 2022
S.L. Herdrich and S. Yount (eds), *Winslow Homer: Crosscurrents*, exh. cat., The Metropolitan Museum of Art, New York 2022

New York 1998
L.S. Ferber and B. Dayer Gallati, *Masters of Color and Light: Homer, Sargent, and the American Watercolor Movement*, exh. cat., Brooklyn Museum, New York; Washington, DC 1998

Philadelphia 2012
K.A. Foster, *Shipwreck! Winslow Homer and 'The Life Line'*, exh. cat., Philadelphia Museum of Art; New Haven and London 2012

Portland 2012
T.A. Denenberg, *Weatherbeaten: Winslow Homer and Maine*, exh. cat., Portland Museum of Art; New Haven and London 2012

Rochester, Chicago, Washington, DC and Williamstown 1990–1
P. Beam et al., *Winslow Homer in the 1890s: Prout's Neck Observed*, Memorial Art Gallery of the University of Rochester, New York, Terra Museum of American Art, Chicago, National Museum of American Art, Smithsonian Institution, Washington, DC, and Sterling and Francine Clark Art Institute, Williamstown, Massachusetts; New York 1990

San Francisco, Portland and Fort Worth 1988
M. Simpson, *Winslow Homer: Paintings of the Civil War*, exh. cat., Fine Arts Museums of San Francisco, Portland Museum of Art and Amon Carter Museum of Western Art, Fort Worth; San Francisco 1988

Sunderland 1988
T. Knipe (ed.), *Winslow Homer: All the Cullercoats Pictures*, exh. cat., Northern Centre for Contemporary Art, Sunderland 1988

Washington, DC, Boston and New York 1995–6
N. Cikovsky, Jr, F. Kelly (eds), *Winslow Homer*, exh. cat., National Gallery of Art, Washington, DC, Museum of Fine Arts, Boston, and The Metropolitan Museum of Art, New York; Washington, DC 1995

Washington, DC, Fort Worth and New Haven 1986
H.A. Cooper, *Winslow Homer Watercolors*, exh. cat., National Gallery of Art, Washington, DC, Amon Carter Museum, Fort Worth, and Yale University Art Gallery, New Haven; Washington, DC 1986

Worcester and Milwaukee 2017–18
E. Athens, B.K. Rudd and M. Tedeschi, *Coming Away: Winslow Homer and England*, exh. cat., Worcester Art Museum and Milwaukee Art Museum; New Haven and London 2017

Books and Articles

Benson 1865
'Sordello' [Eugene Benson], 'National Academy of Design. Fortieth Annual Exhibition. Second Article', *New York Evening Post*, 12 May 1865

Boime 1989
A. Boime, 'Blacks in Shark-Infested Waters: Visual Encodings of Racism in Copley and Homer', *Smithsonian Studies in American Art*, vol. 3, no. 1 (Winter 1989), pp. 18–47

Burke 1998
E. Burke, *A Philosophical Enquiry into the Sublime and Beautiful: And Other Pre-Revolutionary Writings*, D. Womersley (ed.), London 1998

Burns 2002
S. Burns, 'Winslow Homer and the Natural Woman', in T.J. Jackson Lears (ed.), *American Victorians and Virgin Nature*, Boston 2002, pp. 16–38

Burns 1997
S. Burns, 'Modernizing Winslow Homer', *American Quarterly*, vol. 49, no. 3 (September 1997), pp. 615–39

Church 1887
W.C. Church, 'A Midwinter Resort', *The Century Magazine*, vol. 33, no. 4 (February 1887), pp. 499–506

Cikovsky 1990
N. Cikovsky, Jr (ed.), *Winslow Homer: A Symposium*, National Gallery of Art, Washington, DC 1990

Cortissoz 1923
R. Cortissoz, *American Artists*, New York 1923 (18 revised edns)

Downes 1911
W.H. Downes, *The Life and Works of Winslow Homer*, Boston 1911

Foster 2017
K.A. Foster, *American Watercolor in the Age of Homer and Sargent*, New Haven and London 2017

Giese 1990
L. Giese, 'Winslow Homer: Best Chronicler of the War', in Cikovsky 1990, pp. 15–32

Gerdts and Goodrich 2005–14
A.B. Gerdts and L. Goodrich, *Record of Works by Winslow Homer*, 6 vols, New York, Goodrich-Homer Art Education Project, 2005–2014: vol. 1, 1846–66; vol. 2, 1867–76; vol. 3, 1877–March 81; vol. 4.1, April 1881–2; vol. 4.2, 1883–9; vol. 5, 1890–1910

Goodrich 1944
L. Goodrich, *Winslow Homer*, New York 1944

Hannaway 1973
P. Hannaway, *Winslow Homer in the Tropics*, Richmond, Virginia 1973

Harrison 1983
T. Harrison, *Winslow Homer in England*, Ocean Park, Maine 1983 (revised edns 1995, 2004)

Honour 1989
H. Honour (ed.), *The Image of the Black in Western Art*, vol. 4, part 2: *From the American Revolution to World War I: Black Models and White Myths*, Cambridge, Massachusetts 1989

Hyacinthe 2019
G. Hyacinthe, 'The Shape of Humidity: Performing Black Atlantic Theory Making', Performance Philosophy, vol. 4, no. 2 (2019), www.performancephilosophy.org/journal/article/view/237/342

Johns 2002
E. Johns, *Winslow Homer: The Nature of Observation*, Berkeley, California 2002

Kaplan 1966
S. Kaplan, 'The Negro in the Art of Homer and Eakins', *The Massachusetts Review*, vol. 7, no. 1 (Winter 1966), pp. 105–20

Kelly et al. 1996
F. Kelly et al., *American Paintings of the Nineteenth Century*, Part I, National Gallery of Art, Washington, DC 1996

Maury 1855
M.F. Maury, *The Physical Geography of the Sea*, New York 1855

Sampson 1899
W.T. Sampson, 'The Atlantic Fleet in the Spanish War', *The Century Magazine*, no. 57, new series 35 (April 1899), pp. 886–913

Simpson 2018
M. Simpson, '"If you can read this…": Winslow Homer's *The Gulf Stream* and the Viewing of His Pictures', *Panorama: Journal of the Association of Historians of American Art*, vol. 4, no. 1 (Spring 2018)

Simpson 2013
M. Simpson, *Winslow Homer: The Clark Collection*, Williamstown, Massachusetts 2013

Spassky et al. 1985
N. Spassky et al., *American Paintings in The Metropolitan Museum of Art*, vol. 2, New York 1985

Strahan 1883
E. Strahan, 'The Water-Color Society's Exhibition', *The Art Amateur*, vol. 8, no. 4 (March 1883), pp. 80–2

Tatham 2010
D. Tatham, *Winslow Homer in London: A New York Artist Abroad*, Syracuse, New York 2010

Troyen 1984
C. Troyen, 'Innocents Abroad: American Painters at the 1867 Exposition Universelle, Paris', *American Art Journal*, vol. 16, no. 4 (Autumn 1984), pp. 3–20

Valance 2018
H. Valance, *Nocturne: Night in American Art, 1890–1917*, New Haven 2018

Wood 2010
P.H. Wood, *Near Andersonville: Winslow Homer's Civil War*, Cambridge, Massachusetts, and London 2010

List of Exhibited Works

Sharpshooter, 1863, **fig. 24**
Oil on canvas, 31.1 × 41.9 cm
Portland Museum of Art, Maine. Gift of Barbro and Bernard Osher (1992.41)

Defiance: Inviting a Shot before Petersburg, 1864, **fig. 25**
Oil on panel, 30.5 × 45.7 cm
Detroit Institute of Arts, Michigan. Founders Society Purchase with funds from Dexter M. Ferry, Jr (51.66)

The Veteran in a New Field, 1865, **fig. 26**
Oil on canvas, 61.3 × 96.8 cm
The Metropolitan Museum of Art, New York. Bequest of Miss Adelaide Milton de Groot (1876–1967), 1967 (67.187.131)

Prisoners from the Front, 1866, **fig. 27**
Oil on canvas, 61 × 96.5 cm
The Metropolitan Museum of Art, New York. Gift of Mrs Frank B. Porter, 1922 (22.207)

Eagle Head, Manchester, Massachusetts (High Tide), 1870, **fig. 29**
Oil on canvas, 66 × 96.5 cm
The Metropolitan Museum of Art, New York. Gift of Mrs William F. Milton, 1923 (23.77.2)

Snap the Whip, 1872, **fig. 28**
Oil on canvas, 30.5 × 50.8 cm
The Metropolitan Museum of Art, New York. Gift of Christian A. Zabriskie, 1950 (50.41)

A Basket of Clams, 1873, **fig. 31**
Watercolour on wove paper, 29.2 × 24.8 cm
The Metropolitan Museum of Art, New York. Gift of Arthur G. Altschul, 1995 (1995.378)

How Many Eggs?, 1873, **fig. 30**
Watercolour on paper, 32.4 × 23.8 cm
Karen and Kevin Kennedy

Breezing Up (A Fair Wind), 1873–6, **fig. 32**
Oil on canvas, 61.5 × 97 cm
National Gallery of Art, Washington, DC. Gift of the W. L. and May T. Mellon Foundation (1943.13.1)

A Visit from the Old Mistress, 1876, **fig. 35**
Oil on canvas, 45.7 × 61 cm
Smithsonian American Art Museum, Washington, DC. Gift of William T. Evans (1909.7.28)

The Cotton Pickers, 1876, **fig. 34**
Oil on canvas, 61.1 × 96.8 cm
Los Angeles County Museum of Art, California. Acquisition made possible through Museum Trustees: Robert O. Anderson, R. Stanton Avery, B. Gerald Cantor, Edward W. Carter, Justin Dart, Charles E. Ducommun, Camilla Chandler Frost, Julian Ganz, Jr, Dr Armand Hammer, Harry Lenart, Dr Franklin D. Murphy, Mrs Joan Palevsky, Richard E. Sherwood, Maynard J. Toll and Hal B. Wallis (M.77.68)

Dressing for the Carnival, 1877, **fig. 36**
Oil on canvas, 50.8 × 76.2 cm
The Metropolitan Museum of Art, New York. Amelia B. Lazarus Fund, 1922 (22.220)

Promenade on the Beach, 1880, **fig. 33**
Oil on canvas, 50.8 × 76.2 cm
Michele and Donald D'Amour Museum of Fine Arts, Springfield, Massachusetts. Gift of the Misses Emily and Elizabeth Mills in memory of their parents, Mr & Mrs Isaac Mills (36.06)

The Life Brigade, about 1882, **fig. 46**
Oil on canvas, 30 × 44.1 cm
Myron Kunin Collection of American Art, Minneapolis, Minnesota (1997.12.04.1)

Inside the Bar, 1883, **fig. 45**
Watercolour and graphite on wove paper, 40.6 × 73.7 cm
The Metropolitan Museum of Art, New York. Gift of Louise Ryals Arkell, in memory of Bartlett Arkell, 1954 (54.183)

The Gale, 1883–93, **fig. 47**
Oil on canvas, 76.8 × 122.7 cm
Worcester Art Museum, Worcester, Massachusetts. Museum Purchase (1916.48)

The Life Line, 1884, **fig. 51**
Oil on canvas, 72.7 × 113.7 cm
Philadelphia Museum of Art, Philadelphia, Pennsylvania. The George W. Elkins Collection, 1924 (E1924-4-15)

A Garden in Nassau, 1885, **fig. 64**
Watercolour, gouache and graphite on wove paper, 36.8 × 53.3 cm
Terra Foundation for American Art, Chicago, Illinois. Daniel J. Terra Collection (1994.10)

Distressed Boat (Sketch for 'The Gulf Stream'), 1885, **fig. 81**
Graphite on paper, 10.2 × 16 cm
The Metropolitan Museum of Art, New York. Morris K. Jesup Fund, 2016 (2016.1 recto)

Sharks (The Derelict), 1885, **fig. 82**
Watercolour over graphite on wove paper, 36.8 × 53.2 cm
Brooklyn Museum, New York, Gift of the Estate of Helen Babbott Sanders (78.151.4)

Sponge Fishermen, Bahamas, 1885, **fig. 63**
Watercolour, gouache and graphite on paper, 27.9 × 51.1 cm
Private collection

The Fog Warning, 1885, **fig. 52**
Oil on canvas, 76.8 × 123.2 cm
Museum of Fine Arts, Boston, Massachusetts. Anonymous gift with credit to the Otis Norcross Fund (94.72)

Eight Bells, 1886, **fig. 54**
Oil on canvas, 64 × 76.7 cm
Addison Gallery of American Art, Phillips Academy, Andover, Massachusetts. Gift of anonymous donor (1930.379)

To the Rescue, 1886, **fig. 53**
Oil on canvas, 61 × 76.2 cm
The Phillips Collection, Washington, DC. Acquired 1926 (0922)

Undertow, 1886, **fig. 55**
Oil on canvas, 75.7 × 121 cm
Sterling and Francine Clark Art Institute, Williamstown, Massachusetts. Acquired by Sterling and Francine Clark, 1924 (1955.4)

Winter Coast, 1890, **fig. 89**
Oil on canvas, 91.8 × 80.5 cm
Philadelphia Museum of Art, Philadelphia, Pennsylvania. John G. Johnson Collection, 1917 (cat. 1004)

Signal of Distress, 1890–6, **fig. 56**
Oil on canvas, 62 × 98 cm
Museo Nacional Thyssen-Bornemisza, Madrid (1980.71)

Hound and Hunter, 1892, **fig. 57**
Oil on canvas, 71.8 × 122.3 cm
National Gallery of Art, Washington, DC. Gift of Stephen C. Clark (1947.11.1)

Northeaster, 1895, reworked by 1901, **fig. 90**
Oil on canvas, 87.6 × 127 cm
The Metropolitan Museum of Art, New York. Gift of George A. Hearn, 1910 (10.64.5)

Maine Coast, 1896, **fig. 91**
Oil on canvas, 76.2 × 101.6 cm
The Metropolitan Museum of Art, New York. Gift of George A. Hearn, in memory of Arthur Hoppock Hearn, 1911 (11.116.1)

A Wall, Nassau, 1898, **fig. 68**
Watercolour and graphite on wove paper, 37.8 × 54.3 cm
The Metropolitan Museum of Art, New York. Amelia B. Lazarus Fund, 1910 (10.228.9)

Hurricane, Bahamas, 1898, **fig. 67**
Watercolour and graphite on wove paper, 36.7 × 53.5 cm
The Metropolitan Museum of Art, New York. Amelia B. Lazarus Fund, 1910 (10.228.7)

Palm Tree, Nassau, 1898, **fig. 66**
Watercolour and graphite on wove paper, 54.3 × 37.8 cm
The Metropolitan Museum of Art, New York. Amelia B. Lazarus Fund, 1910 (10.228.6)

Study for 'The Gulf Stream', 1898–9, **fig. 83**
Watercolour and chalk on wove paper, 36.8 × 25.6 cm
Cooper Hewitt, Smithsonian Design Museum, Smithsonian Institution, New York. Gift of Charles Savage Homer, Jr (1912-12-36)

Flower Garden and Bungalow, Bermuda, 1899, **fig. 69**
Watercolour and graphite on wove paper, 35.4 × 53.2 cm
The Metropolitan Museum of Art, New York. Amelia B. Lazarus Fund, 1910 (10.228.10)

Nassau, 1899, **fig. 72**
Watercolour and graphite on wove paper, 37.8 × 54.3 cm
The Metropolitan Museum of Art, New York. Amelia B. Lazarus Fund, 1910 (10.228.4)

Shore and Surf, Nassau, 1899, **fig. 71**
Watercolour and graphite on wove paper, 37.9 × 54.3 cm
The Metropolitan Museum of Art, New York. Amelia B. Lazarus Fund, 1910 (10.228.5)

The Bather, 1899, **fig. 70**
Watercolour and graphite on wove paper, 36.7 × 53.5 cm
The Metropolitan Museum of Art, New York. Amelia B. Lazarus Fund, 1910 (10.228.8)

The Gulf Stream, 1899, reworked by 1906, **fig. 84**
Oil on canvas, 71.4 × 124.8 cm
The Metropolitan Museum of Art, New York. Catharine Lorillard Wolfe Collection, Wolfe Fund, 1906 (06.1234)

Natural Bridge, Bermuda, about 1901, **fig. 73**
Watercolour and graphite on wove paper, 36.7 × 53.3 cm
The Metropolitan Museum of Art, New York. Amelia B. Lazarus Fund, 1910 (10.228.12)

Searchlight on Harbor Entrance, Santiago de Cuba, 1902, **fig. 75**
Oil on canvas, 77.5 × 128.3 cm
The Metropolitan Museum of Art, New York. Gift of George A. Hearn, 1906 (06.1282)

Fishing Boats, Key West, 1903, **fig. 74**
Watercolour and graphite on wove paper, 35.4 × 55.2 cm
The Metropolitan Museum of Art, New York. Amelia B. Lazarus Fund, 1910 (10.228.1)

Cape Trinity, Saguenay River, Moonlight, 1904, **fig. 93**
Oil on canvas, 73 × 123.8 cm
Myron Kunin Collection of American Art, Minneapolis, Minnesota (1986.05.19.1)

Channel Bass, 1904, **fig. 95**
Watercolour and graphite on wove paper, 28.6 × 49.2 cm
The Metropolitan Museum of Art, New York. George A. Hearn Fund, 1952 (52.155)

Kissing the Moon, 1904, **fig. 92**
Oil on canvas, 76.8 × 101.6 cm
Addison Gallery of American Art, Phillips Academy, Andover, Massachusetts. Bequest of Candace C. Stimson (1946.19)

Diamond Shoal, 1905, **fig. 94**
Watercolour and graphite on paper, 35.5 × 55.2 cm
Private collection

Driftwood, 1909, **fig. 96**
Oil on canvas, 62.2 × 72.4 cm
Museum of Fine Arts, Boston, Massachusetts. Henry H. and Zoe Oliver Sherman Fund and other funds (1993.564)

Right and Left, 1909, **fig. 59**
Oil on canvas, 71.8 × 122.9 cm
National Gallery of Art, Washington, DC. Gift of the Avalon Foundation (1951.8.1)

List of Lenders, Picture Credits and Acknowledgements

Andover, Massachusetts
Addison Gallery of American Art, Phillips Academy

Boston, Massachusetts
Museum of Fine Arts

Chicago, Illinois
Terra Foundation for American Art

Detroit, Michigan
Detroit Institute of Arts

Los Angeles, California
Los Angeles County Museum of Art

Madrid
Museo Nacional Thyssen-Bornemisza

Minneapolis, Minnesota
Myron Kunin Collection of American Art

New York
Brooklyn Museum
Cooper Hewitt, Smithsonian Design Museum, Smithsonian Institution
The Metropolitan Museum of Art

Philadelphia, Pennsylvania
Philadelphia Museum of Art

Portland, Maine
Portland Museum of Art

Springfield, Massachusetts
Michele and Donald D'Amour Museum of Fine Arts

Washington, DC
National Gallery of Art
Smithsonian American Art Museum
The Phillips Collection

Williamstown, Massachusetts
Sterling and Francine Clark Art Institute

Worcester, Massachusetts
Worcester Art Museum

Karen and Kevin Kennedy

and the private owners who have generously lent their works to the exhibition and wish to remain anonymous

Picture Credits

Andover, Massachusetts
© Addison Gallery of American Art, Phillips Academy, Andover, Massachusetts: figs 54, 92.

Berlin
Nationalgalerie, Staatliche Museen zu Berlin © Photo Scala, Florence/bpk, Bildagentur für Kunst, Kultur und Geschichte, Berlin / Photo Jörg P. Anders: fig. 86.

Boston, Massachusetts
© Museum of Fine Arts, Boston: figs 17, 52, 61, 96.

Brunswick, Maine
© Bowdoin College Museum of Art, Brunswick, Maine: figs 1, 76, 85.

Cambridge, Massachusetts
Harvard University Art Museums, Cambridge, Massachusetts © President and Fellows of Harvard College, Cambridge, Massachusetts: fig. 37.

Chicago, Illinois
© The Art Institute of Chicago: figs 49, 79, 87.
Terra Foundation for American Art, Chicago, Illinois © Photo courtesy of the Terra Foundation for American Art: figs 6, 64.

Deerfield, Massachusetts
© Five Colleges and Historic Deerfield Museum Consortium: fig. 48.

Detroit, Michigan
The Detroit Institute of Arts, Detroit, Michigan © Detroit Institute of Arts / Bridgeman Images: fig. 25.

London
© The National Gallery, London: figs 7, 12.
Royal Collection Trust / © Her Majesty Queen Elizabeth II 2022: fig. 39.
Royal Holloway, University of London © Royal Holloway, University of London / Bridgeman Images: fig. 19.
The Wallace Collection, London © By kind permission of the Trustees of the Wallace Collection, London: fig. 22.

Los Angeles, California
© Los Angeles County Museum of Art, California: fig. 34.

Madrid
Museo Thyssen-Bornemisza, Madrid © Museo Thyssen-Bornemisza, Madrid: fig. 56.

Milwaukee, Wisconsin
Milwaukee Art Museum, Wisconsin © Milwaukee Art Museum / Photo John R. Glembin: fig. 43.

Minneapolis, Minnesota
Myron Kunin Collection of American Art, Minneapolis, MN © Midwest Art Conservation Center: figs 46, 93.

New Haven, Connecticut
© Yale University Art Gallery, New Haven, Connecticut: fig. 15.

New York
© Brooklyn Museum of Art, New York: figs 60, 77, 82.
© Cooper-Hewitt, National Design Museum, Smithsonian Institution: figs 62, 83.
© The Metropolitan Museum of Art, New York: figs 26, 27, 28, 29, 31, 36, 45, 66, 67, 68, 69, 70, 71, 72, 73, 74, 75, 81, 84, 90, 91, 95.

Newark, New Jersey
Collection of The Newark Museum of Art © The Newark Museum of Art / Art Resource/ Scala, Florence: fig. 3.

Paris
Musée d'Orsay, Paris © Musée d'Orsay, Dist. RMN-Grand Palais / Patrice Schmidt: 4; © RMN-Grand Palais (musée d'Orsay) / Gérard Blot / Hervé Lewandowski: fig. 23.
Musée du Louvre, Paris © RMN-Grand Palais (musée du Louvre) / Michel Urtado: fig. 80.

Philadelphia, Pennsylvania
Penn State University: fig. 78.
Pennsylvania Academy of the Fine Arts, Philadelphia © Granger / Bridgeman Images: fig. 58.
© Philadelphia Museum of Art, Philadelphia, Pennsylvania: figs 16, 51, 89.

Portland, Maine
Portland Museum of Art, Maine.
Image courtesy of Meyersphoto.com
© The Trustees of the Portland Museum of Art, Maine: figs 5, 24.

Princeton, New Jersey
© Princeton University Art Museum: fig. 38.

Private collections
Karen and Kevin Kennedy Collection
© Karen and Kevin Kennedy Collection / Photo Joshua Nefsky: fig. 30.
© Private collection / Bridgeman Images: fig. 44.
Private collection © Photo courtesy of the owner: figs 63, 65.
Private collection © Photo Laura Wulf: fig. 94.
Private collection, Seattle © Photo courtesy of the owner: fig. 50.
© Susan Johnson, Cullercoats: figs 40, 41.

Rochester, New York
Memorial Art Gallery of the University of Rochester © Memorial Art Gallery of the University of Rochester / Photo James M. Via: fig. 9.

San Francisco, California
Fine Arts Museums of San Francisco, California © akg-images: fig. 14.

Springfield, Massachusetts
© Michele and Donald D'Amour Museum of Fine Arts, Springfield: fig. 33.

Toledo, Ohio
© Toledo Museum of Art, Toledo, Ohio: fig. 88.

Washington, DC
© Hirshhorn Museum and Sculpture Garden, Smithsonian Institution, Washington: fig. 18.
Courtesy National Gallery of Art, Washington: figs 10, 13, 20, 32, 42, 57, 59.
© The Phillips Collection, Washington, DC: fig. 53.
Smithsonian American Museum of Art, Washington, DC. © Smithsonian Institution, Washington, DC: fig. 35.

Williamstown, Massachusetts
© Sterling and Francine Clark Art Institute, Williamstown, Massachusetts, USA: figs 2, 8, 11, 21, 55.

Worcester, Massachusetts
Worcester Art Museum, Worcester, Massachusetts © Worcester Art Museum / Bridgeman Images: fig. 47.

Acknowledgements

We join National Gallery Director Gabriele Finaldi in offering heartfelt thanks to Max Hollein, Director, Stephanie L. Herdrich, Associate Curator of American painting and sculpture in the American Wing, and Sylvia Yount, Lawrence A. Fleischman Curator in Charge of the American Wing, at the Metropolitan Museum of Art, New York. They have been ideal colleagues in thinking how best to bring this remarkable artist, seemingly known to all Americans, to the attention of a largely new British and European audience, and in securing essential loans for the London venue. We also thank colleagues on both sides of the Atlantic who agree that Homer must be better known here and who have advised and supported us in this exciting endeavour.

This publication, a companion to the scholarly and insightful *Winslow Homer: Crosscurrents*, published by the Metropolitan, has been a collaborative effort, edited with care and attention by Catherine Hooper, designed by Kathrin Jacobsen and overseen by Laura Lappin, Suzanne Bosman and colleagues at National Gallery Global.

Esteemed scholars provided crucial guidance on our texts. In particular, we thank Dr John Fagg, University of Birmingham, for his attentive reading and rigorous feedback, and Marenka Thompson-Odlum, Pitt Rivers Museum, Oxford, who has generously shared her knowledge and advice on the texts and interpretation material that meet the needs of contemporary audiences.

At the National Gallery, we are especially grateful to Jane Knowles, Robyn Earl, Giulia Segreto, Susan Thompson and Joanna Weston for their support and management of the exhibition; and to Belinda Phillpot, Louise Nyborg and Aaron Jones for their sensitive exhibition design. Minnie Scott has been an invaluable aid in adapting the interpretative texts for a European audience.

Finally, we would like to extend our gratitude to the following individuals for their assistance in matters relating to this exhibition and catalogue: Katherine Bourguignon, Terra Foundation for American Art, Paris; David Peters Corbett, The Courtauld, London, Susan Johnson of Cullercoats; as well as, in-house, Caroline Campbell, Jane Hyne, Tracy Jones, Ava Kaartinen, Priyesh Mistry, Daniel Ralston, Alexandra Moskalenko, Lizzie Phillips and John Shevlin.

Christine Riding
Christopher Riopelle
Chiara Di Stefano
The National Gallery, London

Published to accompany the exhibition:

Winslow Homer
Force of Nature

The National Gallery, London
10 September 2022 – 8 January 2023

Exhibition sponsored by

WHITE & CASE

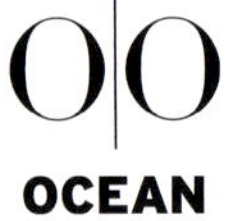

Supported by

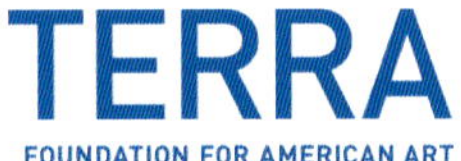

Gregory Annenberg Weingarten

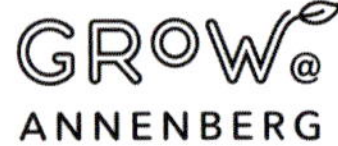

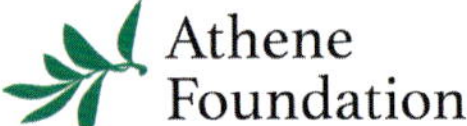

Dr Lee MacCormick Edwards
Charitable Foundation

This exhibition has been made possible by the provision of insurance through the Government Indemnity Scheme. The National Gallery would like to thank HM Government for providing Government Indemnity and the Department for Digital, Culture, Media and Sport and Arts Council England for arranging the indemnity.

First published in 2022 by
National Gallery Global Limited
Trafalgar Square
London WC2N 5DN
www.shop.nationalgallery.org.uk

ISBN: 978-1-85709-687-3
Product code: 1051241

British Library Cataloguing-in-Publication Data
A catalogue record is available from the British Library
Library of Congress Control Number: 2022938379

Publisher: Laura Lappin
Project Editor: Catherine Hooper
Proofreader: Robert Davies
Picture Researcher: Suzanne Bosman
Production: Jane Hyne

Designed by Kathrin Jacobsen
Origination by DL Imaging
Printed in Belgium by Graphius

All works are by Winslow Homer unless otherwise stated.
All measurements give height before width.

Front cover: *The Gulf Stream* (detail of fig. 84)
Back cover: *A Wall, Nassau* (detail of fig. 68)
Pages 2–3: *Northeaster* (detail of fig. 90)
Page 4: *The Life Brigade* (detail of fig. 46)